The Handbook
of Swimming

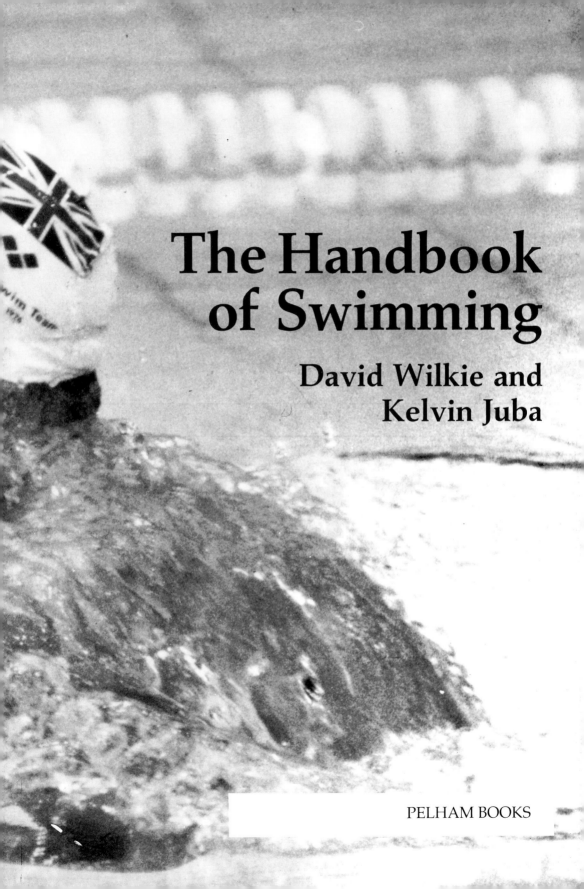

The Handbook of Swimming

David Wilkie and Kelvin Juba

PELHAM BOOKS

Acknowledgements

To Sheila Williams for typing copy; Dr David Hunt for medical advice; June Croft, the late Alan Hime and Barnet Copthall Pool for assistance with photographic sessions; and to the International Swimming Hall of Fame for the use of photos. Also to Celeste Austin, Pat Moy-Bevan, Louise Martin and Christopher Stevens.

Picture credits
The line drawings are by Peter Grinyer and the photographs by Miles Spackman (except where otherwise stated). The photographs on the title page and opposite the foreword are by All-Sport. Designed by Phil Kay.

Contents

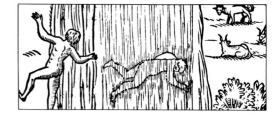

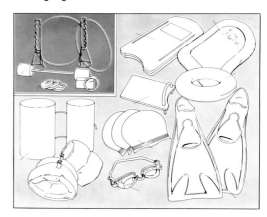

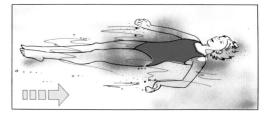

Foreword

by James E. Counsilman

Swimming continues to be one of the world's greatest participatory sports: it is one of the few sports in which people in nearly every country take part. It is hardly surprising that new ideas and improvements take place regularly. The book you are about to read brings together two men who have a wealth of experience in the sport at all levels.

David Wilkie first came to world attention in 1972 at the Munich Olympics. One of my own students at Indiana University, Mark Spitz, won seven gold medals but I also noticed the enormous talent of the silver medallist in the 200m breaststroke.

David went on to be Olympic, World, European and Commonwealth Champion on no less than eight occasions — something unique to British swimming. His outstanding world record, set in 1976 at the Montreal Olympics, lasted until 1983. David is still very much with the sport and I hope that you, the reader, will benefit from his experience.

It was in 1972 that David's co-writer, Kelvin Juba, first came to my attention after two years as Editor of *Swimming Times* magazine. Kelvin, a member of the third generation of the Juba family with an interest in swimming stretching back to the 1920s, has been involved in the sport at all levels as a teacher, coach, journalist, T.V. commentator and sports administrator. His father was a leading swimming writer and a friend of mine for many years.

The mix of these two aquatically experienced young men, allied with the constantly changing nature of our knowledge on the sport, should make this a most interesting volume both for now and for the years to come.

Doctor James E. Counsilman

Former Swimming Coach and Professor of Education, Indiana University, U.S.A., and former Coach to U.S.A. Olympic Swimming Teams.

1 History of Swimming

How swimming started

Only vague records of early swimming exist but they indicate that swimming grew up with Man from the early stages of his appearance on Earth. When early Man needed to move on land he either walked or ran; when early Man needed to move across water he probably waded, and then eventually swam by watching the example set by other primarily landbased animals. The word need is used somewhat cautiously here because there must have been long periods when the climatic conditions made it impossible for people to swim. The ability to swim, however poorly, would probably have been part of the dexterity of early hunters, and the need to hunt would certainly have been a reason to swim.

How the transition was made from an activity of need to a sport and recreation of unparalleled grace and enjoyment, we hope to reveal in the early parts of this book. No statistics exist but probably half the population of Europe now swims.

Lack of written records prior to the birth of Christ make it difficult to be accurate but one would anticipate that, as swimming before this time would have been regarded as primarily a necessity, at some stage it would have been seen as a way of moving armies, both large and small, for the purpose of battle. Soldiers would have first of all been transported across water whilst holding onto their animals, and later have swum themselves. In 2500 B.C. the Egyptians produced the first hieroglyphics which featured swimming. The photograph of the bas-relief shows a swimmer lying flat with one arm out in front and another behind, indicating

The Egyptian bas-relief depicting a swimmer lying on his stomach (Photo: Courtesy of Swimming Hall of Fame).

1

that even almost 3500 years ago people propelled themselves in water with alternating movements.

There are indications that a form of overarm stroke was used by the Assyrians, Greeks, South Sea Island natives, North American Indians and Kaffirs of South Africa.[1] The North African Palace of the Nimrods holds a bas-relief created in 880 B.C. which shows a group of Assyrians swimming through a moat to escape captivity. The Museum of Antique Arts in Munich houses a piece of sculpture made in 460 B.C. which was found in Perugia, Italy, and is thought to be the oldest diving figure in existence. It is some 18 cm (7 ins) high.[2] Through these few existing links we are able to form an impression of techniques employed by swimmers – for example, the diving figure, as you will see from the photo has adopted much the same preparatory position as a diver would today.

Many records in Europe must have been lost during the Dark Ages. This was a time of frequent and persistent plagues and swimming was discouraged because it was generally felt that this was an activity which increased the likelihood of plagues spreading. The first swimming treatise in English appeared in 1595 by Christopher Middleton who translated a Latin original completed in 1587 by Everard Digby, a Cambridge scholar. He was expelled from his Cambridge college six months later and died relatively obscurely whilst working as

The diving figure found in Perugia, Italy, and now in Munich (Photo: Courtesy of Swimming Hall of Fame).

a country parson. Other books were written by Monsieur Thevenot in 1696 on *The Art of Swimming*, based on Digby's work, and by Benjamin Franklin in 1821 when he completed *The Art of Swimming With Advice for Bathers*.

Swimming mythology

The mystical attitude adopted by many ancient writers, particularly the Greeks, has made it even harder to differentiate between swimming fact and fiction. There are some pieces of fiction which indicate that swimming has been held in high regard: for instance, in Persia the Goddess Anahita, the spotless one, was regarded as the course of all waters;[3] Asprasus, an Indian nymph, made her home in celestial waters; and Lakshmi, the Goddess of Wealth and Beauty, was born from the foam and as a result was given the name of Daughter

of the Sea.

Greek legend would not be complete without mention of the water nymphs. Aphrodite, the Goddess of Love and Beauty and mother of Cupid, was born from foamy waters. The Oceanids, the 3,000 daughters of Oceanus eldest of the Titans, were born of the water as were the 200 sea nymphs known as Nereids, daughters of Nereus, Old Man of the Sea. Greek legend also records that Arethusa was startled at her bathing and ran many miles until Artemis took pity upon her and changed her into a fountain. And so the stories go on … with Greek stories finding their way into other cultures. In Jewish history King David spied on Bathsheba at her bath and ended up securing the death in battle of her husband, Uriah, in order that he could marry her.

More often than not, the mermaid was seen as a kind of water temptress. Many of these stories found their way into the next great civilization, the Romans, who treated bathing and swimming as two parallel activities to be encouraged. Roman baths might well have been regarded in much the same way as the public house today: they were social centres that people used daily. The Roman citizen would visit the Lancolium, sweat heavily and be scraped with a strigil blade by his slaves. Men would swim but women would bathe at home. Plato considered a man who didn't know how to swim to be uneducated. The most cutting of insults that one Greek could deliver to another would be 'to dismiss him as a man who neither knew how to run or swim'. Murals of ancient swimmers can be seen in a variety of places including the Vatican, Borgian and Bourbon codices, and the murals of the Tepantitla House at Toetihuacan, near Mexico City, which depicts men splashing about in the waters of Tialocan, paradise of Tialoc the God of Water. There are also mosaics at Pompeii.

The development of bathing and swimming in Europe

The Byzantine Empire developed with Constantinople at its head and this great trading city followed the Roman tradition with regard to bathing. By A.D. 430 there were 150 private baths in the city and hospitals were expected to bathe their patients twice per week. When the Empress Basilissa was married her first public engagement was to take her first public bath, an important social event for the whole country.

In Persia at this time there were 27,000 baths in the city of Baghdad. Meanwhile, the decline of the Roman Empire in Northern Europe meant that colder climates in Europe were a discouragement to swimmers, while the Middle East and Eastern Europe flourished. The nature of power is such that it is never permanent and as each great empire flourished and then floundered, so the fortunes of swimming were reflected.

Early swimming in Britain

Julius Caesar brought with him the first known swimmers in Britain. Plutarch and Suetonius, who wrote biographies of Caesar, talk of his ability as a swimmer. His armies crossed rivers by swimming or on inflated skins. In the winter of 48–47 B.C. at the battle of Alexandria Caesar had to leap into the sea and swim to the safety of a nearby ship with a set of valuable documents in his hand[4] which he kept clear of the water. The distance was thought to be approximately 300 metres. The first recorded swimming situation in British history was by Caesar in his own account of his British campaign. He refers to a battle with English soldiers across marshes in which his centurions were forced to part swim and wade in muddy waters. Tacitus refers to the fact that by A.D. 69 the Romans were using German auxiliaries, called Batavi, who lived near the mouth of the Rhine and were noted for swimming with their horses in order not to break ranks. Under General Agricola the Roman soldiers managed to swim the Menai Straits in A.D. 78 to rout the Britons on Anglesey.

Swimming was created as a reflection of war and peace at this time by the Romans and has continued to reflect in this way ever since: in war it was used to make war; in peace swimming was used for recreation.

After the Roman Conquest, bath houses

were set up at Buxton, Bath and Wells. At Wroxeter, in Shropshire, an open-air swimming pool has been identified beside the indoor public baths. But although the Romans were the first swimming pool builders in Britain, the majority of swimming was probably done in inland waterways because of the relative inaccessibility of swimming facilities for most Romans.

Swimming was seen as the epitomy of manliness and there are numerous references to the activity in records. It was also seen as a pleasurable activity, primarily for men. The Romans taught their young men to swim with the use of cork floats (an idea not revived until the twentieth century) and by laying them on a rush float to help take part of the bodyweight. At this time, swimming was not recorded as a potential vehicle for competition or racing, although some unrecorded races may have been held across the Tiber.

The most famous swimming exploit prior to the Renaissance was recorded by Ovid at this time when Ovid in *Heriodes* and Virgil in *Georice*[5] refer to Leander swimming Hellespont (modern Dardenelles) to meet Hero. Swimming not for the first time was coupled with love and romance. Despite a mention from Ovid, there are no major works on swimming recorded by the great Roman scholars.

It is reputed that swimming races took place in Japan in 36 B.C., during the reign of Emperor Suigiu.

Swimming was a recreation carried out by many men in the Holy Land in Old and New Testament times; the Dead Sea is, of course, well known because of the assistance that its high salt content gives to swimmers. Despite this, the Bible only contains a few references to swimming. The Book of Ezekiel refers to a 'stream deep enough to swim in'. A Jewish commander known as Jonathan swam the Jordan with his soldiers to escape the Syrians and is mentioned in the First Book of Maccabees. A third reference is made in the Book of Isaiah where the downfall of the people of Moab is envisaged. The writer compares the people to a swimmer sinking as he stretches out his hands. This reference was unfortunate because the 'he' referred to was taken as being

God and the more reactionary members of the clergy saw this as a sign that swimming was an undesirable activity. It wasn't until after 1600 that the attitude of the clergy reversed itself.[6]

In the Acts of the Apostles Saint Paul's shipwreck is related and during the course of the story, which takes place in the Mediterranean off Malta, some of those on board the boat swam for shore while others clung to wood and floated to the shore.

Anglo-Saxons

The Roman Empire died in the fifth century and the Romans were replaced by the Germanic race of Anglo-Saxon invaders. Many of the old standards died with the Romans but most interestingly the few existing records show that swimming continued and was accorded a high status in society. The Germani, the Suebi, as well as the Batavi, were all German people strong at swimming before coming to Britain. The Anglo-Saxon poem *Beowulf* refers to swimming in great depth. Written about A.D. 1000, it still exists today, and the implication remains that a great number of people knew of or could swim at that time, although the situation is imaginary.

Viking swimming

The Viking conquest of Britain lasted from the eighth century to 1468 and many swimming incidents are recorded in Viking literature. Once again the references are limited to men swimming. It appears that swimming was carried out in all kinds of open water – ponds, lakes, rivers and the sea – and often naked as in the case of King Sirgurd Jerusalem-Farer.

Norman swimming and on

The Church continued to have influence over the population of the country and the reference in the Bible in the Book of Isaiah led John Lydgate and Robert of Reading, two Benedictine monks, to write adversely about swimming. On the other hand, John of Salisbury in the twelfth, Giles of Rome in the thirteenth and Jacques de Cessoles and William Langland in the fourteenth centuries were all clergymen who wrote without condemning swimming.

Nevertheless, the Norman influence did not bring swimming with it. There seems to be no specific reason for this other than the fact that the Normans were more interested in other physical skills more associated with fighting and combat. However, there was a fillip for swimming in 1408 when Vegetius mentioned it in his work *Epitoma Rei Militaris*, a handbook for soldiers. Medieval knights were encouraged to conquer the skills of swimming in their armour! *Disciplina Clericalis* by Peter Alphonsi, a twelfth-century Spaniard who came to the court of Henry I, also referred to swimming as one of the seven knightly skills.

One of the most striking features of this whole period is how little swimming is mentioned in literature by the standards of people prior to A.D. 1000. When one also considers that there was less literature in general, it makes it very difficult for the researcher. Chretien of Troye's *The Knight of the Cart* of c 1170, creates the impression that knights found swimming difficult because of their lack of mobility! This is borne out in Thomas Mallory's *Tristram de Lyones* written c 1230.

The early-fourteenth-century English illuminated manuscript known as Queen Mary's Psalter shows pictures of swimmers and water jousting. William Langland, one of our most famous early writers, refers to men swimming in the river Thames in *Piers Plowman*. Whilst on the subject of the river Thames, Kingsford's *Chronicles of London* talks of common people taunting the unpopular Cardinal Beaufort by 'saying that they would throw him in the Thames to have taught him to swim with wings'. Nicholas Orme in his *Early British Swimming* notes that the Oxford Dictionary contains no reference to the word 'water-wings' prior to the twentieth century and surmises that with the lack of bath facilities many Londoners who learnt to swim at this time could well have learnt whilst aided with a type of early water-wing.

Up to 1449 there are very few references to women in water, but now the Bishop of Bath and Wells refers to women bathing – but not swimming – in the warm waters of Bath. For hygienic reasons, people were discouraged from wearing clothes whilst bathing, so much so that people were fined if they wore clothes. Bishop Bubwith objected to this on moral grounds. It wasn't until 1576 that a separate woman's bath was built, known as the Queen's Bath after Anne of Denmark, consort to James I. Certainly the men's bath built by the Romans has stood the tests of time and regular use very well.

Four further illustrations of swimming exist in medieval manuscripts. The Treatise of Falconry by the Emperor Frederick II was illuminated in France by Simon of Orleans in the late thirteenth century and shows a falconer swimming in a pool viewed from above. A depicted figure provides an intriguing insight into swimming strokes of the time. It would appear to show a man lying on his stomach swimming breaststroke with his upper body and kicking in a sidestroke manner with his lower.

Queen Mary's Psalter shows two figures in water: one is treading water, a technique probably employed by soldiers who had to take to the water in battle situations; and the other appears to be performing an alternating leg movement or a frontcrawl leg kick, with an outstretched but open-armed breaststroke movement.

In Très Riches Heures a swimmer is seen on his back appearing to kick with a life-saving kick type of movement, but the figure is not clear. This was painted for John Duke of Berry in France in 1413–16 and shows the river Huice by Etampes Castle. All the swimming figures were males swimming naked.

Swimming in Britain during the 1500s continued to be regarded as a minor activity. Although attitudes vary from writer to writer, there were few references to swimming. The curriculum vitae featured high ability in riding, good manners, shooting and fighting but swimming was an insignificant accomplishment.

The attitude remained that swimming was an aspect of war but it was also being more and more seen as an activity promoting health and recreation.

Swimming was practised by youngsters in London prior to 1600 where it was recorded that swimmers swam in Perilous Ponds in north Bunfield.[4] Swimming was also practised at Oxford and Cambridge Universities. However, there were so many accidents that in May 1571 the Vice Chancellor, John Whitgift, threatened the severest penalties on anyone caught swimming. Undergraduates who were first offenders were to be beaten while Bachelors of Arts were to be placed in the stocks for a day and fined 10 shillings. Second offenders were to be expelled. Attitudes were obviously quite different five hundred years ago to our current encouragement of learning.[4]

British swimming after 1550

A new translation into English by John Sadler in 1572 which covered all the original reference material, was written. The most important treatises written during the sixteenth century were by Richard Mulcaster in 1581, entitled *Positions*, and *The Governor* by Sir Thomas Elyot in 1531. Elyot covers swimming in association with wrestling, running and riding but accords it greater coverage. He notes that English gentlemen had not shown a great interest in swimming, but now was the time to do so: he sees swimming as a means of survival and also, unusually, as an aid to health. By comparison, Mulcaster's work, which showed greater originality, felt that the benefits of health were greater than the military application of swimming. Mulcaster was Headmaster of Merchant Taylors' School in London.

References to swimming in literature now increased: they included Spencer's *The Faerie Queene* in 1596; Marlowe's *Dido, Queen of Carthage* written in c 1588 (Marlowe became aware of swimming while at Corpus Christi, Cambridge); and Shakespeare in over a dozen of his plays.

Probably the first reference to a possible swimming race came in 1595 when Sir John Packington, one of Queen Elizabeth I's courtiers, had a wager with three other courtiers that he could swim from Westminster to London Bridge quickest. The Queen forbade the wager. There is further evidence that swimming was practised at both Oxford and Cambridge during the last part of the sixteenth century. However, this did lead to drownings and accidents and on 8 May 1571 John Whitgift, the Vice-Chancellor of Cambridge forbade any scholar from swimming in Cambridge. Anyone caught doing so would be beaten, placed in stocks or, if second offenders, lose their university place. Imagine that happening today! When Everard Digby published his important *De Arte Natandi* in 1587 it was partly because of the number of fellow Cambridge male students still drowning.

Swimming elsewhere in the world

As with swimming in our own country, a lack of documentation exists but it would seem that swimming was still popular in the southern part of Europe as well as in the Pacific Islands and other traditional swimming islands. Many countries continue to suffer from infectious diseases and illnesses and it's our contention that during this period the ethnic problem with swimming began. Black Africans, Americans and Asians do not swim well and this is often dismissed as an inexplicable social phenomenon. But in these times of disease and plague the river or the lake – the only swimming venue for these populations – spelt danger not only from infestation but also from dangerous animals such as the alligator.

Discovery and increased travel brought more people with swimming ideas to Britain and our spa facilities brought foreign visitors to Harrogate, Buxton and Bath. In addition, the relatively settled nature of Britain around 1600 compared to continuous European wars encouraged these richer visitors. The spas depended on their rich clientele because they had their fair share of poor bathers who came to heal illnesses and injuries.

Spa swimming

In 1615 Queen Anne paid her second visit to Bath and declared that it did her good. She prompted her son, Charles I, and his queen to continue this trend a few years later. Charles II and his queen were also visitors in the ensuing years. The discovery of the medicinal value of spa waters can be attributed to Dudley, Lord North, in approximately 1660. North overindulged and had purchased a country retreat, Eridge House, for the purpose of recovering. It was here one day, whilst out on one of his regular long walks, he became interested in some springs which he discovered on common land. He tried the water and maintained that it did him some good – it might well have done as he was 87 when he died!

Spa swimming was reborn – for one can be sure that the Romans had discovered it first! Lord Muskerry, who owned the land which bore the spring, had it enclosed in 1667 and a bath built of roughly ten metres by 3 metres. The 'dippers', as they became known, were charged two shillings and sixpence (12½p) at the start of the course and ten shillings (50p) at the end and six pence (2½p) on leaving.

The spas, of course, suffered when the Puritans came to power but recovered when Charles II became king. Yellow canvas bathing gowns were used both in Bath and along the river Seine, as records in 1685 showed. (The French possibly copied Bath here.) Despite further visits by Queen Anne in 1702 and 1703, the Bath Corporation had become so worried about public morals that in 1737 they insisted that 'no male person over ten years was to bathe without a pair of drawers and a waistcoat, and no female person without a decent stiff'.

During this period it becomes difficult to distinguish between bathing and swimming. The French had three types of baths: étuves, or steam baths, at spas for medical purposes; the bains or baths simply for cleansing; and a third kind – a steaming brothel where the upper classes spent all day being pleasured. There was a British variety of this last one known as the Queens Bagnio in Long Acre, London. This type of open approach continued throughout the Regency period but was slowly reversed and viewed with some disgust by the Victorians.

Bath lost its popularity from about 1783 when the young Prince of Wales went with his uncle to a little known South Coast spot called Brighthelmstone. He introduced his father, George III, to this small place which was soon to become Brighton. Sea bathing was born. Brighton became George's second home for nearly half a century and so became fashionable for sea swimming; visitors came from all over Europe. The South Coast became more and more popular and by 1789 the King was swimming in the sea at Weymouth in Dorset. In the 1820s doctors were exhalting swimming, along with sea air and salt, as of great health value.

Everard Digby

A number of people can claim to have written the first work specifically on the *sport* of swimming. Among the leading claimants would be Nicholas Wynman, professor of languages at the University of Ingolstadt in Bavaria, who wrote *Colymbetes* in 1538. Colymbetes was derived from the Greek word for swimmer or diver. The work is a dialogue between two people, Pampirus and Erotes, with the former being the author. In the book Wynman indicates that he learnt to swim when he was 13 years of age because his mother felt that swimming would help to develop his physique. This work eventually attracted interest in the Netherlands where it was reprinted three times between 1623 and 1644.

Thevenot wrote his swimming treatise in 1696, based largely on Digby's *De Arte Natandi*. In Spain Pedro Mejia covered swimming in a chapter in his work *Silua de Varia Lection* in 1551, and in Italy Tommaso Garzoni wrote a short account in *La Piazza Universale*.

All these works were relatively undeveloped and it is really Everard Digby, who wrote *De Arte Natandi* in Latin in 1587, who can claim to be the first author on swimming. In his work Digby claimed that swimming is an art, like medicine, war, agriculture or navigation. Unfortunately by writing the work in Latin he limited his potential readership to the upper classes.

Digby asserted that the natural tendency of Man in water was for the feet to sink but for the face to rise. He felt that people could remain afloat without arm or leg movements but that they tended to drown because they used their limbs in 'a disorderly way'. He felt that men were even better swimmers than fish, despite fish spending greater amounts of their lives in water. Man could descend perpendicularly, seek and take hold of objects, swim on his back, stand, sit or throw things in the water, to a greater extent than fish.

Swimming in lakes and rivers in Elizabethan times brought its own special hazards and Digby recommended swimming from May to August. The best, warmer winds to swim in are

To swim like a dolphin, from *De Arte Natandi* (*Illustration: British Library*).

from the south and west, the worst from the east and north. He also advised against swimming at night because it was unhealthy and in the rain because it hurt the eyes and reduced visibility both above and under the water.

Digby advised against swimming near overgrown banks because snakes and toads may spoil the swim. Short grass banks with shady overhanging trees were advocated, with clear unmuddied water, preferably sandy or rocky at the bottom. He also advised that the swimmer go with a companion. If this should prove to be impossible then a fishing rod with a weight on the end to measure the depth before entering was considered a good idea. Lastly, the swimmer should not go in the water sweating.

Digby did not describe lifesaving nor speed swimming of any kind. Terms such as striking and thrashing were used which indicates little idea as how to make the best propulsive use of each limb movement. It wasn't until 1595 that Middleton, who translated Digby's Latin work into English, was able to state that sidestroke was the quickest stroke.

Digby produced forty plates with the treatises and it is those which fascinate the modern reader most. He was certainly aware of swimming like a dog, aware of a form of sidestroke, also of floating upright in the water, now known as drown-proofing, and in his final plate of swimming under water like a dolphin. Previously researchers had considered dolphin butterfly to have been introduced into America in the 1930s, in the same way as most people had not been aware that the Romans had learnt to swim with cork floats, nor Londoners with water wings and forms of rings in the 1550s.[5]

The fact that Digby observed that it was possible for someone to kick with a dolphin-like movement is not proof in itself. Thomas Hardy wrote in 1874 in *Far From the Madding Crowd* that Sgt Troy goes for a swim in Lulworth Cove 'well nigh exhausting himself in his attempts to get back to the mouth of the cove in his weakness swimming several inches deeper than was his wont, keeping up his breathing entirely by his nostrils, turning on his back a dozen times over, swimming *en papillon*, and so on, Troy, resolved at last to resort to tread water at a slight incline. ...'[6]

It is worth bearing in mind that Hardy himself was an enthusiastic swimmer and understood the sport well. 'Papillon' indicates that an overarm butterfly was being swum in the 1870s in a butterfly movement, and this coupled with Digby's reference to it means that we can probably assume that some experiments had taken place by individuals in the 1600s and 1700s in butterfly-dolphin. Butterfly could have been swum in Europe in an unco-ordinated fashion before frontcrawl.

Despite Digby's work, swimming was not considered an important activity to the average member of the British population. By contrast, in Japan the Emperor Go-Yoozei decreed in 1603 that all schoolchildren should learn to swim and that there should be inter-school competitions. Inter-college competitions and a three-day swimming meeting were held in 1810. Japan as a country remained fairly isolated and the message wasn't passed around the world.

To swim on the back, from *De Arte Natandi* (Illustration: British Library).

Christopher Middleton

Middleton wrote his 'Short Introduction for to Learne to Swimme' in 1595 as a foreword to his English translation of Digby's work. Now it was available in a language the everyday man could understand. Middleton added very little but noted of sidestroke that 'this kind of swimming, though it be more laborious, yet it is swifter than any of the rest'.[4] This indicates how slow the other strokes were. Middleton uses the words 'beat', 'thrust' and 'strike' the water. He also talks of 'swimming on the back or on the belly' not of frontstroke or backstroke. The word 'stroke' wasn't used for at least another 150 years but it would appear that stroke may well have been a corruption of 'strike'.

The seventeenth and eighteenth centuries

There is a number of documentary records of swimming during this time. Two more treatises were written which both devote a chapter to swimming: James Clelland's *Hero-Paideia* or the *Institution of Young Nobleman* (1607) and *The Compleat Gentleman* written by Henry Peacham in 1622 follow familiar themes. But *Itinerary*, a work written by Fynes Moryson in 1617, brought a change of direction. With the world opening up to travel at this stage, he recognized the usefulness of swimming to travellers around the world, particularly those who travel on or near water.

During the seventeenth century there were some physiological arguments as to whether bathing should or should not be carried out in hot or cold water. Burton in his *Anatomy of Melancholy* written in 1621 doubts whether bathing in cold water is good for you, but in 1623 Bacon in his work *Historia Vitae et Mortis* argues to the contrary.

By 1646 swimming had moved into the scientific realms for the first time. Sir Thomas Browne in his book *Pseudodoxia Epidemica* looks at swimming from the viewpoint of the scientific revolution. Between 1660 and 1682 great scientific strides were made with the Royal Society discussing and publishing scientific works which commented on swimming. One of the founder members, John Evelyn,[7] noted in 1663 that the Royal Society had considered another experiment in diving. He also mentioned that in 1667 Charles II, who was the Society's patron, 'discoursed with me about swimming'.

Another of the Society's members, the Honourable Robert Boyle, disproved the long-held belief that West Indian swimmers, who were considered to be naturals at this time, could stay underwater for an hour. It had been claimed that Sicilians could stay under four times as long. His tests showed a man remaining under water with artificial support for no more than two minutes. We still hear claims today of the vast periods of time that pearl divers are able to remain under water.

William Percey in his book of 1658, *The Compleat Swimmer*, recommended the skill to females for the first time and when talking about swimming on the back he comments that it is easy to splash oneself 'at every stroke'. This is considered to be one of the first, if not the first written reference, to the word 'stroke'. Percey's work more or less follows Digby with few original thoughts. Melchisdech Thevenot's *L'Art de Nager*, written in Paris in 1696, is a little more original than the work of Percey. He comments: 'It is certain that the Indians and Negroes surpass all other men in the art of swimming and diving.' This makes a surprising comparison to modern times. Thevenot's work which copied Digby completed a full circle back into English in 1699 when it was translated as *The Art of Swimming*.

There appears to have been a growth in the use of artificial aids for learners. Corks and bladders were still in use but special girdles had by now been introduced for assistance. Thevenot also describes inventions which closely resemble the swimming ring and flippers. He talks of a 'cylindrical case made of oiled cloth, and kept open on the inside by iron rings, might be contrived as to tie round one's waist, and fastened to keep the water out, and that alone would save from being drowned'. The flippers were apparently made out of small planes of wood with valves.

From 1720 onwards there are increasing references to swimming as it became more and more popular. In 1726 the famous American independence pioneer Benjamin Franklin was on a River Thames excursion when at the request of the company around him, he took off his clothes, leapt into the water and swam from Chelsea to Blackfriars. As he went, he performed tricks under the water as well as above to delight the spectators. He had learnt many of these activities by reading Thevenot. Franklin can be considered to be one of the first great, early swimming experts. He taught a number of friends to swim and was offered the opportunity of running a swim school in England by Sir William Wyndham but returned to Philadelphia because he was homesick.

His swimming repertoire was second to none. He practiced ornamental as well as synchronized swimming, experimented with types of water skis and used a more highly developed type of flipper than hitherto. (Leonardo da Vinci is reputed to have been the first person to design flippers.) He also designed the first hand paddles made out of two oval palettes, about 10 by 6 in (25 by 15 cm) long with a hole for the thumbs.

Franklin said: 'In swimming, I pushed the edges of these forward and I struck the water with the flat surfaces as I drew them back. I remember I swam faster with the use of these palettes but they fatigued my wrists. I also fitted to the soles of my feet a kind of sandals but I was not satisfied with them because I observed that the stroke is partly given by the inside of the feet and ankles and not entirely with the soles of the feet.' It was a great pity that breaststrokers in the early 1950s had not made the same observation — they may well have saved themselves a great deal of time.

The first known swimming bath in this country was Pearless Head in North London which was built in 1743. By 1800 there were five or six pools and all had diving boards. By now ladies participated in swimming, but bathing sessions were still segregated. It was not until around the turn of the century that mixed bathing became socially acceptable. The dog paddle continued to be used and was used by Slav peoples in Europe, but generally most people used breaststroke and sidestroke.

In 1828 a swimming pool was created out of an artificially enclosed area known as St George's Pier Head in Liverpool. We know that swimming races were held in Liverpool around the 1830s and records show that unofficial races in this country definitely go back to 1791. With the vastly increased interest in the sport, the National Swimming Society was set up in 1837 to organize races in London. The person responsible was John Strachan.

The birth of competitive swimming

1844 is a significant year as far as competitive swimming is concerned. A sensation was caused on 2 April in London when a race took place between two North American Red Indians, called Tobacco and Flying Gull, and a breaststroke-swimming Englishman, Harold Kenworthy. The first Indian home, Flying Gull, covered the $43\frac{1}{3}$ yds (39.6 m) in 30 seconds.

The Times reported: 'Their style of swimming is totally un-European. They lash the water violently with their arms like the sails of a windmill and beat downward with their feet, blowing with force and performing grotesque antics.' Nothing quite like it had been seen in Europe before. The most surprising aspect was that no one had ever really noticed this alternative style before, despite the world's continued ability to travel and the greater flexibility afforded throughout the previous 200 years. It would seem that the crawl had been swum by South Sea Island natives, North American Indians and Hawaiians for hundreds

of years. Kenworthy beat the two Ojibbeway-tribe Indians at Holborn Baths and so Britain stuck with the breaststroke for another 40 or so years.

The National Swimming Society now changed names a few times as various factions wrestled for supremacy in the typical manner so familiar with new and emerging sports. It first became the Associated Metropolitan Swimming Clubs (A.M.S.C.), then the London Swimming Association and on 7 January 1869 the Metropolitan Swimming Association, following a swimming congress in the German Gymnasium at Kings Cross under the presidency of Mr R. Ravenstein. Because this group only operated in London, membership was limited and funds small. As a result in February 1874 the name again changed to something more embracing — the Swimming Association of Great Britain (S.A.G.B.).

The Otter Swimming Club, the country's most influential club, broke away in 1884 after further arguments and formed the Amateur Swimming Union (A.S.U.). A great struggle for supremacy took place between the A.S.U and S.A.G.B. before they both finally dissolved to form the Amateur Swimming Association (A.S.A.) in 1886.

Horace Davenport was mainly responsible for resolving the arguments in these early years. He was President of the Swimming Association of Great Britain from 1880 to 1883 and of the renamed Amateur Swimming Association from 1890 to 1894. As well as being a diplomatic administrator, he was no mean swimmer and won the A.S.A. Championship one-mile race in 1874 and in the succeeding five years. The first winner was Tom Morris in 1869 in 27 minutes 18 seconds. The course until 1872 was from Putney Aquaduct to Hammersmith Bridge on the River Thames. After that it was held in still water. Horace Davenport also won the trophy for the Lords and Commons Race outright. This long-distance race was held over five or six miles in the River Thames and the trophy presented by the Members of Parliament, hence the name. Davenport won between 1877 and 1879.

Meanwhile, Australia was also rapidly developing as a swimming nation and the world's first modern swimming championship was organized in 1846 at the Robinson Baths in Sydney. The 440 yards (402 metres) was won by W. Redman in 8 minutes 43 seconds – just over twice the time taken in modern women's 400-metre races.

A World Championship 100-yard (91-metre) race was then held at St Kilda, Melbourne, on 9 February 1858. Jo Bennett from Sydney defeated Charles Stedman of England. (At this time, there was no amateur/professional distinction with prize money available and side bets in evidence.)

Only ten years later the first national record was recognized in this country by the A.M.S.C. when Winston Cole swam the 100 yards in 1:15.0.

Globally swimming continued to expand with the German Federation being founded in 1882, the French in 1890 and the Hungarian in 1896. The newly formed New Zealand Association (1890) cooperated with the New South Wales Association (1891) in organizing championships down under. The U.S.A. held their first championships in 1877 over one mile, the event being won by R. Weissenboth. Their championships were actually organized until 1888 by the New York Athletic Club.

Interestingly, Scotland was the first country to hold a women's championship, in 1892 – a 200-yard (183-metre) event won by E. Dobbie of Glasgow in 4 minutes 25 seconds. In Austria the First Vienna Amateur Swimming Club held two European Championship races over 60 and 50 metres and these continued annually until 1903.

Returning to developments in England, breaststroke finally started to give way in the 1840s to sidestroke. This became the popular racing style because of the greater speed attainable. In 1855 in London, C. W. Wallis demonstrated a new technique which he had observed the Australian aborigines swimming in his homeland on the Lane Cove River near Sydney. Professor Fred Beckwith employed the new single-arm sidestroke with the arm recovery over the water in winning the English Championship in 1859 and in defeating Deerfoot the Senecca Indian in a professional race in 1861. Apparently one of Beckwith's pupils, a man called Gardener, won the championship in 1860 employing the same technique.

The modern era

The next milestone for English swimming came on 11 August 1873 at the Lambeth Baths when John Trudgeon brought both arms over the water in a 160-yard (146-metre) handicap race. He kept his chest high over the water and

his body flat on top. Trudgeon swung his arms alternately over the water and with each alternate arm pull he made one horizontal breaststroke kick.

Trudgeon was reputed to have learnt the

A spacious American swimming pool in the late 1880s. Note the separate pool for ladies (*Photo: National Archives, Washington*).

stroke from the South African Kaffirs when he lived abroad. This new stroke worked well for short distances but the top middle-distance people, Tyers and Jarvis, and the professional champion Nuttall continued with single-arm-over sidestroke.[1]

The Trudgeon stroke later became used by many people in their leisure swimming and is still employed by a few lunchtime swimmers today. Records are unclear as to when and where Trudgeon picked up this technique. It was also recorded that he learnt the technique by watching Indians in South America during the 1880s. Whichever was the case, the result was that the 100-yard (91 metre) record was reduced from about 70 to 60 seconds in a short space of time.

Tyers, who came from Manchester, began to modify the technique and was followed by many swimmers in the north of England.

Instead of drawing his knees up in Trudgeon fashion, he merely opened his legs wide and then snapped them very quickly together. The kick was made when a pulling arm was at right angles to the shoulder.

Most swimmers during the 1890s were using the single-arm-over sidestroke but both in Australia and Britain other swimmers had begun using the double-over-arm. The difference between this and the single-arm movement was that the swimmer moved from the flat frontal position to the side and then back again during each over-arm cycle. The stroke later became coupled with a sidestroke leg action and has since become also known as Trudgeon (or Trudgen as his name was later misspelt).

In Australia swimming had been in evidence since Captain Cook arrived in the Sydney area but the first regular championships were not held until 1889 at the Upper Pitt Street Baths, Sydney. The outstanding swimmer of the period was W. J. Paddy Gormly and attention now switched to Australia where progress was being made at a greater rate than in Britain. The Americans were even further behind.

Australian swimming at this time was dominated by the Cavill family who had a tremendous influence on the world as a whole. In 1896 Percy Cavill, a left-arm-over sidestroker, won the Australian mile championship at Windsor, New South Wales, but not before his brother Arthur (or Tums as he was better known) had jumped in the water and joined in the race halfway through, thus fouling and injuring Paddy Gormly. Tums was disqualified by the officials and turned professional. Competitive swimming certainly lacks that colour these days!

Their father, Frederick, was English and had established himself using breaststroke during the 1870s before emigrating to Australia in 1878 where he built pools and taught swimming. Whilst in Australia, Cavill and his family happened to make a trip to the South Seas and noticed the natives swimming with both arms over the water. He observed that the leg kick was more of an up-and-down movement in the water and decided to try it himself. On his return to Australia he taught the stroke to his sons and in 1902 his son Richard firmly established it when he swam the 100 yards in England in 58.6 seconds. Asked to describe the stroke after the race, Richard said that it was rather like 'crawling' through the water and the word frontcrawl was born.

Another of Cavill's sons, Syd, went to San Francisco where he taught the new stroke to J. Scott Leary who in 1904 became the first American to swim the 100 yards in 60 seconds.

Frontcrawl was to be the stroke of the future. Syd Cavill claims to have been the man who invented it and that Tums, who later died from exposure after trying to swim Seattle Harbour, was the first man to swim it in Australia. Syd Cavill also revealed in the *Sydney Referee* of July 1914 that on travelling to America he had stopped off in Samoa where he had the hardest race of his life in Apia with a woman who swam frontcrawl quite naturally.

Syd wrote home to Tums telling him how he could swim just as fast using frontcrawl arms with his legs tied together. Tums found exactly the same thing. To prove his point Tums challenged Sid Davis to a race at the Davis' floating baths, Balmain. There was a bet of £5 on the race with Tums having his legs tied together and Sid having all limbs free. Cavill won in front of a packed and highly excited house.

The name of Freddy Lane of Australia must also be identified with this period. At 18 years of age he swam the whole of the mile championship in N.S.W. with both arms over the water, the first time that this had been achieved. The famous Australian coach, Forbes Carlile, observed that Lane synchronized the beginning of each pull with the first movement of the scissor kick which only moved about fifteen inches (38 cm) laterally. This contrasted with the double-over-arm swimmers from northern England who were synchronizing this with the middle of the arm stroke. The two styles met one another when Lane swam against Rob Derbyshire in England. The two dead-heated in a world record for 200 yards (183 metres) of 2 minutes 34.8 seconds. In the 1900 Paris Olympics Lane won the 200 metres proving himself to be the master of the double-over-arm stroke.

It is also in Australia that a counter-claim has been made as to who introduced the name of crawl. It is claimed that George Farmer, one of Australia's top coaches at the time, became so excited at watching a young swimmer, Alick Wickham from the Solomon Islands, that he shouted out 'Look at that kid crawling'. I expect we will never know which came first, although Wickham did swim the race first in 1898.

The race was now on to be the first crawler under one minute for the 100 yards (91 metres). Freddy Lane got close when he defeated Derbyshire and Dick Cavill in 60 seconds in July 1902 in Manchester. Two weeks later Cavill swam 58.8 in a handicap race, but it was Lane who finally officially beat the minute in Leicester on 9 October 1902 with 59.6 seconds. On returning to Australia, Lane retired undefeated by Cavill but Cavill, who

Duke Kahanamoku (U.S.A.), one of
the first group of swimmers to be
inducted to the Swimming Hall of
Fame, Florida. *(Photo: Hall of Fame).*

became known in England as 'Splash' Cavill
because of his stroke, captured the imagination
of British swimmers. It has never been established what rhythm both Wickham and
Cavill, those great early frontcrawl swimmers,
swam with. Carlile in his book puts the case for
two, four or six leg beat kicks which we will
describe later in the frontcrawl chapter.

At the 1896 Athens Olympics all the freestylers swam with the single-arm sidestroke,
but by Paris in 1900 the double-over-arm had
become the fastest stroke for the sprint events.
The Hungarian Zoltan De Halmay, who was
second in the 200 metres to London in 1900
and won the 100 metres in 1904, was virtually
swimming frontcrawl at the 1900 Olympics
independently of Australian, American and
English developments. He brought two arms
over and just trailed his legs.

In America Charlie Daniels, a man of powerful physique, watched what Leary, who had a

leg handicap, was achieving. Daniels was the
first swimmer to master the more regular six-
beat kick identified with American frontcrawl.
It served him well. He won four gold medals at
the Olympics and reduced the world record for
the 100 yards (91 metres) in 1910 to 54.8
seconds. Daniels flutter-kicked his legs six
times to every two arm pulls made. The Great
Hawaiian, Duke Kahanamoku, first of the
swimming Hollywood stars, followed Daniels
by winning the 1912 Olympics, but when
asked where he learnt the crawl he stated that it
was by watching his fellow islanders splashing
around in the water. They had indeed used the
stroke for many generations.

When one looks back now, it might be
difficult to understand that double-over-arm
trudgen swimming didn't die an instant death.
In fact the Australians Barney Kieran and Sir
Frank Beaupaire, along with Henry Taylor
from England, kept winning Olympic titles

15

using this technique right through to 1912. Fellow Australian Cecil Healy went on to master regular breathing instead of intermittent breathing with the new crawl stroke in 1911. In Australia the two-beat kick crawl was very much established for the sprinters. In 1920 the American Norman Ross became the first Olympic winner in a distance event not to use the trudgen kick.

The frontcrawl champions from here on are almost too numerous to mention – Andrew Boy Charlton, Arne Borg, Buster Crabbe, Murray Rose, the Konrads, Dawn Fraser, Shane Gould and Mark Spitz to name but a few. Of them all, Johnny Weissmuller in the 1920s and '30s had a greater influence than anyone else because of his size and grace in the water. He set world records in 67 different events ranging from 50 to 880 yards (45 to 800 metres).

Weissmuller swam with his back slightly arched and a high head position in the water. His leg kick was both powerful and beautifully loose with his feet turned in, a pigeon-toed flutter. He set technical standards that everyone tried to emulate.

'Buster' Clarence Crabbe was important not just as the successor to Weissmuller as the film screen's Tarzan but because he was the first exponent of the very high elbow recovery in frontcrawl. The American technique has deviated very little up to modern times. It would be true to say that the six-beat kick is a little looser and less deep and the elbow recovery less high but there was very little basic difference in technique.

The Frenchman Jean Taris, who also swam at the 1928 Olympics, was important to freestyle history as the first man to breathe bilaterally in

The work of Esther Williams reflected here in her role as a show business, as well as a swimming, star. *(Photo: Swimming Hall of Fame).*

a race. Bilateral breathing is the description used for frontcrawlers when the swimmer first breathes to one side on an arm cycle and then to the opposite side on a second arm cycle. The situation therefore created is one in which a breath is taken every three arm pulls. This particularly suited Taris who had an amazingly high lung capacity. When measured at Sydney University in 1934 his vital capacity was measured as being 6.5 litres.

Esther Williams from Los Angeles was more famous as a promoter of the sport than as a swimmer. Her work in films became a major vehicle for making the sport attractive and as a result the sport grew in America as a public recreation for health, exercise, water safety and fun.

Esther won the American National 100 metres freestyle in 1939 in 1:09.0, a time which was not improved on in the next six championships. Her career was interrupted by the war. She may well have won at the 1940 Olympics. Nevertheless, in that year she showed up with 75 other girls for a job as a female lead opposite Johnny Weissmuller at the San Francisco World's Fair Aquacade. Weissmuller picked her because he was looking for a taller female.

Mark Spitz

Mark Spitz of Arden Hills Club and Indiana University is the world's most famous swimmer since the war. He overcame the disappointment of winning only one team gold medal, when he had been expected to win three, at the 1968 Olympics.

In one of the greatest comebacks in sport, in

17

Mark Spitz (U.S.A.), arguably one of the world's most complete swimmers ever. *(Photo: Arena U.K.).*

1972 Spitz became the first ever performer to win seven gold medals in one Olympics. He demonstrated that supreme swimming skills, allied with determination, will win in the end. His seven gold medals were coupled with seven world records. After this amazing success, Spitz retired and, with his good looks, became one of the most commercially promoted sportsmen of all time.

The Japanese were the other major contributors to modern freestyle swimming. In the 1930s they lead world swimming, winning five out of six possible gold medals in 1932. They trained intensely – soaking up some five miles of training in two sessions each day with flexibility work thrown in. The success of the Japanese frontcrawl in the 1930s and again in the 1950s was partly due to their ability to tailor their swimming techniques to their physique. In the case of many of their stars this meant relatively short limbs, rounded shoulders but extremely powerful leg and calf muscles. Their head position was lower than that of Weissmuller. The hip position was also low with a very moderate bend of the knees making up a continuous six-beat action. The kick was so shallow that the feet didn't come below the level of the knees, the lowest part of the body. But most important of all, was the fact that they were the first swimmers to use body roll in the stroke with the shoulders following the arms in their downward movement on entry. This meant driving the arms forward ready for the pull with very little glide or pause. It also meant that the larger muscle groups in the upper body could be employed more quickly and effectively in their case. Fitting the stroke to the physique was to become a feature of swimming in the years ahead.

Backstroke

Backstroke was the third of the recognized strokes being included in the Olympics programme in 1908 for men and in 1924 for women. The first A.S.A. Championship was won in 1903 by William Call. During the period when trudgen was at its height backstroke mirrored this in an inverted form. The top backstrokers were using a double-arm swing with inverted breaststroke legs.

As with frontcrawl, it soon became obvious that an alternating leg action would produce faster results than an inverted action. Again the stroke developed through double arms to single and alternating arms.

Adolph Keifer who won the backstroke at the 1936 Olympics was the outstanding backstroke personality of the early years. He had a low arm recovery, entered his arms wide and attempted to keep his arms straight under the water when pulling. Many backstrokers copied him.

After the war backstroke styles began to change and as these strokes went in to the 1950s not only did it supply Britain with their first Olympic success for 48 years in the form of Judy Grinham in 1956, the technical nature of the stroke also changed. Backstrokers started to drive their arms back deeper behind their heads on arm entry and to pull with a bend at the elbow and a rotation of the forearm at the end of the movement. Experiments took place in which the kick was dowsed in favour of the arm pull but the 1970s saw the return of the heavier flutter which has remained ever since.

Breaststroke

Breaststroke became a separate Olympic event in 1904 when it became obvious that crawl was so much quicker. Breaststroke was swum in the traditional manner on the breast with the hands projected directly out in front of the face and then with the hands pulled wide and round. In the 1930s some swimmers discovered that there was nothing in the rules to prevent them digging into the water with a double overhead arm stroke.

This was the first sign of a change in breaststroke, the first and ultimately most controversial of the racing strokes. There have been arguments on whether a swimmer ducking his head into his own bow wave is swimming underwater,[8] how perfect the arm and leg movements should be and whether the arms can be thrown over the water in recovery.

The coach at Iowa University, U.S.A., Dave Armbruster experimented with both arms recovering over the water simultaneously, or butterfly arms as we recognize it today. One of his swimmers, Jack Seig, moved from swimming with butterfly arms and breaststroke legs to dolphin legs. Although the experiments started in 1935, dolphin leg kick was considered to be too exhausting despite being recognized as faster. Breaststroke competitors stuck to either traditional breaststroke or butterfly arms and breaststroke legs. The latter was so successful that swimmers employing this stroke started to dominate breaststroke races.

Eventually something had to be done and after the Helsinki Olympics butterfly and breaststroke were separated as racing strokes; 1956 saw the first Olympic butterfly race. Meanwhile, breaststroke competitors exploited another loophole in the rules as the Japanese in particular swam for long distances underwater. Obviously this distorted the rules as it was much quicker to swim underwater.

(Breaststroke became known as the 'silent stroke' as a result.) In 1956 the rules were changed so that only one arm pull and one leg kick were permitted at the start of each length, and so the underwater swimming faded away.

Breaststroke underwent one further change in 1961 when Dr James Counsilman of Indiana University, and his pupil Chet Jastremski, developed a wholesale rejig of the stroke timing. The results were amazing with Jastremski slicing over six seconds off the world 200-metre record within eighteen months. Jastremski took his breath after the beginning of the arm pull instead of at the beginning of the head lift. This non-glide, high-revving stroke required the shoulders to be kept low on the surface and the leg kick to be much narrower in its circular and backward projection than before.

Women's breaststroke since the 1970s has been increasingly dominated by Russians and Germans. The Americans have remained a force in men's swimming but their success has been interspersed with European victories.

For a time breaststrokers continued to swim quite flat on the surface with the shoulders and some swimmers also employed the tumble turn with a two-handed touch, but gradually during the 1970s the stroke came to be swum with more rise and fall. The hips have tended to make a dolphin-like movement in being coupled with this up and down movement.

Britain's tradition of good breaststroke which started with Anita Lonsborough winning the gold medal at the Rome Olympics in 1960 continued in the 1970s with David Wilkie in 1976, Duncan Goodhew in the 1980 Olympics and Adrian Moorhouse in the 1988 Olympics in Seoul. Oddly enough, all four swam with completely different techniques and it has been impossible to identify a British 'style' of breaststroke.

Captain Matthew Webb

A swimming history wouldn't be complete without mention of the legendary Webb.

Captain Webb was the first person to swim the English Channel and this was arguably the most outstanding swimming achievement ever. Born in 1848, Webb earned his place in history when he stepped onto the beach at Calais on 25 August 1875 after 21 hours and 45 minutes. It wasn't until 1923 that this feat was achieved again. Webb left from Admiralty Pier in Dover at 12.55 on 24 August, $3\frac{1}{4}$ hours before high water on a 15 foot 10 inch tide. Webb actually swam $39\frac{1}{2}$ miles because of the tides and averaged twenty arm cycles a minute on breaststroke.

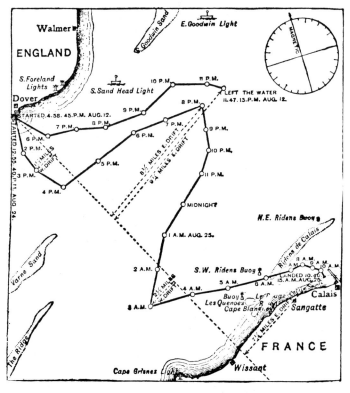

Webb's route compared to the shortest point between England and France (see dotted line). The incomplete line shows a previously unsuccessful attempt. (Map appeared in 'Field' and was reproduced in the 'Badminton Book of Swimming', 1894.)

Webb's achievement made him nationally famous and his feat was commemorated in 'The Hornet' boys' comic.

... and on the matchbox beneath. (Reproduced from 'Captain Webb' by Margaret Jarvis, David & Charles.)

"No one can swim the Channel," said the experts, but to Captain Webb the impossible only took a little longer!

FIRST TO SWIM THE CHANNEL

ON the 24th August, 1875, a small crowd gathered at Dover to see Captain Matthew Webb begin an attempt to swim from England to France, a feat thought to be impossible.

I TELL YOU DOCTOR WILLOUGHBY, THIS IDEA OF SWIMMING THE CHANNEL IS QUITE ABSURD. THE HUMAN BODY CANNOT STAND THE STRAIN!

LATER.

THE CAPTAIN IS SWIMMING STRONGLY.

AYE, LAD, BUT HE'S GOT A LONG, LONG WAY TO GO.

THE HOT SOUP IS PUTTING NEW LIFE INTO ME.

AYE, CAPTAIN AN' THERE'S PIPING HOT COFFEE TO FOLLOW. WITH LUCK, WE'LL SIGHT LAND TOMORROW.

QUITE, PROFESSOR! THE HUMAN FRAME IS NOT CONSTRUCTED FOR SUCH A FEAT!

A JELLYFISH! AAH! I'VE BEEN STUNG!

WEBB IGNORED THE PAIN OF THE STING AND SWAM ON.

THE CAPTAIN IS TIRING. ANOTHER CHAP SWIMMING ALONGSIDE WILL ENCOURAGE HIM.

NO SIGN OF LAND, YET! BETTER GET READY!

LAND AHEAD!

JUST AS WELL, I DON'T THINK I CAN LAST OUT MUCH LONGER!

The weather worsened, but Webb stubbornly plodded on. Encouraged by the shelter of a small boat which put out from Calais, Webb made his last great effort and, finally, at 10.40 a.m., he tottered ashore—the first man to swim the Channel.

The doctors had said it was impossible, but Captain Webb had done the historic crossing in 21 hours 40 minutes of dogged battle against the waves.

Governing bodies

In the early years the work of the A.S.A. covered all aspects of aquatics but some people felt that lifesaving was not receiving the attention it merited and that there was too much concentration on speed swimming. This trend of thought lead to the formation of the Life Saving Society in 1891, later to become the Royal Life Saving Society.

The aims of the Society were announced as being:

(a) to promote technical education in lifesaving and resuscitation of the apparently drowned.

(b) to stimulate public opinion in favour of general adoption of swimming and lifesaving as a branch of instruction in schools, colleges etc.

(c) to encourage floating, diving, plunging and such other arts as would be of assistance to a person endeavouring to save life.

(d) to arrange and promote public demonstrations, lectures and competitions and to form classes of instruction so as to bring about a widespread and thorough knowledge of the principles which underlie natation.

The great pioneers of this new movement were Archibald Sinclair and William Henry.

In 1908 the Fédération Internationale de Natation Amateure (F.I.N.A.) was formed. It was founded in London during the Olympic Games at the instigation of George Hearn, who asked participating nations to attend a meeting to examine problems with the nature of amateurism. Eight nations attended the first meeting: Belgium, Denmark, Finland, France, Germany, Great Britain and Ireland, Hungary and Sweden. The meeting was held at the Manchester Hotel on 14 July.

The purpose of F.I.N.A. at that time was to draw up lists of official world records, organize Olympic swimming and to make a worldwide list of laws to regulate swimming rules in competition.

The Ligue Européenne de Natation was founded in 1927, ostensibly to organize the European Championships. The Championships had been held experimentally for the first time in Budapest in 1926. Nowadays the European Swimming League is responsible to over 40 member countries for organizing the Championships plus the European Youth Championships, two European water polo competitions and a number of diving events.

References
1 *Forbes Carlile on Swimming*, Pelham Books 1968
2 *The Art of Swimming*, Thevenot, Swimming Hall of Fame
3 *Bathing Beauties*, Michael Colmer, Sphere Books
4 *Early British Swimming*, Nicholas Orme, University of Exeter 1983
5 *Swimming Times* March 1953, p 82
6 *Far From the Madding Crowd*, Thomas Hardy
7 *The Diary of John Evelyn*
8 *Encyclopaedia of Swimming*, Pat Besford, Hale 1976

2 Equipment

Swimming is a low-cost sport and very little equipment is needed. You can swim for as long as you want in a public pool for as little as £1.

Because very little equipment is needed, the main expense in competitive swimming is coaching. Many swimmers pay monthly coaching or tuition fees of anything up to £15 for professional coaching – money which in other sports may have been spent on equipment.

The swimming costume

Obviously, the most fundamental piece of equipment is the swimming costume itself. The heavy woollen or all-nylon costumes that we once knew are very much a thing of the past.

Examples of modern swimwear. Women's competitive costumes are designed for ease of movement at the shoulder *(Photos: Arena (U.K.) and Speedo (Europe).)*

Men

A man's costume needs to be lightweight with a cord for tightening the waist. The greater the costume area, the greater the potential for water resistance. In much the same way, a costume which is loose-fitting or fits poorly will create pockets of resistance. The costume should be cut away at the crutch to allow unrestricted leg movements. You should be able to purchase a good man's costume for about £8.

Women

Women's swimming fashions have altered greatly over the years, but there remains a large gap between women's fashion wear and competitive swimwear. It is the competitive swimwear with which we are primarily concerned.

Nowadays there are numerous types of racing costume made by different manufacturers. The costume needs to be free enough at the shoulders for them to be able to rotate and move in any direction. It should be comfortable and not rub on the inside of the armpits and side of the chest, particularly for those swimmers training over distances. (If a costume is rubbing, a small amount of vaseline over the area in question before swimming will help.)

Goggles

Goggles are now an important part of the training bag. Many swimmers find that long training periods in water cause eye irritation and it is therefore important to be able to train with goggles.

On the other hand, they can fall off in race situations. Therefore try to devote some training time to swimming with them in order that this doesn't occur. Always keep a spare pair of goggles in case they break.

Heavy rubber goggles have generally been replaced by lightweight plastic goggles. However, there have been a number of nasty eye injuries, including blindness, which have come about as a result of putting this type of goggle on incorrectly. Never put the plastic strap

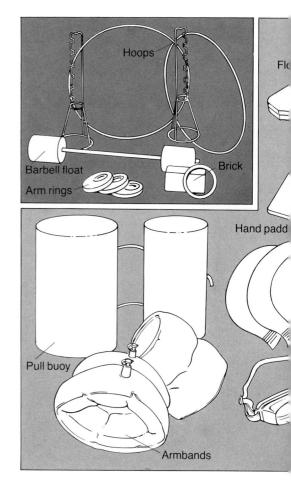

around the back of the head first and the eyepiece on after. The eyepiece can spring back into the eyes. Always put the eyepiece over the eyes first and then whilst holding it over the eyes, stretch the elastic over the back of the head.

Floats

A float is an important artificial aid at all levels of proficiency. Cork floats have now faded out of general use because they are heavier and less manageable. Polystyrene or foam polystyrene are now commonly used and are easy to handle both for legs-only and arms-only drills or attempting lengths or repetitions on both.

It is also possible to purchase foam polystyrene floats mounted on inflatable plastic (the

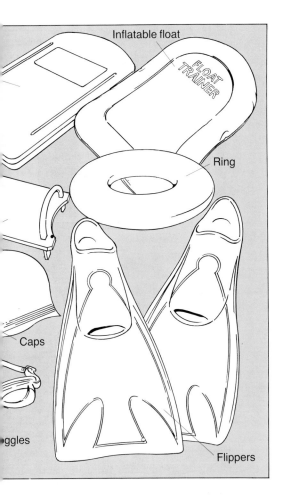

Inflatable float

FLOAT TRAINER

Ring

Caps

ggles

Flippers

same material as that used in armbands). The plastic part can then be blown up (as with armbands) to the level required.

For advanced swimmers the long, originally Canadian-made floats made of foam polystyrene prove to be good for leg practice and aid the correct positioning of both the legs and hips.

Flippers

These are easy to purchase from any sports shop. Some swimmers use them in their training programmes to encourage loose ankles and to strengthen up the ankle region on the alternating strokes.

As with all aids, the use of flippers should be counterbalanced with at least as much practice

again without them. Different sets of muscles are used for the kicking movements and the legs should be given time to adjust to the drop in resistance when the flippers are no longer used and the levers slightly shortened to accommodate this.

Pull buoys

There are numerous devices for isolating the arms for pulling practice – including nylon stockings or tights tied around the legs! A car inner tube section in the form of a 1-in- (2.5-cm-) thick rubber band tends to place the legs lower in the water and to make the swimmer work harder to get the body higher. The result may be that part of the time the arms are not pulling with the body in the normal racing position and therefore different muscles are used.

A pull buoy (see drawing) can be placed either side of the legs and can get the body into the correct position in the water more easily. American swimmers use a tubing system known as the donnut. Either of these aids should form part of the swimmer's kit bag.

Armbands

Arm supports are the province of the learner. They can be bought almost anywhere. Many people prefer to teach learners without armbands or any artificial aids, the argument being that they will have to take them off eventually anyway. Our feeling is that an aid that *encourages* can be of use.

The double-chamber armbands are secure: if one chamber loses air suddenly for any reason, the other chamber can help the swimmer to stay afloat.

Swim belts are made from closed-cell polyethylene and blocks can be removed to reduce buoyancy as the swimmer becomes more comfortable. An adjustable belt is tied around the waist so that the swimmer can freely make arm and leg movements.

This type of aid does tend to make the swimmer a little too vertical in the water.

Earplugs

Earplugs used to be literally plugs. Nowadays, swimmers use plugs which can be moulded to the shape of the individual ears.

Earplugs help to prevent water entering the ears and are most useful for swimmers who find it difficult to balance the pressure of air and water in the ear region. The ears should be dry and warm before inserting the moulding and the swimmer should make sure that the inside of the ear is thoroughly dried after removal.

Noseclips

There is one proprietary brand of noseclips used throughout the world. They consist of a plastic clip which presses in a U-shape over the nostrils and an elastic band which wraps behind the back of the head.

Noseclips are useful for swimmers who are unable to balance the pressure of air inside the nose with the pressure of water outside. The result is that water rushes up the nose. Noseclips can fall off during races and it is better if a swimmer can do without them.

Drag devices

Some swimming squads use training resistances which call on the swimmer to make greater efforts in order to overcome resistances. Some, for instance, use divers' weights belts which make the body lower and the swimmer work harder to get higher.

Other squads use specially made belts with pockets which resist movement through water by increasing the area of resistance beneath the body.

Lane ropes

Over the years the standard lane ropes with cork or plastic buoys have been replaced in many places by the more expensive anti-turbulence lane ropes. These help to reduce waves from lane to lane and are now used at all major competitions. However, unlike back-stroke flags or starting blocks, most local authorities regard them as extras with the onus on the swimming clubs to purchase them. The anti-turbulence lanes help to distribute the water evenly.

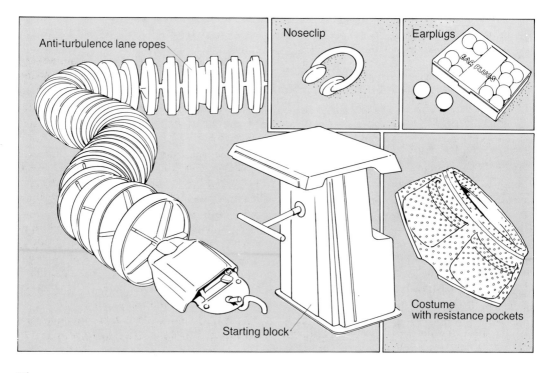

Anti-turbulence lane ropes

Noseclip

Earplugs

Starting block

Costume with resistance pockets

3 Basic Scientific Principles in Swimming

Swimming is a sport where the technical needs of the individual can often outweigh the advantages of the correct mechanical movements in the water. In other words, the sport is not so scientific that a swimmer who is not swimming mechanically perfectly but is swimming with a technique which suits his physique and power cannot still beat another swimmer who employs a technique which is mechanically almost perfect but does not necessarily suit him as an individual.

In such a case, it would not just be stroke mechanics which were important but other basic scientific principles involved with the sport. It is these principles which we intend to examine in this chapter.

Resistance

This can be defined as the forces acting against the swimmer in his efforts to propel himself through the water. One of the major elements of resistance is *drag* which comes in a number of forms.

Overall body drag may be seen as the force which resists the body's forward motion through the water. Overall body or total drag is the sum of three less easily identifiable forms of drag: wave drag, form drag and skin friction.

Swimmers have often felt that shaving the body of hair might help to reduce water friction on the skin, although there has been no conclusive evidence as far as this aspect is concerned. Skin friction is a resistive force which comes about when water moves back along the surface of the skin as the body moves forward.[1]

Skin friction is an important force because the sum total of it stretches over the whole of the body, with the arms and legs as the propulsive limbs being among the major areas affected. We think it is worth noting that a swimmer with a smoother skin appears to move more easily than one whose skin is clearly less smooth. Please note that this is an impression rather than a principle!

Wave drag is caused by waves, large or small, developing on the water's surface in the form of a bow wave as the swimmer moves through the water. The position of the head is an important fundamental here. The head, as the heaviest and first part of the main torso to cut through the water, can have a profound effect on the size of the bow wave. When the head is under the water the majority of the wave drag is reduced; if the whole body is under then the wave drag disappears completely.

The position and size of the wave drag is vitally important to the whole stroke. The bow wave will increase if the head is too high. The barrier of water resistance will also increase in front of the head, if there is too much downward pressure at any time during the pulling and recovery movements of the arms and legs. Obviously, as the swimmer speeds up so the bow wave will increase, and if it is too large

The effect of moving the head on the bow wave. A higher head position leads to a larger bow wave.

The lower head creates a smaller bow wave.

then the fault will be magnified at speed. Bow waves can form against any leading parts of the body that are moving through the point where air and water meet.

The third and most significant type is *form drag*. If one considers that the water is still prior to the swimmer breaking the water in front of him, the area of water displaced by the body is parted and then directed behind the body after the swimmer has passed through it. It therefore follows that the larger the initial area of the body presented to the water, the greater the form resistance. This form of drag is also known as pressure drag because of the differences of pressure between the front and back surfaces of the section moving through that water. High-pressure areas are therefore created at the shoulders, and lower ones around the hips and lateral aspects of the legs. By the time the body has bisected the area of water in this way, there is a fair amount of turbulence at the sides of the body because of this pressure drag. This tends to produce a suction effect in which pockets of water check the movement of the body, particularly the hips and knee areas in their forward movement.

This suction has rather the same effect as in flying when one enters air turbulence.

As the speed of the swimmer increases, the pressure differential increases and the value of the resistance becomes proportionally larger. The level of resistance in this situation can be reduced by placing the body in the correct position in the water. Trying to spear one's way through the water is generally a more efficient approach to that of breaking the water with a large area which is likely to increase resistance. The form drag increases if the legs are considerably lower than the upper body; a

horizontal position is therefore tantamount to good stroke mechanics.

The often-quoted ideal swimming shape of a swimmer with large shoulders, hands and feet and tapering slender hips would appear to increase the form drag because the water is likely to encounter a large area of shoulders. In fact, providing that the swimmer remains on an even axis, the reverse may be the case because this type of body tends to reduce the amount of suction at the hips. A more irregular-shaped body will cause water to flow around these irregular contours at more uneven speeds. The net result is lower pressure on the downstream sides of the body and more suction.

The total body drag represents the resistive force which must be overcome by elements of propulsion if the body is to move forward and maintain a constant speed. To accelerate, the body forces must be less than the propulsive forces. Deceleration comes about if the drag is greater than the propulsive aspects.

The body must be streamlined as much as possible in order to take maximum advantage of propulsive forces. Drag is at its greatest during limb recovery, which is mostly made underwater. It is therefore important that these recoveries are slow and they must account for limbs which face the flow of water which will subsequently increase drag. The use of overarm recovery movements in the three main competitive strokes leave breaststroke at a disadvantage.

Water resistance

Drag therefore creates a great resistance in whatever form. However, water has a natural resistance of its own to bodies moving through it. There is, of course, a fine balance between aspects which propel a swimmer and aspects which resist. A good swimmer can use the natural resistance of water to his advantage in that he can use it to produce greater power, in the same way as a windmill creates power.

The fine balance which can help the body to overcome water resistance can be tilted in favour of the swimmer's efforts to propel himself efficiently by making good use of the hand moving through the water. The hand produces two types of force: propulsive drag force and propulsive lift force.

The propulsive drag force is the resistance encountered by each hand in its effort to pull backwards in order to drive the body forwards. This force is directed forwards if the hand is moving backwards and is at its greatest at the palm, the most stable part of the propelling instrument. The result of the pull backwards is a high-pressure area in front of the palm and a low-pressure area on the back side of the hand.

As with all drag forces, the faster the movement of the hand and the larger the hand, the greater the propulsive drag force. In addition, the greater efficiency with which the muscles of the wrist operate in order to fix the hand in its movement, again the greater the force of the drag. The ideal situation for most arm pulls is for the hand to fix on a certain spot under the water during the pull and for the body to be pulled over and past that point with the greatest power and application. What happens in reality is that the hand moves backwards on the pull and as it moves so the potential for pulling the whole body forward decreases. In other words, backward movements of the hand which are not 'fixed' in the water decrease the potential for moving the body mass forward. Any backward hand movement through the water results in less forward motion of the body per arm stroke. Popular notions may have us believing the contrary, ie if you pull back you will go

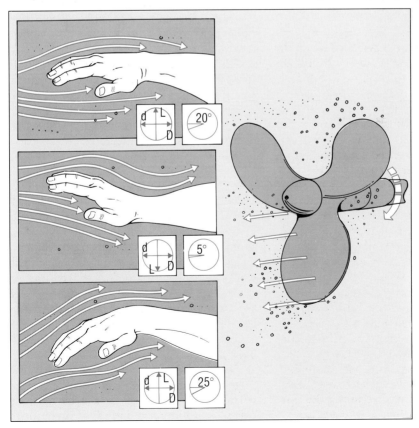

Three different hand positions producing three different flow directions of water past the hand. The propeller, like the hand, uses rotatory movements in order to produce a lift effect and a net movement forward.

forward. In fact the body will move forward more effectively if the hand is fixed and the body pulled over it or past it.

In isolating the movements of the hand, there is a parallel. The drag force against the hand produces some resistance or counterforce, but there must be a hand motion backwards through the water in order to produce the flow past the hand for the drag force in the first place.[1] If the greater drag force was needed to provide a greater counterforce, the hand would have to slip or move backwards even faster, which would result in even less forward body motion by the time the arm reached the end of its stroke.

Propulsive lift force of hand

This type of force is brought about by sculling movements of the hands on such occasions when the use of sculling movements is harnessed in order to propel a swimmer through the water. Typical sculling and lifting movements can be identified during the treading of water. In much the same way as drag force is necessary to increase power on a paddling hand, the hands are required to produce lift force on a blading hand. A hand which is presented to the water at an angle and cuts through large particles of water needs to produce lift force in order to produce this rotation. Lift force is always perpendicular to the path of hand motion.

Bernoulli's principle is probably one of the most important with regard to swimming. It says that where areas of high flow velocity are produced (eg where a limb moves quickly through water) an area of low pressure is also created. Conversely, in an area of low flow velocity, a high-pressure area results. We have already seen an example of this in the case of drag and suction close to the hips. In much the same way, a high-pressure area is created over a lower-pressure area when the hand cuts or blades its way through the water with a small angle of projection between the position of the palm and the direction of the flow past the hand.

If we take the example of treading water, a lifting force can be produced by blading the hands inward and then out in the same horizontal plane without pressing down the water. If we take the arm movements in the sculling situation and lay the swimmer horizontal, the result is similar. The palms of the hands would now face backwards but the blading movements of the hands in a right-angled manner at the elbow produce a similar lift.

If the shoulder muscles contract in pulling the hand and arm back towards the feet, as the hand is blading laterally, the forward-directed lift force would produce a solid pivot and the body would be pulled forward through the water with little hand slip backwards. In other words, the hand once again is better when fixed. Blading the hand through still water at right angles to the direction of body travel, the horizontal lift forces provide a relatively fixed position or counterforce. The body can therefore be moved over a greater distance per arm stroke by contraction of the shoulder muscles. A good swimmer will blade in this way in order to pull in a fixed manner on still water. The result is that the hands don't move directly back through still water but use the best of the still water to their advantage.

Let's now look at the effect of blading in three of the strokes (see diagrams opposite).

In all strokes, the transverse motion blading of the hands coupled with the most forceful contraction of the shoulder muscles takes place when the upper arm moves through the middle part of its range of motion at the shoulder. The applied lift force at this point is able to assist the horizontal movement of the body. It is also when the fixing movement of the hand on the water can produce the greatest power. In frontcrawl and butterfly that point can be seen as being when the elbow is extending and flexing under the body. In backcrawl it is the point where again the elbow is flexing in a vertical plane next to the body at shoulder

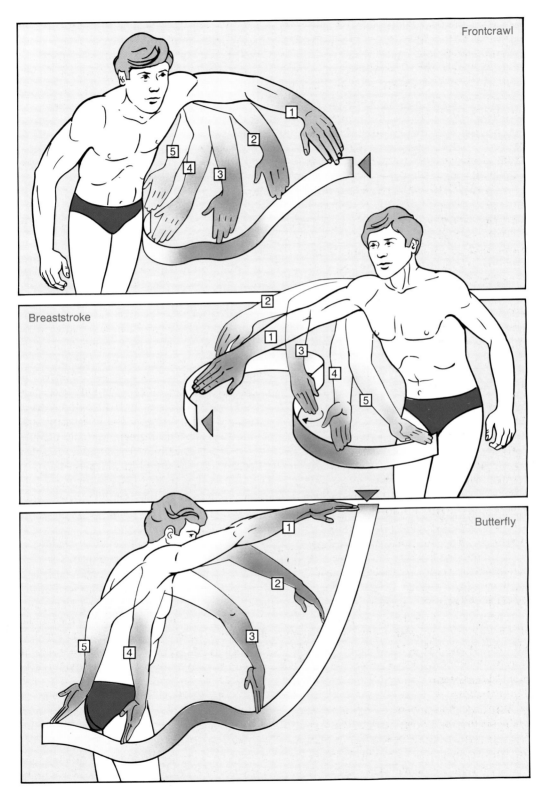

Frontcrawl

Breaststroke

Butterfly

31

level. In breaststroke it is when the hands scull outward and then cut back in an almost hand-clapping movement.

Having identified three forms of drag, we can now also identify three forms of resistance. Firstly, there is viscous drag. Water viscosity may be seen as 'stickiness' or a form of internal friction. It means the power of resisting a change in the arrangement of the molecules. Obviously, it's easier to go through water than through other liquids such as syrup which have great viscosity. The degree of viscous drag is determined by the mass, shape and speed of the body going through the water. It is therefore important that the body lies correctly in the water.

The second form of resistance, eddy currents, is closely associated with form drag. In effect it means that, as water is still and the swimmer is moving through that water, a swirl or eddy currents occur behind the front part of the swimmer.

The final form is surface friction. This comes about because in the case of swimming the surface of one substance, ie the body, is moving over and through the surface of water. A retarding effect therefore takes place.

Buoyancy

When anything is placed in a liquid, upward force or upthrust acts on it. The effect of this upthrust is to make that body apparently lose weight. Stone boulders when put in water have an upthrust on them equal to about four-tenths of their weight. During the Lynmouth flood in 1952 twenty-ton boulders were moved down the main street because their apparent weight was only about twelve tons and they were therefore easily propelled by the force of moving water.

Archimedes' famous principle states: 'When a body is wholly or partially immersed in a fluid it experiences an upthrust equal to the weight of the water displaced.' Water is therefore the necessary medium to measure specific gravity of any substance. The formula used is: specific gravity of a substance = weight of any given volume of substance. Measuring the specific gravity of bodies which float in water is more difficult because a sinker must be employed to immerse that body fully. The weight of the sinker can then be accounted for. For example, in the case of cork, which has so often been used for kick boards in the past, the density of cork is less than that of water so the weight of water displaced is greater than that of the cork itself. Following Archimedes, the cork is affected by an upthrust equal to the difference between its own weight and the weight of water it displaces.

Flotation

When a piece of heavy iron is placed in water it sinks because it is denser than water. But when a piece of wood is placed in water it sinks until the weight of water displaced is just equal to its own weight.

Much the same happens with the human body on diving into the water. The Law of Flotation states that a flotating body displaces its own weight of the fluid in which it floats. The density of fresh water is 62.5 kg/m³ while the specific gravity is 1. The specific gravity of sea water is higher at 1.03, hence the capacity for faster swimming in sea-water pools simply because the body floats more easily in such water.

For a body to sink in water, the force of gravity must be greater than that of the upthrust produced by that water. The degree to which a body remains partially submerged is also determined by the denseness of that body.

Flotation of the human body

The human body has a density fractionally less than water, though this can vary from individual to individual. As the specific gravity of humans is around 1, it should be possible for most people to float with at least part of their body above the water level. Men are slightly more dense and therefore poorer floaters than women.

The capacity of the human body to float can also be affected by filling the lungs with air. In addition, the head and upper legs are more dense than the rest of the body. People who have more fatty tissue tend to float more than people with heavy, dense bones. Flexibility of the human is therefore important because it can affect weight distribution and the capacity to float. The ability to float is in converse proportion to skeletal and muscular density and in direct proportion to chest and abdominal buoyancy.[2]

People with a specific gravity of less than 0.97 should be able to float reasonably well under all circumstances. For competitive swimming it is estimated that as a ratio to overall bodyweight, the amount of fat in a male swimmer should be between 6 and 12 per cent and in females 10 to 18 per cent, with sprinters having smaller amounts than distance swimmers.

Density

Equal volumes of different substances vary considerably in mass. The density of a substance may therefore be defined as its mass per unit volume, which is normally measured in grams per cubic centimetre (gm/cc). Water has a density of about one gm/cc owing to the fact that the kilogram was originally intended to have the same mass as 1000 cc of water at 4° centigrade.

Centre of gravity and balance

Balance is a very important aspect of both poise and streamlining in swimming. The Principle of Moments states that when a body is in equilibrium the sum of the anticlockwise moments about any point is equal to the sum of clockwise moments. This remains important to swimming levers because it means that the force applied at any point multiplied by the distance at which it is applied from the fulcrum must have a balancing force for the body to be streamlined, particularly in the more difficult element of water.

On land, the weight of the body is seen as the force with which the earth attracts it. This does not apply in water because of the upward thrust of water. Out of water, the centre of gravity is therefore the point of application of the resultant force due to the earth's attraction on it. There is, of course, a water equivalent which acts on both the swimmer's stability and ability to roll, known as the *centre of buoyancy*. When an object is immersed in a liquid, its weight acts downwards through its centre of gravity and the upthrust of water acts upwards through the centre of buoyancy. The centre of buoyancy is the same as the centre of gravity of the displaced liquid and is some few inches above the body's centre of gravity, which is normally equivalent in height to the upper third sacral bone in the vertebrae.

When the swimming body is stable the centre of buoyancy is vertically above the centre of gravity. When they are not vertical the body is not stable, but this position can be re-established by rolling. Swimming tends to result in rolling about a horizontal axis or rotating around a vertical one.

In order to retain balance, swimmers constantly have to adjust their limb movements. For example, a deep kick on the right leg in frontcrawl is counterbalanced by a compensatory movement on the left arm and vice versa.

The effects of Newton's Laws on swimming

Sir Isaac Newton's work *The Mathematical Principles of Natural Philosophy*, written in 1687, has formed the basis for laws of motion and their effect on swimming mechanics. They were as follows:

(i) Every body continues in its state of rest or of uniform motion in a straight line unless compelled by some external force to act otherwise.

This means that a body would continue to move at uniform speed in a straight line if there were no forces to oppose it. Unfortunately this does not apply in the case of swimming because the resistance to movement is so great that the human body almost immediately comes to a halt when propulsion ceases. Compare this to the more streamlined fish which seems to glide at the end of movements for longer periods, seemingly without any extra propulsion. This law is known as the Law of Inertia.

(ii) The second law states that the rate of change of momentum of a body is proportional to the applied force and takes place in the direction in which the force acts. When such a force does operate, the consequent change in velocity is directly proportional to the amount of force causing the change and inversely proportional to the mass of the object.

In the case of swimming it means that to accelerate in a swimming race will require a proportional amount of force to create that change in velocity. Both of the first two of Newton's Laws underline the degree to which it is necessary to maintain steady pace and to apply a steady rate of propulsion to all available limbs.

(iii) The third law, which is the Law of Reaction, is considered to have important applications for swimming. It states that to every action, there is an equal and opposite reaction. It is, however, appropriate to remember that this applies in all directions. For example, a freestyler who pushes his head down too far will lift the hips too high, or vice versa. The limits are not just applicable to the arms and legs but to the body as a whole. When a body develops momentum, the supporting surface or other object against which it applies its force develops an equal and opposite momentum. Momentum is the product of mass multiplied by velocity.

A lateral arm pull in swimming will produce a reaction in the opposite direction at the hips and a further reaction at the feet. The movement of the feet will be equal in strength to the movement of the arms. The further from the centre of buoyancy that both the action and the reaction are made, the greater the effect on the streamlining and poise of the stroke. It is therefore important that all movements bear that in mind. We will examine the results of this law and its effect in later chapters.

Theoretical square law

A further law which relates to gases and liquids states that the resistance a body creates in water varies approximately with the square of its velocity. Counsilman points out that the practical application of this law to swimming strokes can be found when a recovering arm enters the water.[3]

If a person throws his arm twice as fast as before, he creates four times as much resistance to forward progress. In the pull phase the swimmer who doubles the speed of arm movement creates four times as much propulsion if he employs the same technique. The energy expenditure trebles with the speed of the muscle's contraction. In the case of the pulling arm, the energy expenditure is increased eight times in order to pull at twice the speed. This is a great amount of energy and, according to Counsilman, explains why so much energy is used and why swimmers tire when windmilling and thrusting with their arms.

It also follows that middle distance swimmers with a higher stroke turnover require great amounts of energy to increase their stroke frequency. This capacity has to be mostly developed through training and the process of adaption.

Force, work and power

Force is a push or pull exerted against something. It can be described in terms of its magnitude, direction and point of its application.

The magnitude of muscular force as applied to swimming will depend on the proportion and number of fibres contracting. As we shall see later, different types of muscle fibres and their ability to contract at different rates are important physiological ingredients.

In terms of swimming mechanics, work is the result of the amount of force expended multiplied by the distance over which the force is applied.

Power, which applies to the sprint events, is the amount of force applied multiplied by the time it takes.

Levers play an important part in the relationship between force, work and power. A swimmer with longer levers stands a greater chance of creating more speed because both force and power can be applied over a greater range. The one important variable is the time it takes.

When a swimming movement or force is applied to a lever, the lever turns about a given fixed point, or fulcrum, and overcomes a resistance or weight. Swimming, of course, presents its own special resistance through the nature of water etc.

We can therefore identify three important points as far as levers are concerned: the point about which it turns; the point at which force is applied to it; and the point at which resistance is applied. There are three arrangements of these levers as shown in the diagram.

The area between the point of force and the fulcrum is known as the force arm of the lever whilst the distance from the fulcrum to the point of resistance is known as the resistance arm. Where the force arm is longer than the resistance arm, force and subsequent propulsion in swimming will result. Less effect is required to overcome resistance here.

A lever of any class will balance where the force arm and the product of the force balances the product of the resistance and the resistance

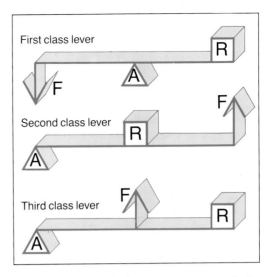

arm. As far as body levers are concerned, the force arm is shorter than the resistance arm. Anatomic levers tend to favour speed and range of movement at the expense of force.

The first and third class levers are the most relevant to swimming. In the frontcrawl and backstroke leg kick, for instance, the thigh, lower leg and foot act as a series of individual levers. By creating a series of levers, the force arm remains greater than the resistance arm.

Strength in swimming

Often we talk about a swimmer being strong in the water; what we are usually saying is that that swimmer is fast. How is this swimming strength developed? Frequently, it is a combination of power and endurance and it is difficult to identify greater proportions of either in a given swimmer.

In common with all sport, swimmers develop specificity in their conditioning. In physiological terms, specificity is regarded as the area where the effects of training are specific, or limited not only to muscle groups being used but also to the way in which those muscle groups are used. This specificity is heightened because of the degree to which swimming levers are subjected to the resistance of water − a feeling that one wouldn't get in most other sports.

Even in relaxation, there are always some muscle fibres in a partial state of tension, known as *muscle tone*. Muscles contract after receiving messages from the nervous system informing them to do so. The fibres then create a tension against the tendons attaching the muscle across a joint and, by the use of one of the three levers already described, they pull the bones of the joint closer together. The amount of weight that this particular tension can hold against gravity determines the strength of the contraction. Such a movement is known as an *isotonic contraction*. Obviously during such a contraction the amount of force that a muscle can apply is dependent on the length of that muscle and on joint angle, which increases as the muscle length increases.

The shortening of levers against the resistance of water and the hands often results in greater strength within the movement.

Swimming power

This type of force has particular relevance to the sprint events. From the point of view of mechanics, power equals work divided by the time it takes to perform that work. There is, therefore, an important difference in swimming as in any other activity between force and power. Force is the measure of strength being applied at any given point during a stroke.

If we take the breaststroke arm pull as an example, force can be measured at any time from the parting of the hands from the extended position to the end of the pull in front of the face, and a reading can be given which would demonstrate the amount of tension at any one stage. By comparison, work is the force applied during the whole of the arm cycle, while power is the speed or rate at which that work is done.

Swimming power can be developed in the weight room, but the ability to overcome drag or resistance requires efficient stroke mechanics and plenty of time in the water. Power is the major component of physical strength in swimming. Work and force play lesser roles. Tests have shown that as swimmers increase their power on dry land so their speed has increased in the water, all other factors being equal.

References
1 'Swimming Biomechanics Resistance and Propulsion', Katherine Barthles, *Swimming Technique* Autumn 1977
2 Noel Bleasdale in *Swimming Times* May 1952
3 *The Science of Swimming*, James Counsilman, Pelham Books 1968

4 Learning and Improving

Unlike many sports, swimming is an activity which can be learnt and enjoyed at almost any age. There are literally no barriers – not even ill health.

Learning as a baby

Great success has been achieved in the last twenty years with teaching babies and young children to swim. Some people, though, mislead themselves into thinking that a baby of six months who is taken to the pool and acquainted with it will remember what he learns on returning to the pool at five or six years old.

These early stages should be seen as a first taste but not really as a means of getting babies to swim long distances. It should be fun, the movements easy and relaxed with as little strain on the breathing as possible. All babies possess a certain amount of natural buoyancy and can make small propulsive movements. They can't unfortunately keep their heads above the water – they simply lack the strength. Many can move short distances intuitively on their backs or on their stomachs, slightly under the water with their faces in. There is no great point in placing pressure on a baby by getting him to swim distances underwater on one breath.

At a very young age a baby picks up messages which are automatically transmitted by the parents when they are holding the baby: a parent who can swim and is confident is therefore less likely to transmit fear.

Start in the bath at home – the bathroom is a familiar surrounding for the baby and the atmosphere is warm and comforting without the noise of diving boards, shouting, splashing etc. Go in the bath with your baby. Fill the bath up to about threequarters full. Support your baby by holding him under the armpits from behind. This is best done with the parent lying or sitting on his back; the parent can then wrap his hands under the armpits so that the thumbs rest just above them in front of the shoulders.

The baby is now ready to be submerged or to submerge himself. The baby will often make automatic kicking movements so that the knees are bent and the lower legs bicycled along the surface. Slight propulsion can result. During the first nine months of life the baby will be able to adapt naturally to the breathing, but don't extend your baby with regard to breathing, either in the bath or in the pool. Toys can be a useful attraction in the bath, particularly if the same toys are transferred to the learner pool later on.

Unfortunately it is difficult to get the baby used to swimming on his front in the bath. If you've been lying on your front, get out of the bath and then from the side of the bath gently hold your baby under the chin and let him move in any way (providing it's horizontal) that he can. You'll find that you don't encounter the problem of your baby suddenly bending his knee and curling up as when he is on his back, but you will have the difficulty of controlling the neck and head when the chin drops suddenly.

If you're going to wean your baby on armbands, it's a good idea for him to wear the bands in the bath in order that he can get used to them before moving to the main pool. Breathing is another thing which can be helped by time spent in the bath. Although this happens naturally in many cases, try to give your baby some idea by letting him ape you. Blow on his face and then blow bubbles lightly yourself in the water. Then blow on his face again and release your grip from under the armpits so that he slowly sinks just a little way under the water. Hopefully he will have associated with the breathing before sinking.

It is also possible to control your baby in a puppet-like fashion while he lies on his stomach in the water. Take two tea towels: place one in a U-shaped manner so that it is slung under the hips, place the other in a similar manner under the chin. Be very careful with the towel under the chin in order to ensure that the towel doesn't slip under the throat and restrict the breathing.

Transfer to the pool

These early breathing, kicking, and hand-splashing movements should now be transferred to the pool. It is important that you go into the water with your baby and go back to the blowing-on-the-face type of activity. Lightly jumping your baby up and down can be fun too. Try blowing on the face and then submerging your baby's body. Bob him under and then lift him again (obviously you can't do this with armbands).

When this has been accomplished, the up-and-down feel through the water should alter to a horizontal propulsion through the water. This can only be achieved with the help of a second adult so that the baby can be projected from one adult to another. A very light forward push is then followed by the baby making walking movements through the water until it sinks and has to be picked up by the other adult.

This will help your baby with his forward movements. If you prefer him to be in his armbands most of the time then it's wise to give him a taste without in the above manner and to try both swimming with and without them at each session.

Swimming on the back, first attempted in the bath at home, can continue in the pool with the parent holding the baby behind the head. This will get your baby used to having his ears under the water and it is again possible for a baby to swim submerged for short distances by splashing his knees and feet. After nine months of age you may find that your baby may lay curled but rigid on his back without moving. Don't worry about this – it is quite normal. Persist in a gentle manner until kicking recommences.

Finally, we'd like to give you a few points to bear in mind when teaching babies:

1 Make sure both the pool and the swimming pool air temperatures are warm enough.
2 Take your baby out if he becomes unhappy for any length of time.
3 Don't stretch your baby to the limits of the effort he can make. Remember you are only preparing for the future.
4 Take your baby at least once a week but not more than twice. The period of the swim should not be greater than half-an-hour.
5 Try to always talk to your baby throughout and remember to encourage.
6 Doctors recommend that young babies of less than six months shouldn't swim in a public pool until they've had all the standard inoculations, but swimming in the bath tub can be a help at this age.

Learning between 1 and 4 years

Continue to try to encourage your child. Regular swimming on the basis of a little often will do no harm. In the early years, a half-hour session during the lunch hour will be sufficient.

Lunch times are normally less crowded and therefore better for little children.

Breathing remains one of the great difficulties simply because it requires strength in the neck and upper body and most children do not possess the necessary strength until they are at least three-and-a-half years old. There's nothing to stop a child swimming with his face in the water in the meantime.

Nervous children should be allowed to get in the water steadily and to stand in very shallow water or to sit over the edge with their feet splashing. Each new step should be introduced gradually. Getting the face into the water can be a problem and an ability to do this may hold up the introduction of dog paddle. It might be worth returning to the wash basin or bath at home. Try exercises like the child counting the number of fingers you are holding up or submerging on the pool steps to collect strategically placed coins.

Introducing new movements and strokes

The frontcrawl leg kick

People of any age may wish to start by learning the dog paddle or frontcrawl leg action and this section, although it is related to the young swimmer, is applicable for any age group.

Young children often find that kicking whilst holding on to a float actually sends them backwards in the water until they get the knack of getting the body in a position where the legs can kick propulsively. Floats can be difficult to control, therefore try to go to the pool during an off-peak period. Take a float and stand in the shallow part of the water. Hold the float at the end so that the thumbs are positioned on top.

Now kneel in the water or crouch so as to lower the shoulders down to the level of the surface of the water. Stretch the arms out in front and very gently push yourself, either with your knees or feet, off the bottom so as to straighten the body along the surface. Try this with or without armbands according to your standards. If this feels comfortable and balanced, try it again, stretching out further.

If you don't feel confident enough for this, start by kneeling on the bottom and aim to merely stretch the feet backwards without pushing the body forwards. This can be achieved by lifting the knees off the bottom first of all and by feeling water pressure on them. Put them back on the bottom. Then keep lifting the knees until you feel confident enough to point the toes. You will then find you can glide forward in a balanced manner.

Now you can start to kick by pointing the toes and then straightening the knees. Try to shake the feet off as well as point the toes, so that the ankles are loose and relaxed. The power of the kick should come from the upper leg as described in our frontcrawl chapter.

The dog paddle

Children of four years and above should be able to make pulling movements with the arms. The dog paddle is a useful all-purpose stroke for children because they don't have to recover the arms over the water.

Get the swimmer to stretch out with his fingers in a dog-like swimming manner. The arms should be straightened at the elbows on the recovery and the swimmer should aim to pull with his hands and forearms, not just with the hands. The pull should continue back to the stomach and then recover forward again. The stroke can be swum with the head up and head down.

The glide

When the swimmer has mastered the frontcrawl legs and dog paddle and has dispensed with the armbands by releasing air bit by bit, he is now ready to master the glide.

The glide is an important movement in the swimmer's future development. It can be taught whilst the swimmer is learning to kick, but it is more effective to wait until he has more balance and is more streamlined. You can glide faster than you can swim and that provides the rationale for making the movement in the first place. It is therefore important to try to lengthen the glide as far as possible.

Start with the shoulders and chin on the water surface. Stretch the arms out behind and hold the gutter or rail with the hands palms downwards. The knees are bent and the feet brought up under the body so as to rest parallel with one another against the wall.

The first move the swimmer makes is to release his hands from the wall. He then drops his hands under the water and draws them, palms facing down, in a semi-circular pattern until they are close to the ears. In the meantime, the swimmer has dropped his head under the water. The arms continue on their forward path by straightening at the elbows. As they begin to straighten the swimmer pushes from the wall by squeezing the wall with his feet. The hips have dropped lower in the water in the time that it has taken to draw the hands up to the head.

This should mean that the push is made with the body about half a metre under, where the water is less disturbed and the movement stronger. The hands are brought together during the push to make a hole for the head and to streamline the movement.

Other early fun

Floating movements such as a star-shaped float, mushroom float or floating in a star shape on the back help to develop confidence as does diving down for a brick or a surface dive.

The backstroke leg kick

Normally a swimmer will start by mastering the prone movements of the dog paddle and its kick. A few swimmers will be more comfortable the other way up because of the fear of having their face near the water.

If we begin once again by kneeling in the water, or by standing with the knees bent so that the shoulders are down on the surface, then the body can quickly get to the correct position without disturbing the surface too much.

First rest the head back on the water so that

Survival jump

Float

Float on back with aid of armbands

the middle section of the back of the head rests on the surface. There should be no strain on the neck and the weight of the head should be carried by the water. When you can feel the weight of the head being carried by the water, bring the knees up to the surface and point the toes. Try this several times until you are confident.

You are now ready to introduce the leg action. Throughout the kick, concentrate on blowing out through the mouth more than on breathing in. The leg kick should be made from the hips by way of an alternating up and down kick. The recovery or down kick should move down until the feet hang diagonally from the

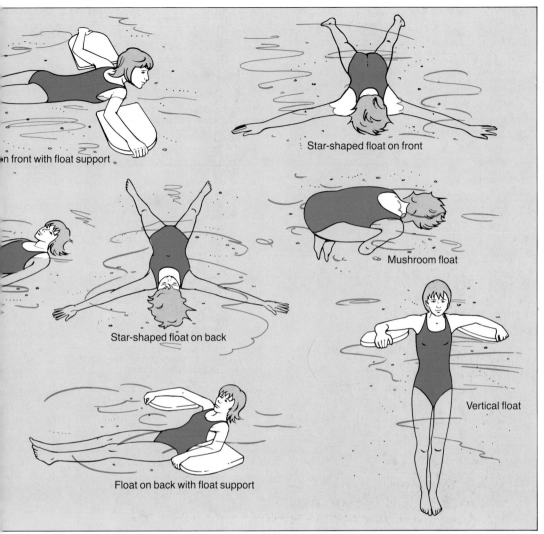

n front with float support

Star-shaped float on front

Star-shaped float on back

Mushroom float

Vertical float

Float on back with float support

knees towards the bottom.

Meanwhile the other leg should be pointed at the toes with the knee extended as it drives upwards. The kick should be strong but only the toes should break the surface. The youngster should be told to try to kick a football off the surface and to a point about 30 centimetres into the air. The knees should not bend on the up kick and should stay under the surface. The ankles should remain loose on the down kick and flexible on the up kick in order to achieve a whipping movement.

If the swimmer is still not confident about floating or kicking on his back, he can try floating with a float under each arm. This can be managed by wrapping the lower arms over the floats in order to provide greater buoyancy. The arms are held out straight at either side in order to stabilize the body around the shoulder joint. Alternatively, the swimmer can carry a float behind the head but this tends to make it difficult to adopt a good head position in the next stages of development. It's better to hold one float in both hands with the arms held out straight so that the float rests over the pelvic girdle on the surface.

As the swimmer becomes more confident, he can adjust his head which can be made more streamlined by tucking in the chin and looking slightly towards the feet.

Watermanship and confidence development

The backstroke and frontcrawl leg actions along with the dog paddle have now developed but the young swimmer should continue to develop in confidence, either by working in a group or as part of a team.

In recent years we have been involved with the development of asthma swimming groups. Young asthmatics have become much more confident and more able to cope with life in general through swimming. Many of the groups play games and take part in watermanship activities to break up any monotony which might build up as a result of just practising their swimming.

There are literally hundreds of such activities but we have listed just a few examples. Most of the games are used by swimming groups whether asthma sufferers or otherwise. We are, however, grateful to Sheila Dobing and Win Hayes of Dunfermline College of Physical Education and Charles Ramsey of Edinburgh Royal Commonwealth Pool, for producing the following examples[1]:

Practical activities for building confidence, watermanship and endurance [2,3]

Group activities

Musical hula hoops	*Use and observations*
Coloured plastic hoops are floated on the surface of the water – one less than the number of participants. Players swim/move about the activity area, shallow or deep water being used according to ability levels. When the music stops each player ducks under water and into the hoop. One hoop is removed each time.	In normal circumstances the player without a hoop would be eliminated, but this reduces participation and creates disappointment. Allow all children to continue to participate. Only those who get into the final hoop become the winners. More than *one* child may get into any activity. Useful activity because children can participate within their own limitations: work at their own speed, swim or tread using any method of choice.

Simon says	
All players form a circle with one designated leader. Different participants should become leaders. Leader calls out activities to be performed eg 'Put your hands on your head and jump up and down'. Participants should only begin the activity if the instructions are prefaced with the words 'Simon Says'. Any watermanship skills may be used.	With teacher guidance or intermittent guidance, regulation of the physical demands of the skills is possible. Every energetic command followed by subsequent calming activities = minimal physical demands. Wide range of challenges may be included.

Obstacle courses

Obstacle courses are regulated by the types of equipment readily available and must be devised accordingly. The course could include:

(a) Suspended balloons to be touched

(b) A post, on upright coloured cones placed on the bottom of the pool which the participant is required to go round.

(c) A series of ropes attached the width of the pool, to go under, over, under etc.

(d) Hoops suspended under the water, held by metal skittles or weighted ropes. In and out activities.

Changing demands on breathing, inhalation, breath holding, portable trickle breathing, during some under water activities. Good movement exploration activity.

Poison

Participants join hands in a circle. Some floating object is placed in the middle of the circle, anchored on a weighted rope. The group attempts to pull the circle in such a way that some player touches the 'poison'. When a player touches the poison he is eliminated. The last player remaining in the game is the winner.

Participants may grasp a rope rather than each others hands. Good stabilization game. Can be played by the less-confident swimmer – head may if necessary remain above the water throughout the activity.

Number retrieve

Participants form a circle and are given numbers around the circle. The leader calls a number and simultaneously throws a slow-sinking object into the water in the centre of the circle. The player whose number was called must retrieve the object before it reaches the bottom of the pool.

This may be played by beginners in standing-depth water, or in deeper water by those with greater skill.

The game can be played for points or on a time basis.

Traffic lights

The teacher holds up a large red, orange or green circle, or orange/red. The swimmers move about the pool responding appropriately to the demands of the respective colours: red stop, red/orange prepare to move, green travel, orange slow down to stop.

Varies the speed of activity required. Allows for rest periods. Demands full attention. Any stroke may be used.

Tread tag

Players swim about in deep water with one player designated as 'it'. A player may be tagged while swimming and before he begins to tread water. If a player is tagged while not treading water he or she becomes 'it'.

Good activity for development of endurance. Different methods of treading water may be encouraged. Development of the understanding of the necessity to only use the required degree of effort in relation to specific activity.

Treasure hunt

A variety of objects, each assigned a point value, are sunk or floated in the pool. (Heavier objects and those which sink should be allocated higher point values.) The games may be played with a group or with teams.

At a starting signal players leave the poolside and retrieve as many articles as possible before a stop signal, or until no further objects remain to be retrieved. The points value of the treasure is counted for each individual or team; the player or the team with the highest score wins.

Matches different ability levels. Participants may submerge to different depths (some objects may be chosen which sink more slowly).

Musical statues

Players move about a set run, using any stroke or method of propulsion. When the music stops they must establish a position in which they remain very still until the music restarts.

Teacher can control the duration of rest. The method of propulsion between each rest may also be stipulated to create specific demands or variety.

Dive and collect relay

Variety of sinkable objects tossed into the pool. This may be played by swimmers sitting on the bottom or surface diving to collect as many objects as possible before the signal to stop. The swimmer with the largest number of objects is the winner. Alternatively, the team members may enter the water individually, competing against another team, and return to the side bringing only those objects which they have retrieved by submerging once only. Second team member enters the water.

Small teams should be used: 3 or 4 participants. This game affords opportunity for three swimmers on the side to have a recovery period without it being perceived as such.

Log roll

Mark off spaces for goals at opposite ends of the pool or the sides of the pool. One player – 'the log' – floats on his back in the centre of the playing area midway between the two goals. All other players swim in a circle around the log. The log without warning suddenly rolls over and chases the players. Players attempt to reach one of the goals without being tagged. All players who are caught must join the log and float in the middle of the pool, with the original log. The last player caught becomes the first log for any subsequent game.

Variation in energy expenditure: periods of greater rest, others eg 'the chase' with increased activity. Potential within the game for periods of learning.

Team games

Tug of war

Provide a rope about 8 m (30 ft) long and attach quoits for a number of swimmers on each side; 4 v 4 or 6 v 6 are appropriate team numbers. The game is played exactly like tug of war on land. Players hold onto the quoits. They are not permitted to wrap the rope round their bodies

Requires steady, sustained exertion or if feet off the bottom, repetitive energetic input. Useful physiological demands.

Volleyball

Any number of players may participate. They are divided into two groups, one group on either side of the net. Players should rotate from shallow to deep water, or alternatively if not too large a group is involved the game may be played across the width of the pool. A net is hung so that the bottom is 60 cm–1 m (2–3 feet) above the water. Players bat the ball back and forth over the net using their hands. A side loses the ball if it fails to return it or bats the ball outside a limit line. The side winning the ball becomes the serving side. If the serving side wins the ball it gains a point. Only the serving side scores. If it loses the ball it simply fails to score.

Number in each side should allow for maximum participation by players. Players may regulate their own involvement. Group competitive activity.

Over and under

Teams form columns in chest-deep water, all the participants face the same direction. On the starting signal the last person in the line leaps over the member ahead and then goes between the legs of the next participant and continues in this manner 'over and under'. The new person who was behind him originally goes through the legs of the participant ahead of him.

Numbers in each team should not be large, six would be appropriate. A fairly active game which may be used for team competition when the skills have been accomplished. Allows for regaining breath control during the 'over' period.

Leap-frog

The participants line up in small lines, probably not more than 5 in any line. Players line up from the shallow to deeper water. Those in the deeper water adopt treading support. The end player on each line puts his or her hands on the shoulders of the person in front, pushing that person under the water while leaping over with legs widespread. Continue until the first in the line becomes last.

Allows for activity and rest as well as breath control potential within the submerged support position. All aspects of breath control may be anticipated.

Touch relay

The teams line up on opposite sides of the pool. The leader calls out an object and the teams must enter the water, touch that object and then return to the starting place. Eg touch all cones on the bottom of the pool, using any body part to touch them; touch head, bottom, knees and feet; Touch the floating mat on all sides/edges.

Starting place may be in the water holding rail if participants have a great deal of difficulty in leaving the pool. Fast activity, competitive, quick short burst of energy.

Quietening games

Electricity

Players stand in shallow water and hold hands. The helper, or named child, squeezes the hand of his neighbour and passes him a sponge. Each participant as they feel the squeeze and take the sponge submerges.

To help the children feel totally relaxed in the water and to develop ability to submerge. The game may be played without the use of the sponge, but the sponge helps eliminate response to any small adjustment of neighbour's hands. Breath-control game.

Still pond

Game for any number of players. 'It' stands on the side of the pool and on the signal 'Go' players swim the length or width of the pool according to ability. 'It' shuts his eyes, counts up to ten aloud and then says: 'Still Pond – no more moving.' He opens his eyes and when he looks up everyone should be floating motionless. Anyone he sees moving is sent back to the starting point. The game is continued until all have swam the length. Variations can include specific floats, treading water or sculling skills instead of motionless floating.

Participants can regulate own speed of swimming, useful as a concluding or contrasting activity in the lesson. Teacher should make variations as appropriate to the specific group in the class.

Will-o'-the-Wisp

This game is best played with 6 to 8 swimmers. All participants are blindfolded except the person who is 'it'. This person submerges and swims underwater. Every time he surfaces he must ring a bell and the blindfolded participants attempt to tag the bell-ringer. The player who tags the bell-ringer becomes 'it'. The tagged player joins the blindfolded group and the game continues.

The game should be confined to the water. Nature of the blindfolds makes the game tentative, with rather cautious swimming. Participants can regulate their involvement.

Learning (5 years and older)

There is no strict order when learning but the regular swimmer should by now be able to swim dog paddle, kick on his back, float and carry out other watermanship exercises, such as sculling.

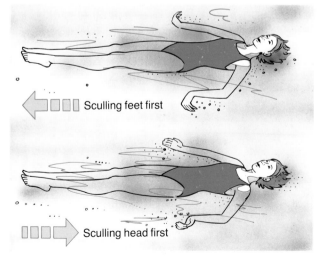

Sculling feet first

Sculling head first

Sculling

From the age of five, more complex movements can be built up. Butterfly legs can be taught quite soon, but breaststroke legs require great coordination.

Butterfly legs

Butterfly legs are best taught without the use of a float. Get the swimmer to float facedown in the water with the arms and legs stretched out. It might be a good idea to give the swimmer the mental idea of swimming down a cylindrical tube so that he doesn't overemphasize the hip and knee movements. The movement should be one of gentle undulation from the chest downwards; overkicking will lead to a loss of power and the swimmer's body hitting the outsides of the tube.

Try to get the swimmer to bounce his stomach lightly up and down, wriggle or shake his feet off. All will help to trigger off the correct early movement. The power should come from the feet on both up and down movements as well as the frontal and outside surfaces of both the upper and lower legs. Many swimmers when first learning simply bend their knees too much and so kick air. Toes should be under the surface at all times.

When the feet are driven down the hips should be automatically forced up and when the feet recover, the knees should bend as the feet relax and the water presses on the toes. At this point the stomach should be driven down. This will help to maintain an up-and-down movement.

Breaststroke legs

The movement here is much more complex. Some young swimmers lack the ankle strength for the movement, and there is no point in pushing a youngster to swim breaststroke if it is clearly a stroke which he is not equipped to swim. It's better he swims another stroke.

If, however, the swimmer can make even rudimentary movements of this nature, it is well worth following up. Start out of the water with the person lying over a seat or bench and run through the leg action with him. Then get him to try it in the water whilst holding onto

the scum trough with his elbows against the wall. With the use of his elbows he can lever his feet up closer to the surface.

When he has mastered both practices, it is time to get him to try it with a float.

If we try it with him holding on to the rail, start with the feet and legs straight out behind. The toes should be stretched out. The first phase is to bend the knees and to lift the heels towards the surface so that the lower leg is lifted and above the general height of the upper leg. The knees are turned slightly outwards so as to be approximately 40° from the vertical.

As the knees are steadily bent more and more, the heels are squeezed up to the behind, and on reaching the behind the feet are rotated outwards at the ankles 45° from the vertical. The soles face backwards away from the line of direction. The soles then push backwards. As the knees begin to straighten, the feet not only kick back but continue their outward rotation with the toes adopting a curled position. Meanwhile the upper leg has stayed fairly still so as to prevent the knees being drawn up under the body.

The heels are finally brought together in a whip-like manner by changing the emphasis at the toes from a situation where they are curled to one where they are pointed. Some young swimmers have problems with drawing up their knees, which may be drawn up too far at the sides or brought too far under the body. Get them to wear a rubber band across the knees to prevent this movement.

The kick can be strengthened slowly by getting the swimmer to place two and then three floats between his arms for kick practice. This has the effect of placing great strain on the ankle region.

Lifesaving kick

The learning phase of the breaststroke leg kick can be coupled with the learning of its supine counterpart: the lifesaving kick. The swimmer should try to use his soles to a great degree and should also try to employ part of the insides of the leg for the kick. The knees should be kept underneath so as not to slow the movement.

The arms and early coordination

Backcrawl

You really need a good strong leg kick before introducing backstroke arms. The legs can be strengthened by varying the position of the body in the water to increase resistance. This can be achieved by moving the arms to various positions other than kicking with the arms by your sides. Get the swimmer to lift both arms up so that the hands are held together above the head which lowers the hips and legs, or, alternatively, kick with one hand above the head on the water, or with both hands above the head on the water with the arms outstretched and thumbs linked. This lifts the hips but still makes the kick more difficult.

When the kick has been fully mastered the arms, which alternate and orientate backwards, can be added. For a youngster, they should be likened to two paddles in rowing a boat. Get the swimmer to come out of the side, stand and go through the feeling of the backwards alternating movement. Get him to turn his hands to face outwards at his sides before swinging them with the elbows straight backwards.

Now employ the same arm movements in the water. The little finger enters first on one hand as the hand turns outwards. It should go in between 1 and 2 o'clock, but the swimmer needs to be encouraged to stretch out and keep his elbows straight. The fingers are then driven backwards until they are about 40 cm under the water, before the hand is turned in line with the surface and cupped for the pull. Try to give the young swimmer the windmill type of feeling.

You may find that the swimmer has difficulty in fitting in the arms in the first instance. The swimmer may appear to overkick, taking as many as eight kicks to each arm cycle. Don't be too concerned at this. It's all a matter of developing the strength in the trunk muscles for the arm pull. The breathing, however, remains important: continue to concentrate on pushing bad air out with the mouth. The breathing movement should be carried out so that it is regular and continuous.

Frontcrawl

A more complex description of the frontcrawl arms and timing can be found in that chapter. Our main concern here is in introducing the swimmer to the stroke as the next step from dog paddle.

The frontcrawl should merely be an extension of the dog paddle with the arms being recovered over the water instead of under. This is achieved by lifting the arm out of the water when it has finished pulling just beyond the hips. The thumb should be kept by the side of the body as the hand is lifted out.

Once again, get the swimmer to practise the arm motion either on the side of the pool or in a mirror at home. The arms should operate like bicycle pedals. On returning to the water, get the swimmer to push off and glide and to try to operate the arms over the water with the head in to the front. Ask the swimmer to go as far as he can on one breath so as to get him pulling the arms without interruptions. He should be encouraged to bend the elbows when recovering the arms over the water.

If a swimmer still has difficulties with feeling his arm movements, get him to fix his feet into the swim channel while you hold him lightly under the stomach. Now he should try to recover the arms without pulling hard under his body whilst his face is in the water. You are in close contact and able to guide him by talking to him even with his head under.

The breathing is tied up with the co-ordinatory movements of this early frontcrawl. It can first of all be rehearsed at the rail. Most learners have difficulty in balancing the pressure of air inside the nose with the pressure of water outside it. Therefore get the swimmer to stand and put his face in the water so that the head is looking straight in front. Place your hand on the top of the head and twist it lightly to the most comfortable side through an angle of 90°. When half of the face is clear of the water, the mouth should be turned a little further, so as to be able to take in air. The swimmer should be encouraged to twist the mouth back towards the shoulder for protection. Then twist the head back towards the centre and tell the swimmer to blow out through his mouth.

This should now be tried with the swimmer standing with knees bent in the water. The face should once again be dropped into the water. The swimmer should experiment so as to ascertain which is the most comfortable breathing side for him. If it looks as though the right side will be the best, the head should turn every time the left hand enters the water and the face should be centralized prior to the right hand entering.

When this has been tried whilst crouching in the water, the swimmer should try it whilst swimming. In the first place he might like to start with his face in the water and to try it every four strokes. Many swimmers at this time breathe in too much water by mistake. This normally comes about because they mistime the beginning of the breathing out phase.

The young swimmer often imagines he is breathing out early enough when his nose returns to the water but that is often not the case. In the period when he imagines he has begun blowing out the water shoots up his nose. The problem is compounded because the swimmer is already slightly confused over the change of pressure as the face moves through air pressure back to water pressure. This particular timing problem can be overcome by the swimmer actually exhaling before the nose and mouth have re-entered the water.

Swimmers who still don't have the idea of the correct position to which they should turn their head should be asked to 'bite an apple on their shoulder'.

Breaststroke

The swimmer who has mastered the breaststroke legs with a float should find it easier to pick up the arm pull. The pull should be circular and wide but never straight back. For a young swimmer, get them to go through the pulling movements on the side of the pool first. These movements are described in the breaststroke chapter. Possibly a partner's arms acting as a resistance will help the feel for the pull. Then the swimmer should try the pull in the water with the legs trailing.

As the wider pull becomes easier the swimmer adds the leg kick and feels the backward and downward drive of the feet. Take two arm pulls to one leg kick at first, or vice versa, until the swimmer feels balanced enough for one pull, one kick.

By progressive steps the swimmer should be able to get to a stage where he starts to pull and then kicks afterwards. Slowly he will learn to add the breathing by lowering his head and aiming in the first place to blow his fingers away as they move forward and away from the face. Finally, he will learn to breathe in when he has pulled back until his hands are immediately in front of his chin.

Butterfly

Having learnt the legs, the swimmer has to learn to cater for the much greater amounts of strength needed in the arm movements of butterfly.

Start by jumping off the bottom of the pool and throwing both arms forward together whilst lowering the head. This should be coupled with at least three kicks of the legs. If the arms can now be pulled over the water without having to stand, three more kicks can be made. The number of kicks and jumps from the bottom can be slowly reduced until the swimmer is making two kicks to each pull and pulling consistently. The swimmer can eventually get used to the feeling of taking a breath when he has pulled his arms to their rear-most point.

It must be emphasized that the swimmer should aim to enter his arms softly, trying to avoid splash. Power needs to be applied during the pull underwater by aiming to bring the hands under the stomach as though the young swimmer is pulling his or herself out on to the poolside.

Learning to dive

Overcoming the early fear of the head crashing through the surface is a problem which should be tackled in stages. Start the swimmer off by getting him to push and glide. The surface dive (see diagrams below), seal dive (see diagram on the right) (or diving through a hoop held over the water surface) and a jump off the bottom followed by ducking through the surface are all good ways of overcoming the psychological as well as physical impact.

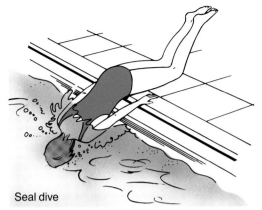
Seal dive

Surface dive

Then start with the swimmer sitting on the poolside with his legs wrapped over the edge. The feet should be placed flat on top of the swim rail. His arms should be placed around his head with hands together, elbows straight and the ears covered by the insides of the arms. At first the fingers should be pointing diagonally up towards the roof at an angle of 45° to his torso which sits vertically. The swimmer now lowers the fingers so that the hands point towards the water and then pushes with his feet on the rail or swim trough.

As he pushes, he should aim to straighten his legs and to get his hips as high as possible behind so that the body makes a parabolic curve and then enters the water half a metre in front of the starting position. The body should go into the water in one straight line, fingers first with all other parts following vertically.

Sitting dive

When the sitting dive has been mastered, the swimmer can transfer to a crouch dive where he would follow the same pattern of movement but start by kneeling on one knee

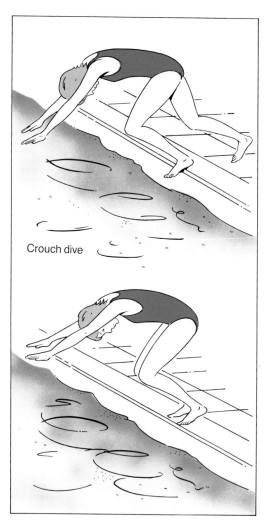

Crouch dive

with the other foot flat on the pool deck. Again he should try to get the hips up high and enter the water with feet together in a straight line. When confident with this, he can move from the kneeling dive to a crouching dive in which the body is slightly bent in the back with the feet together but about 15 cm (6 ins) apart.

Slowly but surely, the swimmer can stand up and extend the kneels, uncoiling the back, so as to eventually stand with the arms above the head and the knees 5 cm (2 ins) apart. Practice with a hoop helps the entry (see diagram).

The plain header

The swimmer is now ready for the plain header. If you are diving for distance or speed then the racing dive is the obvious dive to employ; if you are going for smoothness and diving appearance then use the plain header.

The stance to be adopted is one with the feet roughly 2 cm (1 in.) apart, the body vertical with the toes over the edge of the pool, the face looking straight across the pool directly and the arms diagonally pointing away from the shoulder line at an angle of 40° from the vertical, ie Y-shaped.

The knees now bend to about 90° with the elbows accompanying this flexion. The body, however, remains straight. The feet drive the body upwards towards the roof and simultaneously the arms are brought together so as to wrap around the ears. The hips are now

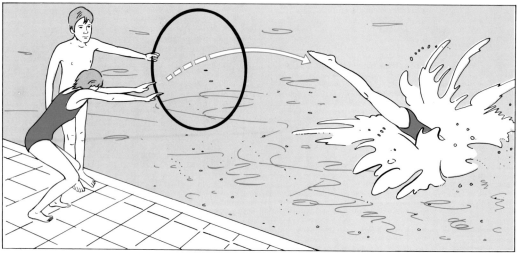

Plain header

thrown forward as the eyes cease to look directly in front and look down at the surface.

The aim should now be to get the fingers entering first with the body following perpendicularly and the feet entering the original hole made by the hands. Don't tuck the head in too much or the legs will go past the vertical and produce a splash.

The follow-through in the water is just as important with the diver needing to keep the arms and fingers as stretched as possible until the whole body has entered. When this has been achieved the swimmer can look up towards the surface, arch his back and move his fingers from pointing diagonally down to stretching back to the surface.

References
1 *Activity and the Asthmatic*, by Sheila Dobing, Win Hayes and Charles Ramsey, Fisons plc, 1984
2 *Adapted Aquatics*, American Red Cross, Double Day New York, 1977
3 *A Practical Guide for Teaching the Mentally Retarded to Swim*, Council for National Cooperation in Aquatics and American Association for Health, P.E. and Recreation, 1969

5 Frontcrawl

Frontcrawl, or freestyle as its competitive counterpart is generally known, is the fastest form of unassisted human propulsion through the water today. Nowadays, it takes the form of a range of alternating movements made with the limbs in a series of right angles at the joints. The alternating movements make the stroke continuously propulsive and this propulsive aspect, aided by the advantageous position of the larger, pulling muscles of the body and the streamlined effect of much of the torso, combine to make the stroke some four seconds faster over 100 metres than the next fastest stroke, the butterfly.

The modern freestyler is encouraged to keep his body centre on a long axis in line with the direction in which he is moving. The larger, pulling muscles are brought into play by a rolling action of the shoulders which occurs during the arm recovery. Frontcrawl has changed quite considerably since the Second World War. For instance, immediately prior to the War swimmers were encouraged to swim with a flat elbow recovery, ie one in line with the wrist[1] and to swim with little roll as it spoilt the balance of the body.[2] Attitudes were starting to change going into the War. There

was a general move towards a higher elbow recovery. A more lateral recovery had been handed on to the frontcrawl by the Trudgen stroke. It meant that a low, lateral armswing could employ the relatively large upper trapezius muscle as well as the anterior and posterior deltoids in assisting the forward movement of the arm. By comparison, the more pendular high elbow recovery felt less easy because the recovery of the arm was accomplished by the anterior fibres of the deltoid muscle, a small muscle in relation to the movement required.[3]

Slowly people were beginning to realize that the higher elbow recovery resulted in less lateral movement throughout the rest of the body and less resistance as a result.

The world record for the 100 metres in 1960 stood at 54.6 by John Devitt of Australia. In relation to other strokes the improvement of the world record by six seconds is not that great. Frontcrawl being the fastest stroke has been the hardest to improve. The greatest areas of improvement have come about with conditioning and training for the distance events and in starts and turns on the 100 metres.

Body position

The body needs to lie flat on top of water, the position of the head being adjusted to bring the hips and feet into the most streamlined position. The weight of the head needs to be carried by the water in order that there is no strain on the neck. This can normally be achieved by resting the hairline on the surface

of the water.

When travelling at speed the shoulders and head need to be high in the water. This creates a greater amount of resistance at the shoulders because of a larger bow wave but it helps the leg kick by moving the feet lower in the water. The range of the leg kick is increased as it becomes harder in order to produce the effect of lifting the body up and over the water.

The higher head position during sprinting needs to be attained without placing any extra strain on the neck muscles which will be needed for general deportment and the breathing function. It's therefore a bad idea to merely lift the head with the aid of the neck muscles. Instead attempt to move the whole of the upper body into a slightly different position by arching the back lightly so that a small amount of pain can be felt in the small of the back. This will have the effect of getting the head in a higher position.

Swimmers competing and training in middle-distance events will not want the head so high. A high head brings greater resistance at the shoulders and therefore requires greater leg power to overcome it. The legs would become too fatigued if this amount of leg power were still required over 400 metres. The buildup of lactic acid in the body as a result would be disproportionate to the extra speed that could be achieved and its continuation.

In middle-distance events the eyes need to be centred on a point approximately five metres ahead of the swimmer on the bottom of the pool. This, of course, refers only to when the head is brought back to the central breathing position.

The general position of the feet should be such that the heels and rear part of the toes just break the surface of the water on the upkick and drive to a position of about 45 cm underneath. The hips at their uppermost point need to be approximately a metre under the surface. The shoulders should rest immediately on top of the water. When breathing to the side takes place, the uppermost lateral aspect of the hip on the breathing side needs to be about 15 cm (6 ins) under the surface.

The whole body movement should be almost screw-like in orientation, moving through a lower plane of 180°. The concept of the perfectly flat body position produces a smooth body surface moving through smooth particles of water, in much the same way as a screw failing to grip. A body which rotates laterally through water will act as a screw would on a rawlplug, producing a breaking up of fairly still water particles and a greater grip of the body on the water as it moves through it.

Timing of stroke

The stroke timing is dependent on the type of leg kick employed by the individual. The various leg actions are as follows:

Six leg beats to each arm cycle

Taking a situation where the right hand is entering the water, first the left leg should be fully extended in a straight diagonal line through the knee at an angle of about 45° from the horizontal at the hip. The right arm should be fully extended so that the arm is parallel but approximately 15 cm (6 ins) beneath the surface of the water when stretched out in front. It should also be level with the shoulder.

As the right hand begins its pull backwards, the left foot lifts as the left knee is bent. In the meantime, the right foot begins a downward movement as a counterbalance to the movement of the left foot upwards. The right hand has by now reached the halfway point in the pull, ie the hand has been pulled to a position where it is bent at a 45° angle at the elbow and is almost under the face. At this point the first downward kick of the left leg should be complete with the toe more or less pointed.

While the right hand has pulled to a position parallel with the head in a lateral plane, the left hand should have begun its recovery over the water and should now be hanging in a pendulous manner immediately under the bent elbow over the water having just cleared it at the end of the pull. When the left arm is halfway through its recovery over the water, ie the hand is over the water but level with the shoulder line, the right foot should be driven through a vertical plan towards the bottom in the pool. The left leg bends at the knee at the same time in order to facilitate a third downward kick timed to coincide with the later part of the pull.

The pattern is then repeated on the other side where the left hand enters the water. The right leg should have completed a fourth downward kick. The alternating action of the legs continues as the left leg makes a fifth downward movement and the right recovers by bending at the knee and by being lifted so that the heel is within a centimetre or two of

the surface. The final and sixth downward movement of the legs is made by the right leg during the final phase of the left arm pull — in other words, when the hand tract is in the process of being made under the left shoulder.

Here we see Olympic bronze and Commonwealth gold medallist June Croft.

D = Drag
d = direction of movement
L = Lift force
R = Resultant force

The left hand has just entered the water whilst the right is half way through its pull.

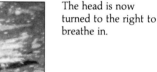

The head is now turned to the right to breathe in.

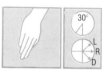

The head is now returning to the front, whilst the left hand pulls.

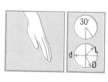

Now the head is centred and the right hand enters the water.

The right hand starts its pull whilst the left is about to go into the final propulsive stage of the pull.

Note the right elbow is kept up higher than the hand during the pull.

Here we can see the right hand about to fix very firmly on the water.

57

Four leg beats to each arm cycle

This particular timing would normally be used by a middle-distance swimmer who preferred to work without the powerful sprint six-beat kick rhythm. It's worth noting that the six-beat kick need not be limited to the sprints and has been used successfully by middle- and long-distance swimmers over the years.

The four-beat leg kick lacks the power but requires less from the body system because less oxygenated blood needs to be pumped to the legs. As in the six-beat kick, there may be individual differences in the timing of the kick but these will not vary widely.

If we start once again with the right arm entering the water in line with the shoulder, the left leg projected diagonally towards the bottom of the pool as in the opening description of the six-beat sequence. Once again the right hand begins its pull backwards. On this occasion, the hand would pull back until level with the shoulder. During the period of this pull, the left leg would have been bent at the knee and the right foot then driven towards the bottom of the pool.

During the second phase of the right arm pull – from a point roughly in line with the shoulders to a point where the hand completes the pull by the righthand side of the swimmer – the left leg makes a second kick towards the bottom whilst the right leg bends and recovers. In the meantime the left arm has recovered over the water, with the swimmer trying to keep the armpits open by showing more and more of them, and is now in a position to enter the water in front of the head. As the left hand enters the right foot now begins its kick downwards and the left leg recovers. The pull with the left arm continues and, as with the right arm, a fourth kick is made by the left leg during the final phase of the pull.

Two-beat kick

This kicking tempo is nearly always used in middle- and long-distance events. There have been periods where world-class middle-distance swimmers have used it in turning to the sprint events. This has normally resulted in success, not because of the kick used but because of the relative paucity of top six-beat leg-kicking sprinters at that time.

The kick is normally used by a high-floating swimmer (who has light legs). The downward movements are normally made with great power to balance a hard shovel-like pull of mainly arm-dominant swimmers. The right leg kicks down to time with the catch of the left hand on the water. The left leg is kicked to time similarly with the right hand entry. When the legs are separated the bottom part of the body is stabilized and excessive rolling, which prevents forward movement, is reduced. Swimming coaches have defined two leg beats to each arm cycle in two aspects: active and pure. The active version sees a great deal of propulsion from the kick; the pure kick involves a great degree of stabilizing and less propulsion.

This type of kick can have an effect or be brought about as a result of other stroke variations to the six-beat kick. The two-beat kicker will often have a wider hand entry position, sometimes wide enough to be outside the shoulder line on entry. As more power is required from the arms, the arms tend to bend quicker and earlier to catch hold of the water sooner than in a four- or six-beat stroke. This, in turn, means that the pull is often shorter and slower in moving back.

The number of strokes taken per length will be greater than the more economical six-beat kick. Many good swimmers utilize both kicking techniques, switching from two leg beats to six when they want more speed at the expense of greater energy output and vice versa.

Kicking variations

In modern-day swimming one sees a number of kicking variations which are tailormade to suit the individuals making the movement. These are always of erratic tempo but all have a balancing effect leaving the swimmer on an even keel.

Broken-tempo or flutter kicks occur even in the traditional up and down movement of the legs. A two-beat leg kick might be followed by a trailing of the legs or the rhythm of four further equivalent kicks. The tempo may be less broken than this, with a moment's pause used by four- or six-beat kickers at the end of every second or third down kick respectively. This helps the body level off and again brings it on to an even keel.

As we shall discuss later, frontcrawl is accompanied by a fair amount of hip rotation as well as shoulder roll. These two aspects combine to provide lateral movements, which are greater in some individuals than others. As the stabilizing and balancing agents, the legs counteract these lateral movements by crossover kicks. This is very rarely a deliberate act on the part of the swimmer but occurs naturally during the course of his attempts to kick straight up and down in a vertical plane.

Swimmers with a tighter shoulder girdle will throw their arms wide of the body during the recovery. The result is known as a two-beat crossover kick. If we start with the right arm entering the water once again, the left kick drives downwards whilst the right foot moves laterally to a position where it crosses the right leg at the calf muscle. It is then driven laterally bringing the foot back in line with the thigh. At the end of this sideways movement the foot is then driven downwards. This is accompanied by a similar crossover of the left leg over the calf of the right leg as it completes its downward movement. At this point, the left hand should be entering the water.

Arm stroke

The general movements of the frontcrawl arms should be angular with the arms working in a counterpoise relationship. To keep the body in perfect alignment the swimmer needs to ensure that as one arm is pulling the other arm is recovering, and the recovery arm should be opposite the pulling arm in order to follow Newton's Third Law of Motion.

Let's imagine a situation in which a swimmer is lying with his face in the water on his stomach, the legs kicking alternately. The right arm is halfway through its pull and the left arm is halfway through its recovery. The left arm is bent at the elbow so that the elbow is carried higher than the hand. The fingers relax and point diagonally downwards and forwards in relation to the surface of the water. The lower arm is positioned so as to be in line with the upper part of the arm, the elbow being bent at an angle of $120°$ to the vertical.

At this stage, it is very important to ensure that there is a fair degree of relaxation which can be encouraged by shrugging and rotating the shoulder as the arm is swung forward. Stiffer swimmers will tend to throw the arm in a pattern where the hand is recovered well outside the horizontal line of the shoulders. A looser freestyler will recover the arm with the elbow at a higher peak and the hand pointing down (palm backwards) in line with the shoulders from the front.

As the arm comes over the water the elbow tends to fix at the mid point in its orbital path and the arm straighten as the fingers enter the water. The hands slide into the water with the fingers creating a hole through the surface; the fingers, shoulder and elbow drive into the water through the same hole. The hand would normally enter between a line with the shoulder and the body midline at a $45°$ angle to the surface from a vertical aspect. The right arm continues to straighten in front of the head. The hand needs to enter about 30 cm (12 ins) in front of the head with the thumb side down slightly, but the swimmer should continue to extend the arm to its maximum. By continuing this extension, which is made in line with the shoulder and approximately 9 cm (4 ins) under the surface, the swimmer increases the potential range of his backward pull (ie force × distance determines the propulsive power in this instance). In the meantime, the right arm has completed its pull and is positioned about 20 cm (8 ins) lower than the right hip in an opposite position.

When the left arm has reached maximum

extension the lower arm begins a rotation at the elbow. The swimmer exerts pressure at the fingertips in the first instance in a downward and then backward direction. The pressure starts at the fingertips and is then systematically applied by the rest of the hand with the heel of the hand employed last. The downward movement of the hand takes it to about 30 cm (12 ins) under the surface. At this stage the arm is still outstretched in front of the hand. The right arm has meanwhile been lifted from the water at the start of the recovery.

The catch

There are still some air bubbles under the hand from its entry in to the water. The job of the hand is to now overcome this air cushion, grab hold of larger molecules of water and to fix on the water in order to move that water in a backward direction towards the swimmer's right foot. A swimmer with a good 'feel' for the water will now be able to use his hand to purchase on the water as early as possible in the pull. The earlier you can 'catch' hold of the water the better the potential for propulsion. The elbow should be kept up and not dropped beneath the level of the hand as it pulls backwards.

When the arm was at maximum extension before the pull it was hook-like in shape. As the swimmer begins to catch hold of the water the elbow fixes. It isn't pulled backwards at this point. The elbow remains the fulcrum and the hand moves backwards towards the feet. The aim of the swimmer at this point will be to pull with the forearm as well as with the hand. This is one of the prime reasons for the swimmer keeping the elbow above the hand. Obviously, if the elbow was allowed to bow to the

Left to right:
The elbow bends slightly in a lateral plane simply because the muscles of the shoulder region are not generally strong enough to hold all the water.
The lower arm continues to rotate under the elbow in its backward movement and the hand is pulled to a position where the angle at the elbow between the lower and upper arm can be anything from 45° to 75° in a lateral plane.
The aim now is to pull the body over the arm and hand as they fix on the water. The greatest point of application is when the water is pulled back immediately under the face at a depth of about 60 cm. At this stage the right arm has reached the mid point of its recovery, which keeps the body balanced.
The hand of the swimmer should ideally point towards the bottom of the pool as the arm is being pulled back towards the feet. In reality the hand is often bent so as to face sideways to the surface with the thumb slightly upwards.
The pull phase ends at the highest point of elbow flexion under the mid body. The swimmer now pushes the rest of the way back towards the feet.

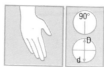
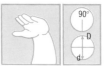

pressure of the water and dropped to the level of the hand, the forearm could play no part in the pull backwards. Try to catch and press from the outside inwards, with the wrist flexed. There should be pressure on the fingertips and palm but turn the hand in from the outside or little-finger side.

The pull

The pull commences when the hand in the water finally fixes and appears to move in a backward direction towards the feet. When the right arm has reached a position where it is some 60 cm (2 ft) under the water and is being pulled along a central path which could cut the swimmer into two equal parts if one were to consider the body both horizontally and vertically, then the pull is at its most important.

The push

This can be identified by change of hand direction in search of 'new' water. This backward movement can be identified as the push. It starts when the right arm has been moved to a position where it is level with the face and continues until the arm has been lifted from the water. The elbow now rotates inwards with the hand facing sideways to the surface, thumbs uppermost.

The swimmer should aim to keep his hand as close to his body as possible and the push should finish with the arm fully extended and straight at the elbow. The palm of the hand finishes facing up. The arm should be in juxtaposition to the upper leg with the fingers fully extended. At this point, the left hand should be just entering the water, the right hand 2 cm (1 in.) under the surface.

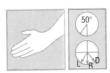

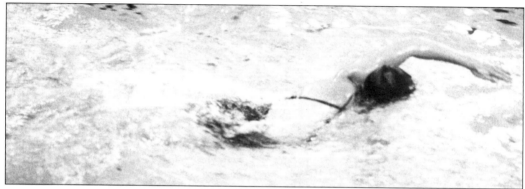

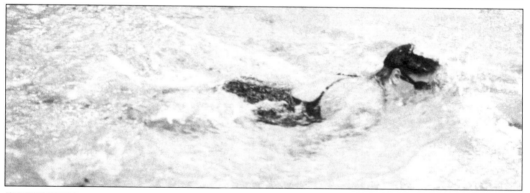

The recovery

The head remains central as the left arm recovers over the water (see photos opposite). Notice the shoulder rotating as the left arm is brought forward to enter fingers first. At the point of maximum extension, the swimmer will have ensured that the pull has been made through the greatest range possible bearing in mind the length of his levers. The right elbow now bends and is released from the water first. The elbow is followed by the hand which hangs perpendicularly from the elbow. The hand is now brought quickly forward with the aid of shoulder rotation to the front position.

To encourage the correct position during the recovery, the swimmer should be asked to show more and more of his armpit as the arm is lifted over of the water.

The mechanics of the arm stroke

There is considerable variation in the amount of elbow bend when the arm is perpendicular to the body in the pull of most champion swimmers. The reason for this is simply that as each has different levels of strength at different points, they all bend their elbows to different degrees in order to create a situation where greater power can be applied.

Studies have shown, however, that there is no regular pattern as far as middle- or long-distance swimmers are concerned. However, all top swimmers pull with a type of inverted question mark, and during the mid section of the pull on each of these swimmers the hand is positioned halfway between the midline and the opposite shoulder. This crossover type of pull is counteracted by the legs, eg with a crossover leg kick.

Experiments were carried out by Susanne Higgs and Harry Gallagher on 36 swimmers aged 10 to 17 at the Regina Optimists Club, Canada, in 1979 using a Pacific Scientific Company T5 cable tensionmeter. The swimmers were placed in prone positions facing a pulling assembly attached to the wall. The midstroke position was defined in this test as being adjacent to the line of the shoulders. Strength was tested in the six positions shown diagrammatically opposite.

The effects of fatigue on the stroke were overcome by rotating the start position through five separate points with each of the subjects. They found that the two righthand positions were much stronger than the two lefthand as in the results opposite.

Although the mean age of the males was nearly a year older, the average pull applied in mid stroke was 34.08 lb in terms of the males and 31.56 in terms of females. Higgs and Gallagher suggested that in view of their findings it might be wiser for coaches to advocate their swimmer's hand pull being wide

125° Shoulder up

M L

125° Shoulder down

M L

120° Shoulder up

M L

120° Shoulder down

M L

95° Shoulder up

M L

95° Shoulder down

M L

of the centre lines and even for the hands to be placed wide of the central axis. They did however note that strength is not the only criterion for speed through water. For instance, when the arm is pulled straighter and wider with a more obtuse angle at the elbow the forearm can present less of a surface area for pulling because of distortion. A sharp edge rather than a flat pulling surface is presented.

Their findings resulted in their recommending a wide pull with an angle of 125° at the elbow because the area for pulling and pushing against the water is flatter, and this position gives a more acute feel of the water. They also, however, recognized individual differences here with Johnny Weissmuller and Dawn Fraser swimming in a shoulder-up position and wide pulls whilst Mark Spitz pulled down the centre line in the mid pull phase.[4]

These types of tests are, of course, not new. In April 1939 the British coach W. H. Downing introduced the 'swimagraph' which he termed the swimmers' X-ray. The instrument was controversial at the time; the A.S.A. refused to buy it. Nevertheless, it demonstrated an increased desire by the swimming fraternity to develop a scientific approach to the sport.

The swimagraph was placed on the poolside, attached to a belt worn by the swimmer. The value of each movement, rate of each stroke, falling off period due to fatigue was recorded on a graph on a revolving drum.

The swimagraph was employed on front-crawl stroke variations, and on early test cases competitive swimmers recorded an average of 17.8 lb during the pull on crawl, 16.9 lb on trudgeon crawl, 9.6 lb on bilateral frontcrawl, 8.3 lb on crawl considered to be affected by excessive breathing, 8.8 lb on crawl affected by over reaching, 19.2 lb for an erratic crawl with a lot of twisting and 18.7 lb for an arm-dominant crawler. Whereas the situation for the two tests is quite different, the average strength difference does provide part of the reason as to why freestylers have been faster over the years.[5]

The leg action

As with the arms, the leg action is angular, alternating and the propulsive concentration made in the vertical plane by oscillating movements. The up-and-down action of the legs emanates from the hips. The hips tend to roll from side to side in keeping with movements of the shoulder and arms. The result of this is that the leg movements are not made straight up and down but at a slight angle to the vertical as the hips alter their position.

The aim of the swimmer should be to shake the feet during the kick downwards. This should assist in straightening the knee and leg at the end of the kick which encourages greater power. The muscles of the leg should be in an extended state at the end of the kick without the toe necessarily being completely pointed.

As the left foot reaches this position, the right leg should have completed its recovery. In other words, the knee should have bent slightly, facilitating the upward move of the heel towards the surface. The sole of the left foot should just break the surface of the water. Any further lifting of the leg will result in the freestyler merely kicking air on the downward thrust which in turn will result in negative propulsive power. On the upkick or recovery the lower leg should be completely relaxed allowing the water to press on the toes as they move towards the surface. The result is normally a pigeon-toed effect with the toes turned slightly inwards.

The depth of the kick is dependent on limb length but would generally be about 2 m (6 ft). A common fault in younger swimmers is to bend the knees too much, thereby losing a lot of power from the kick.

The eddies of water of columns created by the up and down movements of the legs can interact on one another (see the diagrams opposite). This integration can have a positive influence on the kick. Two disturbed areas of water can interact in this way and produce the friction required for forward movement.

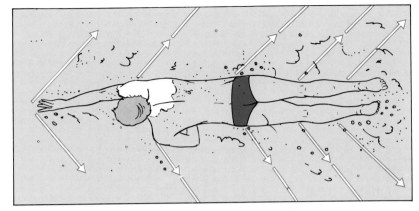

The position of the head during the frontcrawl can affect the eddies produced by the body. Here, the head is up and the eddies come off the shoulders and knees.

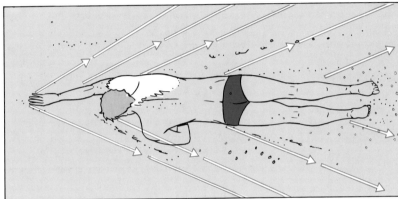

The head is lower in this figure and the result is more acute, eddies being directed from the shoulders, hips and legs.

Breathing

A swimmer normally inhales in a race situation when under a fair degree of strain. He is usually tired and has difficulty grabbing air. It's therefore important that some of this strain is removed by developing a breathing mechanism which is reasonably relaxed and comfortable.

Some swimmers breathe to the left, others to the right. Some swimmers breathe to the left once every four strokes and others employ the same technique to the right. Bilateral breathing is often used to encourage a more balanced stroke. Here the swimmer might inhale breath first to the left shoulder, make three arm pulls and then inhale to the right shoulder and so on.

The mode of breathing is purely individual but of paramount importance. If we accept that water is not the natural human environment,

the one aspect above anything else that divides us from fish or other water-based animals is the breathing. It therefore follows that the breathing has to be exactly right in each swimmer for maximum race performance, and yet it is the most neglected area. Breathing is neglected by most swimming coaches simply because it is so difficult to identify and analyse whilst the face is underwater.

Experimentation seems to be the only course, particularly in the early years. Most of the problems come about because swimmers either take in too much air or too little, or because they let it out too early or too late when the head comes back to the centre point in the stroke. In these days of large squads there isn't normally the opportunity for this type of individual experimentation.

If you start from the premise that the breathing you are using is not either fully effective or comfortable, then experiment by swimming single lengths, altering your breathing pattern and combinations on the following basis:

1 Take in a larger breath than normal and then do *one* of the following:

(a) retain that air until your head has reached the centre line. Then expel the air in the period between the head leaving that centre line and return for another breath (see the diagrams above).

(b) blow the air out in steady phases from the time that the face returns to the water through to the centre point and back to the breathing-in position at the side.

(c) retain that air and then attempt to blow it out in the mid point, between the centre point and the point of inhalation.

(d) attempt to explode the air as soon as it feels comfortable to do so.

(e) let the air trickle as soon as it feels comfortable to do so.

(f) attempt to push the air out hard when the head reaches the centre line.

2 Now attempt all of the above but take in a smaller breath.

Further experimentation can take place, with the size of the breath being larger or smaller as desired. As we would consider this breathing to be of vital importance to the stroke later in the swimmer's life, it's well worth spending the time on it at an early age. As you grow older, the body forms neuromuscular patterns and they prove difficult to alter.

In general terms, the air should be inhaled to the left or right when the hand attached to the opposite shoulder to the direction in which you are facing is entering the water. As far as timing is concerned this is the optimum position. The water surface should be positioned somewhere between the hairline and the eyebrows. The breath should not be snatched but taken by moving, twisting the neck muscles in the first instance and then by moving the mouth back towards the shoulder during the final phase. Although the head is held up partly by the water, the neck muscles are already being used for general positioning of the head and it's therefore important not to overtax it by using it for all facets of the breathing.

During the final part of the inhalation the mouth should move so that it turns back towards the shoulder. By doing this both the head and the mouth won't need to turn so far because the area in front of the shoulder will already be protected by the bow wave created by the head. The result of this is that an air pocket forms behind the head and creates a greater potential area from which air can be obtained.

Most swimmers remember to take in air but only the good ones remember to blow out fully, ridding themselves completely of carbon dioxide. If a heavy residue of carbon dioxide is left in the lungs at the end of each exhalation, an unnecessary lactic acid buildup may result.

The final movement on returning the head to its centre position should be to edge the chin past the centre line as the opposite hand pushes. This will improve the balance of the stroke.

The drawing shows one example of the six suggested breathing patterns. In this instance (point b in text) the swimmer breathes out on a regular basis throughout the movement.

Vertical body movements

Obviously not all the body movements in frontcrawl are made in the lateral plane. Many are made vertically as a result of rotations at pivotal positions. A shoulder rotation made in a forward and upward direction takes place on entry of either hand. The result is a corresponding lowering of the hips.

Further rotations take place at the hips at the end of the pull with each arm. At this point one side of the hips is lifted and then rotates forward and the hand is released from the water.

These four rotations in each arm cycle produce considerable movement alone. The body is never flat on the surface but it is the responsibility of the trunk muscles to adjust the body in order to retain a streamlined position.

Muscular analysis of freestyle

During the first part of the pull to the centre line, the latissimus dorsi, teres major and pectoralis major play an important part in both adductive and horizontal flexion. The same muscles are responsible for the push phase as the hand is brought to the side of the body.

The part of the pectoralis muscle closest to the sternum plays a major part in this movement whilst the long hand of the biceps muscle, situated to the rear of the upper arm helps to stabilize the joint.

During the pull the scapula close to the shoulder blades rotates downwards to aid the push of the arm and the downward movement of the hand during the catch.

The biceps, brachialis, brachoradialis and pronator teres are the muscles responsible for flexing the forearm until the elbow fixes for the pull. The pronator teres and quadratus keep the forearm slightly prone. The flexor muscles of the wrist and fingers along with the palmaris longue hold the fingers in an extended state against the pressure of the water. During the last part of the pull and the release from the water the fingers flex at the wrist. The fingers are adducted by a palmar interossei and the adductor and opponens pollicis.

During the recovery the lifting of the arm is achieved through hyperextension at the shoulder joint by the posterior section of the deltoid muscle along with the large latissimus muscle and the teres major. As the arm recovers in front of the face, the movement changes to adduction and horizontal extension. The middle deltoid, supraspinatus, infra spinatus and teres major combine to bring this about. The middle deltoid is increasingly employed as the arm reaches forward; the posterior part is used less and less as the arm moves to an extended position.

The rhomboid and middle trapezise muscle lift the scapula which is adducted during the lifting of the arm. The elbow is flexed at first but slowly extends forward. The triceps, assisted by the anconeus, bring this about. The supinator helps the forearm to become less pronated and finally the fingers extend before hand entry.

As the head enters the water, the adduction of the humerus in the upper arm is completed. The arm now moves slightly forward and depresses downward. Slight inward rotation takes place at the shoulder joint. Again the latissimus dorsi, teres major, pectoralis major, posterior deltoid and triceps muscles are responsible for the movements at the shoulder joint. The shoulder rotation continues until hand entry. The catch and downward rotation of the shoulder are achieved by the scapula also rotating by means of the rhomboids and pectoralis minor acting on them.

The hands and fingers remain in extension, whilst the triceps, assisted by the anconeus, extend the forearm, until the elbow is completely extended.

The hip, knee and ankle joints are all involved in the frontcrawl kick. At the start of the kick, which comes from the hips, the knee and hips are flexed slightly and the feet plantar flexed.

As the kick is made downwards the psoas major and iliacus, fasciae latae and pectineus flex the thigh along with the sartorius muscle. The extension of the knee and the majority of the leg is carried out by the quadriceps femoris. The ankle and tarsal regions remain plantar flexed throughout. The soleus, peroneus tongue and brevis tibialis posterior are supported by the flexor muscles of the ankle.

There is a moment of relaxation before the upkick begins. The knee flexes at the knee at the start of the recovery phase. The thigh now extends and the hamstrings, adductor magnus and gluteus maximus contract. The foot moves to a position where it is flexed and higher than the knee at an angle of about 130°. The sartorius, gracilis, poptiteus and gastrocnemius assist the hamstrings in the continuation of flexion.

At the end of the upkick, the sole of the foot comes under pressure from the water. The plantar flexors have to work hard to overcome this pressure. At the completion of the upkick, the leg is then adducted and slightly inverted.

Further advanced frontcrawl mechanics

In frontcrawl, as in all strokes, greater propulsive power can be generated when the hand is pulled through an area of still water. A swimmer's hand will have an area of turbulence around it. If it moves so as to push against water that has similarly been recently moved, it will generate less propulsion than if pushed against an equal area of still water. A large amount of water moved over a short distance is more important than vice versa.

There is, obviously, a larger amount of propulsive power if the swimmer pulls more deeply with the arms because the water is still, but there is less control around the shoulders in making that deeper movement. The pulling power increases linearly with the length of the resistance arm. The modern top freestyler tends to attempt to swim with a balance of these two facets.

The propeller is used by ships and boards because it makes efficient use of water. It is interesting to note that very few water-based animals use the water in this way. Man doesn't follow this pattern. Propeller blades always pull on still water because as they revolve they move forward, whilst the rotation of the blades in a lateral direction produces a forward force without pushing the water backwards.

As explained earlier, Bernoulli's principle results in different pressures bringing about a lift in the movement. The lift force is directed at right angles to the direction in which the blades are moving.

The sculling type of effect seen in the diagram opposite demonstrates the lift that can result.

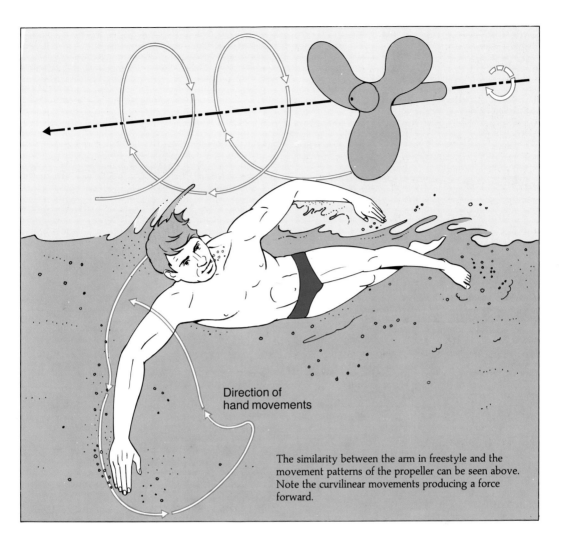

Direction of
hand movements

The similarity between the arm in freestyle and the
movement patterns of the propeller can be seen above.
Note the curvilinear movements producing a force
forward.

Hand movements

A slow-motion film of a frontcrawl swimmer
observed from the side may give the impression of the hand fixing and pulling backwards. The net motion of the hand is however
forwards. The freestyler overleaf show that the
hand is lifted from the water at the end of the
pull in front of the original point of entry
because of the forward movement of the hand.
Where poor purchase is made by the hand, ie it
slips, there is very little movement either
forwards or backwards. Despite this it is
important for the hand to keep as close to
pulling along the midline as possible.

As the hand quite naturally searches for
more still water on, or just over, the centre line,
the pull forms a three dimensional curve. The
fine balance between the level of resistance and
the power applied to the movement by the
hand, determines the speed of the hand. In
swimming a maximum speed of hand can only
be achieved for a fraction of a second. The hand
must then alter direction in order to attain a
speed of movement either anywhere near this
velocity or without the hand slipping in the
water. A high velocity over a long period
results in the hand slipping. A highly skilled

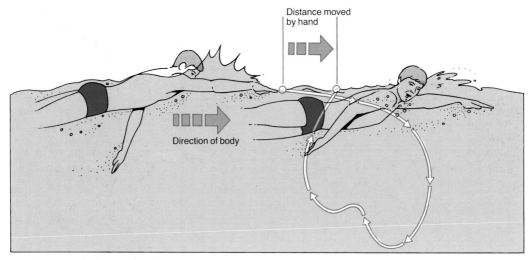

Distance moved by hand

Direction of body

The figures demonstrate net hand movement. The right hand actually moves forward considerably less than one might at first believe.

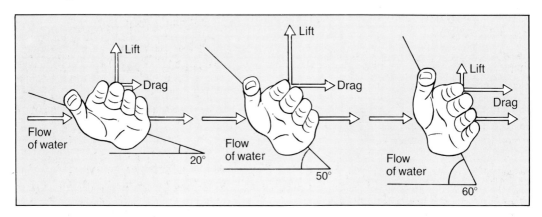

Lift

Drag

Flow of water

20°

Lift

Drag

Flow of water

50°

Lift

Drag

Flow of water

60°

swimmer will be able to alter and vary hand speed in order to get the best out of the pull. Cinematographic analyses demonstrated that the hand velocity of Mark Spitz varied between 3 and 10 feet (1 and 2.5 m) per second, but he was able to make all parts work to very close to maximum propulsion.

The position of the hand on the frontcrawl hand entry is also important. In order to produce the necessary lift force, the hand must be positioned correctly. The diagrams above also demonstrate how this can vary with the position of the hand either as it enters the water or as it pulls.

The diagram opposite shows the close balance between lift and drag forces in the

pulling hand. The resultant force, which comes about because of the two interacting, determines the direction in which the body will move. The pitch of the hand must therefore alter during the crawl in order to keep the body moving in the right direction. The overall picture is one in which the parallelogram of forces is constantly changing.

Body roll

Body roll is a further advanced element to be examined in freestyle. One can imagine the body to be operating rather like a chicken spit without going through the 360° motion, ie it stays prone throughout. Body roll not only

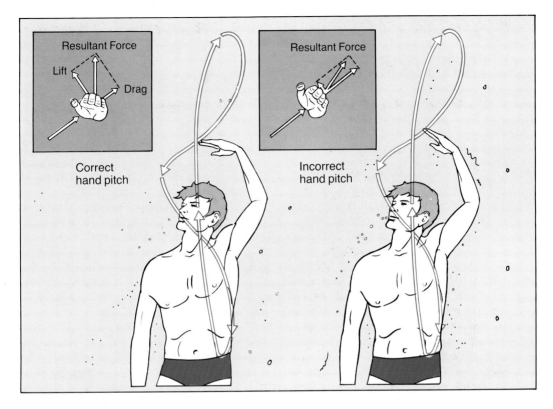

Correct hand pitch

Incorrect hand pitch

helps to make the stroke look effortless but the correct amount of torque keeps the movement continuously streamlined.

It's easier to achieve with the six-beat kick. The two-beat kick sees the lower half of the righthand side of the body balancing the movements of the upper side of the left and vice versa. The chicken spit works on a long axis right down the centre of the body. General momentum should always be maintained with no start, end or interruptions.

Considering the stroke as a whole, it's important to go into the catch at the right time. If it starts too early then some of the power from the other arm will be bisected. The catch-up frontcrawl where one arm enters the water before the opposite, pulling arm has even passed a point parallel with the face, is still used by mostly buoyant freestylers. It was used and encouraged by the top Japanese stars between the wars but it does create a lack of fluent propulsive action. The longer the arms are extended in front, the greater the leg kick required to accommodate this.

The figure shows the interaction of lift and drag forces in the pulling hand, which determines the direction of travel.

The hand is a very important agent in the frontcrawl. It acts as a type of sensor in hunting for the right water to pull on and in telling the arm when to apply power. To achieve this the fingers need to spread slightly, the hand be cupped and the movements should be completed with alertness and sensitivity, because of the smooth adjustments it makes in order to give the swimmer lift.

References
1 'Swimming Hints for Boys and Girls', Janet Bassett-Lowke, *Swimming Times* Sept 1938
2 'How to Swim the Crawl Stroke', T Hayashi (Bournemouth), *Swimming Times* February 1939
3 'The Dynamics of Arm Recovery', Norman Cox (Vancouver), *Swimming Times* Sept 1939
4 *Swimming Technique* Spring 79 'Effect of Arm Position on Strength of Pull on Free and Back'
5 'The Swimagraph' *Swimming Times* April 1939

6 Backstroke

Introduction

For swimmers who are just learning, backstroke has the advantage of their being able to keep the face away from the water and they therefore find it easier to breathe. In just about every other respect backstroke remains a very hard stroke to master: swimmers require a great degree of flexibility and strength.

Backstroke standards are continuing to rise throughout the world. The Americans and Australians were dominant in the twenty-five years after the Second World War but the Australians have lost their prominence and the European nations have passed the American women whilst honours are equal in the men's backstroke events. Roland Matthes, the East German ace, stood out above all other backstrokers in the post-war era. He possessed the flexibility, height and agile approach to the stroke which made him known as the 'Rolls Royce' of backstroke swimming.

The diagram below indicates the progress of backstroke in relation to other competitive strokes. In terms of world records, backstroke was the second-fastest competitive stroke until 1957. Backstroke was then passed by butterfly, although this was partly disguised by the fact that after being separated from breaststroke butterfly inherited the 200 metres event from breaststroke as its standard racing distance whilst backstroke remained a 100-metre distance stroke until the mid 1960s.

Increasingly backstroke events are swum underwater with the swimmer lying on his back, arms out above the head, and the traditional alternating kicks being replaced by upside down dolphin kicks. This was highlighted at the Seoul Olympics where the American swimmer David Berkoff swam over half the race underwater. To encourage a return to surface swimming, FINA introduced a rule which limited the underwater element of each length to a maximum of 10 metres.

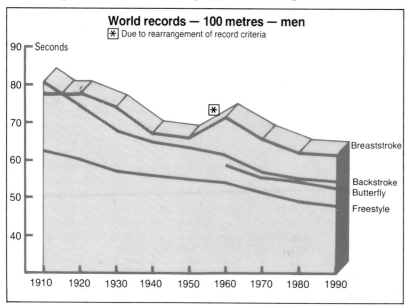

The graph to the left shows a gradual improvement in world backstroke records.

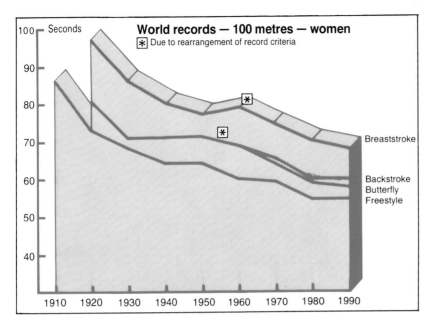

World records — 100 metres — women
⊠ Due to rearrangement of record criteria

This graph shows the improvement in world backstroke records for women.

Breaststroke

Backstroke
Butterfly
Freestyle

Basic ingredients

In backstroke the head should be well back in the water. There is a fine balance as far as the head position is concerned: on the one hand, the neck needs to be straight to allow the air to easily reach the lungs; on the other hand, the head should not be forced so far back that it increases surface resistance. The guides to this resistance are small jets of water that spurt over the head as it moves through the water (as in the diagram). It is therefore important to have the chin tucked fractionally in towards the chest to avoid that situation.

The head position therefore needs to be comfortable, relaxed and the weight of the head should be borne by the water so that the head is never carried above the surface.

A good way of ensuring that the water level is in the right position is to make certain that it is positioned just under the chin and over the ear lobes. The position of the head tends to be partly dictated by the power of the kick, which in turn partly determines the position of the rest of the body. The head needs to be absolutely still and this tends to hold the body on an even keel whilst the shoulders and arms produce body roll at the extremes. The rolling movement at the shoulders tends to generate greater power by bringing the larger muscle groups in the shoulders and chest into play. The fact that the head is kept still controls the whole projection and ensures that the power is generated along a straight line.

It is difficult for a swimmer to over-roll whilst the head is kept still. In addition, a swimmer can't over-reach with the arms because the head position will prevent this. To aid the breathing, the mouth should be open as much as possible but the mouth should also be relaxed. Tension in the shoulders, particularly in the recovery over the water, can come about as a result of this lack of relaxation.

As far as the torso is concerned, very little water should run over the chest and abdomen with the swimmer attempting to get his rib cage up towards the surface. He should also attempt to get the hips as high as possible in order that the stroke shouldn't have a sitting feeling at the hips. There shouldn't, however, be an over-concentration on pushing the hips up. The position of the hips is the responsibility of the feet and hands.

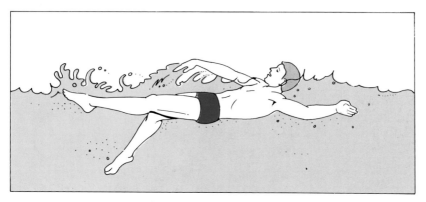

Note the relaxed but controlled head position as the left hand (positioned higher than the elbow) fixes on the water.

The left hand begins its final movement of the pull towards the hips.

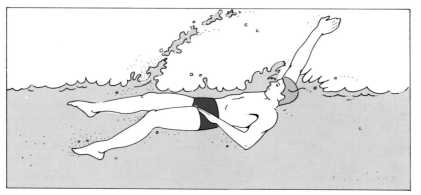

The right hand is forced upwards as the hand pushes back by the flow of water.

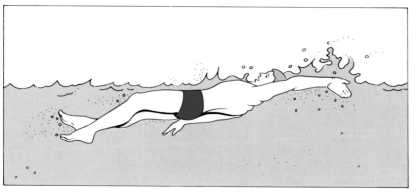

Notice how the shoulder has rotated, extending the elbow whilst the hand is driven back towards the feet.

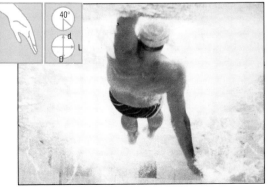

The pitch of the hands on the backstroke pull is out and then backwards towards the feet. The hands enter the water powerfully behind the head and this is achieved by accelerating the hands through the recovery.

(The photographic and drawing sequences show different starting points.)

The arm pull

This consists of a number of straight and bent arm movements which drive the water in the right manner in order for the body to move forward through the water. The pull consists of: the entry, the catch, the finish of the pull and the arm recovery.

Hand entry

The position of entry is either directly in line with or slightly outside the shoulder line. The little finger should enter first. Over the years a number of coaches have encouraged their protégés to enter with the back of the hand or in any manner that feels comfortable simply because they feel that a large amount of tension is created by constricting the muscles of the shoulder in a fairly unnatural movement in order to ensure that the little finger goes in first.

These movements do however create a greater area of resistance as the hand enters the water. The capacity of a backstroker to hyperextend the elbow joint will aid this movement. Hyperextension, or the capacity of joints to extend beyond reasonable degrees of movement therefore making them exceptional, is an important ingredient for both the elbow and knee joints in order to extend the range of limb movements during the pull.

As the little finger enters first, the hand should face outward at a 45° angle to the horizontal plane with the forearm. The palm slants towards the water at an angle of about 60° from the water's surface. It is important that the fingers enter before the hands and forearm and this can be ensured by slanting the hand towards the water by about 35° to the vertical plane.

Swimmers who have less shoulder mobility will probably attempt to enter the hand outside of the line with the shoulders. The more mobile the shoulders, the more the capability of the swimmer to rotate them and to therefore enter the hand with little finger first. The hand should be driven into the water and steady pressure applied. Generally the catch will take place at a depth of between 10 and 15 cm (4 and 6 ins). But this should allow a swimmer to catch hold of the water without drawing air under the hands and into the water. The depth of the catch will depend on the height of the swimmer and is difficult to determine. In backstroke the catch may be defined as the point at which the thumb enters the water (the rest of the hand having already entered) and the defined area of movement is from the downward pull of the arm behind the head to the beginning of the backward movement.

The catch

The catch describes the position of the hand prior to the pulling part of the stroke. When the hand has entered at a point behind the head, the swimmer now has to get his hand into a catch position before it reaches the maximum depth behind the head. The hand needs to be flexed in order to achieve this. The palm of the hand now needs to be in a position where it is perpendicular to the oncoming line of the pull.

At this stage the elbow remains straight and extended in order to give maximum range to the pull. The deeper the catch, the better the purchase because the water is more still at depth. This results in greater resistance and greater power as a result of the catch. The aim must therefore be to try to drive the hand during the catch back to a depth of about 50 cm (18 ins) before bringing the palm perpendicular to the pull.

The pull

The arms are now ready to go into the pull phase. This can be achieved by bending the elbow to a more acute angle and by applying steady pressure along the heel of the palm as

well as at the fingers in a general direction back towards the feet. More specifically, the hand moves from that deep position to a point adjacent to the rib cage but at a depth of approximately 15 cm (6 ins) beneath the surface.

The hand moves parabolically in its backward direction because of the different currents of water moving around it. As the hand starts to move back in parallel with the surface, fast water moves over and between the hand and the surface of the water. The swimmer's hand therefore tends to move automatically up a little in an attempt to keep the power of the pull constant.

The elbow continues to bend in towards the body. As it does so, the hand rotates from an entirely open position with the fingers in line with the rest of the wrist structure to a position where the thumb is uppermost and the hand slightly cupped. In terms of levers, the wrist must remain firm as it plays an integral part here as the fulcrum. The rigidity of the wrist will determine the degree to which more water can be pushed backwards because of the capacity of the wrist and forearms to be used here for pushing water back.

The elbow continues to play an important part. During the first part of the pull it leads the hand, but the aim of the swimmer must now be to reverse this. As the arm is drawn to a 90° angle with the shoulders, the hand is now pushed on in front of the elbow. The elbow is automatically lowered to allow this hand movement, although it's important to keep the elbow at an angle as close as possible to 180°. It is more likely to be around 120° because of water pressure and the optimal point of propulsion from the upper body.

The push

The hand should now be parallel with the rib cage. The function of the arm movement so far has been to set the hand up in order that it can apply the push from the very best available position for that particular swimmer. The push is vital to the whole stroke. If one were to look at the backstroke in a 'freeze frame' from the side, one would observe that the hand now fixes on the water and the body is now pushed forward on that point, rather like rowing a boat. A general observer might previously have viewed the backstroke as pulling his body continuously through the water, but forward movement only takes place on the fixing of this hand twice during every arm cycle. It is therefore vital to get it absolutely right as all movements to this position will have been wasted.

It is estimated that approximately 85 to 90 per cent of the backstroke power occurs at this stage. The push can be defined as being the part of the arm stroke which lies between the hand trajectory point reached by the average swimmer when it passes a point of movement in line with the rib cage to the conclusion of the propulsive hand movement prior to the arm being lifted out of the water for recovery.

The pull phase has ended with the palm facing towards the feet and the elbow bent to about 90° in a fixed position. Intrinsically, the palm now needs to be pushed towards the feet. The arching movement of the hand during the catch phase of the stroke is now reversed to a U-shaped trajectory. The drag created by the body form has created an area of disturbed water close to the hips and the hands need to get under this to make good purchase. In the meantime, the wrist has increased its hyper-flexion in order that the palm of the hand can lie perpendicular to the line of the pull. The elbow, which has been bent, now extends as the hand nears the hips on the push backwards. The swimmer should push right the way through to about halfway across his mid thighs. The hand should face downwards at the end of the push phase as this will assist in lifting the shoulder in the oncoming recovery over the water.

It is important to concentrate on accelerating the hand throughout the pull phase.

Continuation of the movement will have meant that the hand is flexed downwards to a position of 30 cm (12 ins) in depth. The aim should be to press or dab the hand downwards before lifting it out of the water.

This movement should occur as naturally as possible without an over-emphasis on the roll at the expense of the arm pull.

The recovery

The release of the hand will be assisted by a correctly balanced arm stroke. In other words, as the swimmer puts one hand in the water to begin the pull, it should be balanced by the other hand coming out of the water for the recovery. The hand-down movement will help the lifting of the shoulder. At the downward movement of the hand the shoulder should be kept close to the head and lifted ready for the arm movement. The arm is rotated outwards so that the little finger is lifted first from the water.

Many backstroke authorities believe in lifting the hand with the thumb first and for the shoulders to rotate the hand through 180° until the little finger is ready to enter first. The theory here is that again the blade stays clean of water on the initial lift and that the shoulders are able to rotate in a more relaxed manner than the wrist. It remains very much a matter of personal choice.

Top backstrokers do feel that by the second method they can retain a higher body position and bring about a quicker recovery because of the lack of resistance during the mid-air movement. The rotation takes place as the vertically recovering arm reaches eye level. This keeps the blade clear and discourages unnecessary water from running off the back of the hands. The fingers should be as relaxed as possible at this point. The recovery movement is now made in a vertical arc back behind the shoulder with the elbow and whole of the arm kept as straight as possible simply to increase the potential range of the arm stroke.

The hand moves at right angles to the surface of the water to the point of entry behind the shoulder. During the first part of the recovery the hand trails slightly behind the rest of the arm which is moving in a straight line. By the time the arm is immediately above the head, the whole arm is level. At the point of entry it has to be level in order for the fingers to enter before anything else. At the point where the hand is immediately above the head, the rotation of the shoulder should be complete so that the palm of the hand faces away from the body. Shoulder roll is important here.

Shoulder rotation

The great American backstroker John Naber referred to his backstroke body roll as a corkscrew-type movement. The shoulders rotate in order to facilitate a high hydroplaning action. This reduces drag as the body cuts its way through the water. The shoulder bearing the entry arm rotates backwards on entry and the opposite shoulder rotates forwards and upwards as the opposite arm is being lifted from the water. When the catch takes place your shoulder has rotated right back and your hips now follow the pattern of the stroke in rotating backwards. At this point the opposite side of the hips is substantially lower than the rotating aspect of the hips. During the first stage of the recovery the shoulders rotate upwards and the body moves with them. Rolling the recovery shoulder upwards will allow the pulling shoulder to roll downward, providing for a strong power phase during the pull.

Common faults and their correction

1 Over-reaching. This can normally be ascertained if the arm entering crosses the centre line of the body behind the head. This tends to affect the hand entry because the elbow touches the surface before the little finger, setting up a greater area of resistance on hand entry and encouraging the wrong hand position.

It can be overcome, as with so many things in swimming, by over-correction. The swimmer should be encouraged to put his or her hands in at a diagonal of about 10 and 2 o'clock from the head with the head regarded as the centre point of a clock.

2 Hand pulled too shallow at the start of the pull. The result of this is that the hand starts deep at the beginning of the pull and goes deep instead of the other way round. The problem can be solved by encouraging the swimmer to complete the stroke in the first place in slow motion, with the concentration on pressing down before pulling back. The stroke can then

increase in speed as the swimmer gets used to the deeper position.

3 The swimmer keeps the arm too straight for too long. The effect here is for a lot of lateral movement in hips and feet to take place. A swimmer who snakes his way through the water can be encouraged to pull with his arm straight until his hand is parallel with his shoulder. He can then press his hands directly towards his feet. This two-phase feeling should help greatly.

4 Under-reaching. This normally occurs when the swimmer begins pulling before the hand enters the water; the elbow is often bent before the hand has entered the water. The result is that the swimmer misses part of the pull and therefore wastes quite a large part of the arm pull. The panacea is for the swimmer to ensure that the arm touches the ear before entering the water.

5 Slapping the water. This happens when a swimmer fails to control the arm on entry. Again the swimmer will have to slow down the whole stroke. Pulling with the arms pausing at the entry point while two extra kicks are made has proved to be a remedy because it heightens the swimmer's knowledge of his arm position on entry.

6 Elbows drawn in to the body. A further common fault can be seen when swimmers pull their elbow in towards their body too early. This can best be overcome by explaining to the swimmer with the aid of diagrams on a board. Many swimmers simply bend their elbow and pull the arm with the elbow leading instead of attempting to lead with the hand and to rotate the elbow.

7 Failure to rotate the hand fully at the end of the arm pull. The final amount of power from the arm pull is lost because the hand is pulled out of the water too early. This can be solved by getting the swimmer to lie on his back and to then lift the arms, either alternately or at the same time, as far as a point in line with the shoulders. The swimmer then mimmicks the last part of the normal pull, gliding at the end of each movement and trying to feel the position of the hands at the end of the pull.

8 Hand slipping. This can occur at any time during the arm pull if the wrist isn't held firm. At the start of the pull it can, as already mentioned, lead to the pull being too early or for the catch to be partly missed. This is normally signified by frothy water close to the surface. It can lead to the hand slipping during the pull. This can be partly overcome by getting the swimmer to attempt to press his fingers in front of the heel of the palm whilst the hands are cupped during the pull.

Resistance also tends to be created at the thighs by the hand pulling water in towards the body at the end of the movement. This can be alleviated by rotating the palm of the hand over the original side-facing hand position and for slight downward pressure to be exerted at the side of the thighs.

The leg action

The legs in backstroke are there essentially to stabilize the body but they can also be extremely propulsive, particularly in the 100 metres (or less) events.

The legs should be allowed to move naturally, using the resistance of the water to its best possible effect. On first learning to swim the kick tends to be straight up and down. This doesn't happen as a swimmer becomes more advanced simply because of body roll: the kick tends to follow the line of the hips as they roll from side to side. The kick should be fairly shallow but strong. From a hydrodynamic point of view, the kick should lie between the surface of the water and the deepest part of the swimmer's body as he moves through the water. Generally speaking, the kick tends to be deeper and stronger during the sprints than in the 200 metres.

The backstroke leg kick emanates from the hip, the knees bending slightly in recovery. The knee shouldn't break the surface of the water. If we take one leg on its own, the ankles should remain extended on the upkick. The toes should be pointed but not rigid. This will have the effect of bringing the whole of the leg into play on the upkick. Mechanically the leg is now at its most efficient. The larger muscles of the upper leg can now drive the toes towards the surface. The toes should merely break the surface of the water on the upward movement, no more.

Water resistance will mean that the feet are slightly pigeon-toed on the upkick. The range of the kick should be shallow enough for both legs to not be more than 30 cm (12 ins) apart at any one time. When the foot has reached the top let the knees give slightly on the downward movement. The leg action as a whole should be used to get the hips a little higher and the chest very high in the water.

The right hand with fingers outstretched enters the water. Notice the chin tucked slightly in and the hips slightly under the surface.

1 The right arm remains straight during the first phase of the pull.

2 This arm has now completed its pull and the left arm catches hold of the water.

3 The forearm, as well as the hand, pulls on the left arm.

4 Here, the left arm finishes its pull with the hand pressing slightly downwards.

Common faults and their correction

1 The feet are too loose. This will lead to a lack of power. Simply, concentrate on pointing the toes on the upkick.

2 Bending the knees or knees breaking the surface. This will lead to the power of the leg kick being halved. Again, it's important to point the toes on the upkick.

Backstroke timing

The rhythm of backstroke is important to balance and breathing. As a general rule, a good competitive swimmer will use the timing which allows him to employ the most comfortable and yet powerful movement.

Six leg beats to each arm cycle (or every two arm pulls) is normally used on the 100 metres event in order to attain a higher body position. A typical arm cycle might be identifiable from the entry of the right hand. As the right hand enters the water at a position in line with the right shoulder and approximately one metre in front of the head (where the arm is outstretched), the left foot should be just breaking the surface by approximately 2 cm (1 in.) at the toe. The pull then takes place as the right foot begins its upward movement. The right foot should be moving from a depth of about 1 m (3 ft), where the right leg has been moving from an angle of 90° at the hips. By the time the right hand has pulled level with the shoulders the right foot should have touched the surface on the upkick.

When the right hand has completed its pull by pushing back towards the thigh, the right and left legs should be parallel with one another – the right leg halfway on its path downwards and the left in the same position on the way up. Throughout this period the left hand has been recovering over the water in an almost opposite position to the right when the two arms are viewed through 360°.

The left hand now enters and as it does so the right foot should be completing its drive

back to the surface. Four of the six upward, propulsive leg kicks have now been made. The left hand, as with the right, now pulls parallel to the shoulders while the left foot returns to the surface as the fifth of six beats. The complete cycle terminates as the left hand completes its pull at the hips and the right enters. When these two movements coincide the sixth and final beat, or the drive of the right foot, takes place.

The regular movement of the legs in this way pushes the upper body, particularly the chest, to the surface. It can produce a tendency for the head to be forced back in the water to match the chest movement. A good backstroker will reduce surface friction created by the head in such a situation by tucking the chin in towards the chest.

Four-beat kick

As the name implies, this type of backstroke is propelled by four upward leg movements to each arm cycle, or two pulls. It is normally employed by backstrokers who either find it more comfortable to lie low in the water because they lack the necessary trunk strength for higher poise, or those who lack true leg strength. A lack of angle flexibility can also lead to a swimmer adopting this technique.

In such cases, a four-beat kick is a good compromise. It can be employed successfully at any level over 200 metres and, at least at international level, over 100 metres.

Without repeating the description of the alternating movements of the arms and legs, as in the six-beat kick, I will summarize as follows:

1 Left hand enters; right leg kicks
2 Left hand pulls; left leg kicks
3 Right hand enters; right leg begins kick
4 Right hand pulls; left leg almost completes kick.

With some swimmers, the pull creates lateral movements at the hips, knees and feet. The result can be a crossing movement, called a crossover kick. This can be more evident in a two-beat kick where there is even more time for the legs to deviate laterally.

Two-beat kick

The two-beat kick is used by 200 metre backstrokers who have strong arms, are frequently heavily boned, particularly in the upper body, but lack leg power. This type of kick is now very rarely used at top international level over 100 metres because the legs in backstroke are seen as agents of speed whilst the arms are principally responsible for stamina.

The legs act as elements of balance. The left leg kicks up as the right hand enters and vice versa. The relatively lengthy period between these two leg kicks can lead to a range of compensatory movements in the interim period.

For instance, if the pull is not made directly backwards and part of the arm power is applied across the front of the body and hips, the legs, when parallel with one another (one halfway through the upkick, the other halfway through the recovery), may move slightly sideways in tandem to compensate. A further compensatory action may be made by the opposite pulling arm during its pull.

Timing and breathing

Although this is not always observed as being so, the timing is often related to breathing. The most comfortable method of breathing on six-beat leg kick is usually to breathe in on one kick and blow out on the other because it fits in with the faster rhythm of the legs. It is, however, somewhat difficult to ascertain whether the legs fit in with the breathing or the contrary. Our feeling is that it is the breathing that can partly determine the timing of the legs and arms.

The aim of the backstroker should be to expel air which he has used. The head needs to be in a good position from where to take in air but, as a broad rule, there are very few problems with the inhalation because a swimmer will very quickly tire if he fails to take in the air he needs for the swim. Most swimmers, therefore, take in all the air they need without further prompting.

The average backstroker doesn't, however, expel air fully. The lips need to be pursed and a puffing movement made with them. Failure to expel air on a regular basis can lead to a lactic acid buildup and the legs tiring quickly. It is a common fault for backstrokers to mouth the movement and forget to actually drive air out. This may occur once in, for instance, six exhalations, but on a regular basis it can lead to the body tiring more easily and is something to look out for.

Training for backstroke

Like all events, the backstroke, whether it be 100 or 200 metres for which you are aiming, needs early season planning. Technique is important and there should be a period in the season which is set aside for technical improvements. Technical corrections made during this period can then be reinforced through constant reminder during the racing season.

Correct backstroke turns should be employed during training and the use of backstroke flags in permanent position will assist trainees in their turns. A fair proportion of each workout should be devoted to backstroke legs because of the different muscle groups used here by comparison with other strokes. The pattern of the season as far as training is concerned will vary from country to country but will basically be as follows:

Phase 1 – Develop good stroke mechanics; iron out faults. Improve quality of starting, turning and finishing.

Phase 2 – The bulk of the training programme during the winter; build up stamina by distance repeats. Swim plenty of front-crawl in order to get greater distance covered in training in the time available.

Phase 3 – Transfer the training base on allround strokes to concentrate to a greater extent on backstroke. Yardage per day here would be between 14,000 and 18,000.

Phase 4 – In season would bring about an overall reduction in the distances completed and a honing of the starting, turning and finishing skills developed in Phase 1.

In Britain swimmers are now confronted with a two-season year, that is a two-peak season: one for short-course competition (less than 50-metre length pools) and one for long-course competition (50 metres or more). The average swimmer, particularly those involved in age group swimming, should be planning their season to peak at the National Age Group Competitions. Let's take the example of a backstroker of 14 years of age who has a best time of 70 seconds for the 100 metres in the previous season.

He should start the new season with a positive target in mind and must realize that if he is peaking correctly he will only achieve that target once in the coming season, hopefully at the National Age Group Competitions. His target times might look something like this:

September	1:11.0	
December	1:10.0	
March	1:09.0	
April	1:08.0	1st Peak
June	1:08.5	
July	1:08.0	
August	1:06.0	2nd Peak

The training should be designed in order to bring a relatively large drop in time at the most important period of the year. Swimmers are only human and there will be variations throughout the season but time targets on this broad basis would point the swimmer in the right general direction.

Backstroke stroke drills

Backstroke, in common with all other strokes, can be improved with the aid of stroke drills. Some swimming squads seem to suffer a kind of stroke drill paranoia: they spend the majority of their sessions working on drills. The problem with drills is that whereas they break a stroke down in order to help a swimmer to concentrate on the improvement of a particular aspect, they also tend to dislocate the stroke mechanically and the drills themselves are not sufficiently aligned with the strokes to help overall performance. Constant drills can therefore be of little assistance after a certain level of skill acquisition has been achieved. There is nothing quite like swimming the stroke for improving the stroke.

Below are some of the more helpful stroke drills.

1 Single-arm backstroke. This drill helps the correction of hands which are regularly entered in the wrong position. The swimmer can even take his head off the water and look back to check where the hand is being placed.

2 Double-arm backstroke. The idea behind these drills is to ingrain into the swimmer the correct position at which to bend the elbow during the pull in order to apply the backward movement. With two straight arms it is extremely difficult to control the stroke and drive the body forward. Recovering and applying the pull with two arms at the same time will develop the correct movement for this. In addition, it will encourage the chest to be kept high in the water and demonstrate the importance of a good strong kick.

3 Single arm with overhead pause. This drill will help in catching hold of the water at the correct time and finishing the push properly. A single arm is used for the drill, the arm not being used is recovered to the entry position and held above the head there whilst the other arm pulls.

4 Recovery with pause. Here the swimmer merely lifts his arm over the water in the recovery phase but pauses when the arm comes level with the eyes. Two extra kicks are made whilst the swimmer ensures that the hand is rotated so that the little finger enters first.

The muscles employed in backstroke

The bent-arm type of backstroke pull brings into action the muscle groups of the upper shoulder and particularly those of the upper arm. The deltoid muscle lies on the outer side of the shoulder; it overlaps the front and back of the limb and exists in the same plane as the pectoralis major, which passes from the clavicle and upper ribs to its insertion in the upper humerus.

When the shoulder joint is rotated, as in backstroke, the arm is also rotated on its long axis and the shoulder joint moved to the most favourable position. The glenoid fossa is brought into use by gliding the scapula over the surface of the chest or rotation upward or downward to face the right direction. The scapula is firmly anchored to the trunk, which makes the glenoid fossa a solid fulcrum on which the arm may swing as a lever.

The force is applied here when needed to keep the axis in place during this movement.

The shoulder joint (scapulohumeral articulation) is formed by the articulation of the spherical head of the humerus with the glenoid fossa of the scapula. This joint capsule is reasonably loose; it can permit up to 3 or 5 cm ($1\frac{1}{4}$ or 2 ins) of separation between the bones. As the backstroke arm lever meets the pivot here, the looser you are the more effective the range of the arm action. The circumlocutory movement of the arms is cushioned at this joint by cartilage called glenoid labrum.

The deltoid is a triangular muscle located on the shoulder with one angle pointing down the arm and the other two bent around the shoulder to the front and rear. The deltoid is elastically attached to the humerus, therefore controlling the movement as the arm is outstretched above the head. The anterior (or front) fibres pull on the humerus at a fairly large angle (as much as $20°$) and this angle of pull diminishes as it passes back to the acromion, where the pull is directly in line with the humerus.

The middle fibres of the deltoid muscle are responsible for lifting the arm in the first part of the pull. With the average swimmer the arm recovery would be higher over the water were it not for the action of the deltoid. The scapula is rotated downward by the pull of the deltoid and the weight of the arm which brings the lower angle back well towards the spinal column, depressing the acromion and making the posterior edge of the scapula stand out from the chest wall.

The pectoralis major group of muscles are a large group situated just under the skin at the front of the upper chest. With the arm having reached the thigh, the whole of the pectoralis major is now able to pull the arm forward. The upper fibres lift the arm during the first part of the recovery, the lower fibres pull at a smaller angle which diminishes as the arm approaches the head during the recovery.

It is therefore the upper half of the muscle group which plays a role in backstroke. These muscles swing the arms forward and inward, lifting the acromion which tends to help the second trapezius in bearing the force on the shoulder.

Probably the most important muscle in backstroke is the latissimus dorsi which is situated, as its name suggests, on the lower half of the back. The latissimus muscle is responsible for pulling the arm down by the side at the end of the pull. The lower fibres can also assist when the arm is high, pulling at a right angle when the arm is almost horizontal. When the arm has been lowered to within $45°$ from the side, the upper fibres adduct the arm and the scapula, working with a long lever arm. This is the best point of leverage for the muscle as a whole. The muscle pulls the arm to the end of the lateral plane, ie the end of the pull, whilst the pectoralis acts in opposition in pulling it forward.

The teres major, which is the muscle that operates antagonistically to the deltoid, is responsible for rotating the arm inward. The teres major also assists in the action of turning the wrist during the arm recovery so that the little finger can re-enter the water first. The infraspinatus and the teres minor help the arm to swing backwards as well as rotate.

The total backstroke arm movement may be seen as circumduction, a movement in which the arm, starting with the position of the arm hanging at the side of the thigh, moves through 360° finishing in a position vertically upward.

The lower arm bears a hinge joint and a rotary union of the radius and ulna in the forearm, ie the wrist can be rotated about a horizontal axis. The upper arm also has a large involvement with the stroke. The triceps, or muscle positioned at the back of the arm, is used merely for extending the arm throughout the elbow. By comparison, the biceps at the front is used as the pulling oar of the arm once the hand is in the water. Whilst the bicep is applying power on the pull, the degree or bend at the elbow is partly dictated by the brachialis muscle which is responsible for simple flexion.

This is supported by another elbow flexor, the brachioralis. These muscles are not really strong enough to provide a straight arm lever at the elbow, which is part of the reason for a bent-arm movement.

The pronator teres, which lies obliquely across the elbow, assists the biceps in flexion at the wrist and elbows.

The trapezius lies immediately under the skin in the upper back and may be seen as a flat sheet of muscle. It has the ability to assist in adjusting the position of the head in back-stroke. In addition, it plays an important part in lifting the arms above the head and moving through a lateral range when recovering them. The rhomboid, which lies beneath the middle of the trapezius, has a different role: it plays a powerful part in the first stage of the underwater pull.

7 Breaststroke

Breaststroke was the first competitive swimming stroke and it therefore follows that there have been more changes to this stroke than any other. The latest change, which allows the head to be submerged under the surface of the water, has not changed the stroke as much as I envisioned. It does, however, allow the swimmer to extend the stroke much more. When I was swimming this rule was not in place. We always had to be aware that if our head was to fall below the surface level we faced disqualification. This was a rule that I felt held back the development of my particular swimming style. It prevented me from fully extending my stroke and this would certainly have been an advantage for me. Breaststroke started life as a relaxed form of swimming with the head up, and as a stroke which could be used for swimming distances. It was popularized in the UK by the feats of well-known swimmers like Matthew Webb who completed most of the Channel crossing on the stroke.

In the more than a century since Webb's achievement numerous attempts have been made to adapt the stroke in order to keep it within the laws and yet develop its maximum potential speed. The law-makers have had the problems of controlling the situation so that the essence and original spirit of the stroke remain. In the 1940s and 1950s there was no limit to the distance that could be swum underwater. The result was that many top world stars, particularly the Japanese, swam for enormous distances in this manner because it was much faster. Eventually a rule was brought in which limited swimmers to one pull and one kick underwater for each length of the pool completed.

Butterfly-breaststroke then became common in the breaststroke events. There was no rule to prevent a swimmer bringing his arms over the water and, again, the world stars swam with the overarm recovery because it was faster. This was accompanied by breaststroke legs at first and dolphin leg kick later. After the 1952 Olympics the much-faster butterfly arms combined with breaststroke legs was divorced from breaststroke and at the 1956 Olympics they were swum as two separate events.

Breaststroke had just begun to settle again when Doctor James Counsilman and his famous Indiana breaststroke star, Chet Jastremski, revolutionized the stroke and very quickly had America, and then the world, following them. Up to and including the 1960 Rome Olympics, breaststroke had always been swum with a slightly swan-like approach: the head was lifted and a breath taken as the hands began pulling. The Jastremski technique saw the pull take first place with the breath being taken at the end of the pull, immediately before the recovery. The timing of the stroke therefore changed completely from pull and breathe, kick to pull, breathe, kick. The result was a drop of over six seconds in the world 200-metre record in 1961 alone.

In the over 30 years since then, the stroke has managed to avoid any wholesale changes but most breaststrokers tend to take their breath halfway through their arm pull. In the late 80s the Hungarians introduced a new aspect to the stroke. I refer to it as the 'roll over', where the hands at the beginning of the recovery stage of the stroke flip out of the water and stretch forward until the arms are at full extension on entry. This has developed as a natural progression for some swimmers rather than a positive change for everyone.

Wilkie breaststroke

My particular breaststroke technique was developed to suit my physique. As I mentioned earlier, the change which allows the head to submerge on each stroke came too late for me. Had it been introduced earlier I feel that I would have improved on my times in the 200 metre race. However, it would have made little difference in the shorter race, the 100 metres, as the stroke has a much faster turnover and allows little time to reach full extension. My main competitor, John Henken of the USA, had a faster revving technique and a flatter approach to the stroke so the present rule change would probably have been of little advantage to him. Many swimmers at that time swam quite flat on the water. Notabuka Taguchi of Japan, who won the 100 metres, swam in a fairly similar manner.

I had a higher longer stroke than either of these swimmers. As I pulled back I used to lift my shoulders clear of the water in order both to facilitate the first part of the arm recovery and to help get a good stretch into the final phase of that recovery. I have relatively long limbs and this helped in my particular case. I also managed to kick right through at the end of my recovery which helped to overcome any drop in propulsion before going into the next pull.

In 1973 I won the 200 metres breaststroke at the World Championships. However, it was felt that my technique still didn't turn over quickly enough to generate assistant arm speed for the 100 metres. This was borne out by my wins over 200 metres in 1974 and 1975. In the early part of 1975 my coach at the time, Charlie Hodgson, suggested that if I was going to win the 1976 Olympic 100 metres or have the necessary acceleration on the last length of the 200 metres, I was going to have to shorten my arm stroke slightly but try to retain a similar cadence as far as the rest of the stroke is concerned. The change of technique was hard to live with at first.

The modern idea of breaststroke would seem to be one in which there is a fair amount of rise and fall. This shows a complete reversal from the attitude of top coaches in the world twenty years ago who were advocating that resistance would be reduced by remaining as flat as possible.[1]

If we look at the difference between men and women swimming the breaststroke we see a great variation, with there being much more undulation in the women's stroke than the men's. The greater flexibility in women allows the dolphin kicking action to be much more evident in their stroke. I for one think this is an integral part of the 'modern' breaststroke. The ability to force the hips downwards on the propulsive part of the kick and then upwards on the recovery creates even more propulsion and therefore increases speed. A dolphin kick is not permitted in the rules of breaststroke so care needs to be taken that this movement is not construed as illegal.

General timing of the breaststroke

Continuous propulsion is hard to achieve in breaststroke because it has more natural 'dead spots' than other strokes. The movements should, however, slide over one another so that there is a continuously propulsive element. For the breaststroke to be continuously propulsive the body needs to be in a straight line at least once in every arm cycle.

In ideal terms, it would be much better for the body to move in a straight line fractionally under the water's surface. The net result of this is to bring about a situation where much of the body is moving through already disturbed water and the propulsive factor is therefore increased. However, the overall body tilt on breathing shouldn't be too great. It is, therefore, important to offset this by the correct timing.

If the stroke starts from a position where the arms are stretched out in front approximately 4 cm (2 ins) under the surface of the water, the body in a straight line behind, the hands start their circular pull outwards and backwards. At this stage the swimmer's head should remain in the water. When the pull has reached a stage where the hands are about to be brought back in front of the face, ie when the hands are almost in line with the shoulders, the head should be lifted and air inhaled.

The hands now cut in front of the face and the heels lift in time with the bending of the knees so that the kick can take place. The kick should not be timed so that the backward movement of the feet matches a corresponding forward movement of the arms – the two would cancel one another out. The forward movement of the hands from the chin starts first. As the elbows begin to straighten the swimmer should start his kick backwards.

A slight pause, but not a glide, should take place at the end of the kick so that the body comes into a straight line. If the hands start their pull again too early, the power of the kick will be reduced and much of it lost.

The arm action

The general movement of the arm action is wide, lateral and circular. It differs from the other strokes both in direction and the relative inability to counteract a pull which is out of alignment, by body or other limb adjustments. It is, therefore, important to get it right at the start of each movement.

If a swimmer assumes the straight-line position once more with the head in the water, eyes fixed about 8 m (30 ft) in front of an imaginary perpendicular line created by the nose and the bottom of the pool, then the hands and arms should be extended to their maximum with the hands facing the bottom of the pool. The hands should be together with the head in between, the ears being covered by the inside of the arms.

The first movement is for the hands to part. The palms are turned to face outwards so that the thumbs are nearest to the bottom of the pool and the little finger uppermost. The hands should not press down but pull round in a circle. The forearms should be encouraged to pull as well as the hands at this point. They should remain facing outwards with the elbows straight. The shoulders move forwards into the whole movement which helps the elbows to remain straight whilst the pressure of the water increases on them. As the slight lean starts, the lower arms drop slightly in the water. The hands are now pulled wide of the shoulder line on each side and when brought to a position where they are about 10 cm (4 ins) wide of the shoulders on each side, should be approximately 30 cm (12 ins) under the surface. Meanwhile, the shoulders remain close to the surface.

The catch

Most breaststroke swimmers would not catch hold of the water early in this pull. The hands would probably be pulled until approximately level with the shoulders before real grip took place. The deltoids and bicep muscles have a considerable influence on the powerful fixing of the arm as a lever at the shoulder.

The body starts by being stretched out.

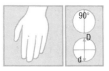

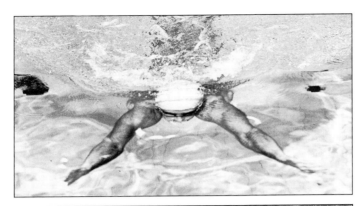

The hands pull out wide of the shoulders but are kept just under the surface.

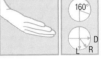

They are then sculled back in. Here the hands are facing down prior to being rotated at the wrists.

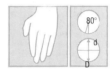

The head is now lifted whilst the hands are swirled together in front of the face.

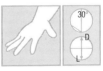

Finally, the hands are extended forward again.

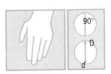

The pull

Unusually for swimming, this first phase of the pull isn't directed backwards. It's almost like parting the water for the head and torso to follow. The pull is out and then in; the breaststroke arm movement is a direct extension of sculling.

The two columns of water created around the hands are moving far enough away from the central axis of the body in order for the pull to be fixing on 'new' water until the hands start to cut back in under the face.

Having pulled until the hands are almost level with the shoulders, the elbows should now bend and the lower arms cut in. They literally make a minor swirl or clap. The hands, which previously faced outwards, rotate at the wrist. The upper arms should remain fairly still.

The hands now move from their outward-facing position, first to a situation where the fingers are pointing down towards the bottom and then round to a position where the middle fingers diagonally face one another in front of the face.

The hands are not more than 30 cm (12 ins) under the surface at this point. The movement of the hands together can be assisted by a shrugging effect of the shoulders or a high lift of the head to breathe.

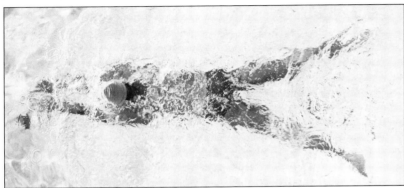

The hands should not be pulled back too far. They should always be kept in front of the face. The elbows should not be drawn backwards but should remain fixed in order that the hands can cut in. If they are drawn back extra resistance will be created.

The recovery

The effects of blading with the hands

Bernoulli's principle plays a greater part in breaststroke than in the other strokes because of the lateral movements of the arms. He said that pressure is reduced in a gas or liquid where the speed of a flowing fluid is increased. If we imagine that the breaststroking hands are blades then a change in the flowing speed of water comes about as the blades cut through the flow at right angles to its direction.

A greater pressure is created on the back of the hands as they blade their way outwards as this is a low-velocity surface, whilst there is less pressure across the palms of the hands as this surface is travelling outwards at a higher velocity. The net result is a lift force which is at right angles, ie forward to the identifiable fluid flow.

The hands act a little like propellers blading the water outwards which propels the body

forwards. They then blade back in at about 135° with the rest of the body and, unlike the upward movement, the thumb is up and the rest of the hand down. Interestingly, experiments have shown that there are two maximum points of hand velocity which are soon lost: the first, about two-thirds through the blading movement outwards, and then another just over two-thirds of the blade back inwards. At this point the hands are creating their greatest amount of forward force towards the body's total propulsion. Concentration on accelerating the sculling movements does the stroke no harm at all.

The hands are now returned from this praying type of position to the stretched position at the front. The palms of the hands should now face down towards the bottom of the pool and the elbows straighten as the fingers stretch out in front. The straightening of the arms tends to bring the stroke to a peak in that it concentrates the propulsion of the stroke along one central path towards where the swimmer ultimately wants to head.

The leg action

The multijointed and triangular-shaped leg action works partly on the basis of a parallelogram of forces and partly on the propeller-like movement of the feet in a manner of displacing water to create propulsion.

For many years it was believed that a great deal of power was created by two movements which were later shown to generate very little. We will explain these in order to create a better understanding of the current leg actions. Until 1960 the top breaststroke swimmers had started with their legs together, stretched backwards and in line with the central axis of the body. They had then bent the knees and turned them outwards and sideways. The knees had then to be drawn up under the body and kicked diagonally outwards at a 45° angle at the hips on either side and then brought together on the body's central axis.

It had been considered that both the diagonal kick backwards and the squeezing of the legs generated propulsion. The net result was not great. The kickout to the sides had made it difficult for the feet and lower leg to really become involved in the movement. The leg extensors in the upper leg did most of the work (like a frog). It was also later shown, using an area of coloured water placed between the lower legs of a swimmer in a static position ready to bring his legs together, that this merely displaced water upwards and not backwards. When coupled with the fact that the low position of the lower leg created extra resistance, particularly when the upper knee was drawn up, it became clear that this was not Man at his highest level of aquatic efficiency!

Slowly the modern techniques evolved. At first the upper leg was held fairly still, bent a little with the knees turned out in order to reduce the resistance factor. The next stage was to realize that a much narrower kick would aid the movement. The lateral extent of the leg kick was therefore reduced, the stroke losing its diamond sequence shape. This was brought

Once again, the body starts in a straight line, the toes pointed.

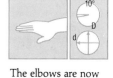

The elbows are now bent and the hands brought together under the chin.

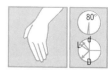

The knees start to bend as the hands are directed forward.

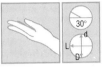

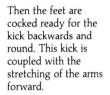

Then the feet are cocked ready for the kick backwards and round. This kick is coupled with the stretching of the arms forward.

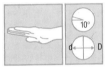

The kick is completed with a rotating of the ankles and the return of the face to the water.

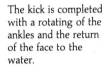

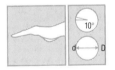

about by the knees being made to face the bottom of the pool. Finally the knees were bent so that the heels were brought up towards the surface of the water.

The ultimate result has been a leg kick in which the upper legs are more or less in the same position but the lower legs have reversed themselves from a position where they are lower than the upper legs to a situation where they are higher. Whatever would Captain Webb have made of it all! He swam a very different breaststroke in crossing the Channel.

The leg kick today

Let's now have a look at the leg kick as it should be swum today. If the swimmer starts with the body in a straight line, the legs stretched out together behind, the toes pointed, the legs should be in a state of extension right through from the hips.

The first movement is for the knees to bend and the feet to part, with the heels kept close together. The bend of the knees produces a diamond shape at the knees. The soles of the

feet face upwards at this point, the toes don't face backwards but are turned out at an angle of about 45° from the heels.

The knees continue to bend in a manner where the heels are lifted towards the behind and the water's surface. Obviously, the more flexible the swimmer is in the hips and the knees, the greater the potential length of movement and kick. The knees shouldn't bend so as to bring the upper legs under the hips. In addition, there should be very little forward movement towards the hips by the knees. They should stay relatively fixed.

When the heels have been lifted and drawn towards the behind to their maximum range, the swimmer is ready to kick. At this stage the feet remain dorsi flexed, ie the toes curled forward. The heels should also be in close proximity to one another. The kick backwards now takes place, matching the circular and backwards movement of the arms in direction. The heels of the feet press backwards first, then the instep and finally the inside surface of the lower legs. The ankles rotate to facilitate the movement which creates a large part of the propulsion (breaststroke is often considered to be the only leg-dominant stroke).

The feet kick back more or less in line with the hips. As the ankles rotate to provide the correct position for the kick backwards, the feet are turned sideways so as to remain fully curled at the toes. The instep presses on the water as the feet move backwards in a sideways-on position. As the knees begin to straighten, the feet rotate around the ankles so as to bring more of the sole into the rotatory movement as the feet begin to travel back and down at the extension of the knees. The final part of the kick sees the insides of the lower leg brought together in a whipping movement which is triggered off by the pointing of the toes. Throughout the kick backwards the knees are turned slightly but not fully outwards.

Firby[2] found that all parts of his propeller foot or a propeller take the same amount of time to rotate. 'The farther the point is from the centre, the larger the circle it travels and, therefore, the faster it moves through the fluid.' He concluded that if the foot propeller were to scribe larger semi-circles in the same time, much faster foot blade speeds and greater amounts of thrust should come about.

The pressure of the feet backwards on the water does not provide propulsion in the breaststroke kick. Like a propeller, there is a number of different blades within each foot which rotate to produce the correct effect. During the recovery the feet and these blades relax which separates the knees, and the movement helps the toes to turn in and stay close together. The feeling is one of lightness as they relax and are lifted by the disturbed water which the body has just travelled through. This, of course, creates a low-pressure area. They relax to the extent that they are close to the behind but stay under the water on all occasions.

The body will be more streamlined if the swimmer lets the hips sink a little. The feet now dorsiflex, ie toes curl, and the lower legs rotate forward slightly and then outward. They should aim to catch the water as high as possible in this rotation which will help to bring about a lift force similar to the blading movement of the hands. This scull or blading movement if made at speed will create great lift force. All the top breaststrokers have this characteristic known as 'fast feet'. The sculling effect is enhanced because the feet are pitched into still water which creates even greater lift. The thighs should be still during the catch and rotating only during the recovery and final scull of the legs which are by then extending backwards.

With every foot movement, the flow of water is faster over the upper surface which is convex in shape than the lower surface which is more concave on the sole. The result is an upward and forward lift from the underside where pressure is greater. On the top pressure is reduced. The Canadian Coach, Howard Firby, carried out tests at the Hall of Fame pool,

Fort Lauderdale, U.S.A., in which a wooden two-feet-shaped propeller was attached to a long shaft on a simple boat shape. It was driven by a round model airplane flight rubber. He found the results were staggering in terms of the lift produced.

The screw kick

Many swimmers do not have the necessary ankle makeup to be able to swim good breaststroke. In these cases there is little point in spending hours and hours trying to get them to kick according to the textbook – better to let them get on with a stroke to which they are more suited. However, many young swimmers just suffer from lack of ankle strength which causes the most common of all swimming faults, the screw kick.

With the screw kick, or dropped knee, the legs are not symmetrical due to the pressure of the water on the feet as the toes are curled during the recovery of the legs. This pressure tends to result in one toe being bent back in a pointed manner or the foot being flipped back with the toe almost pointed. The problem is often compounded because the young breaststroker can't see or feel the position of the arms.

The problem can be overcome by the swimmer turning his knees further to the side than normal and then aiming to keep as much of the soles or heels together as the feet are drawn up. The swimmer can now feel where his feet are and has his toes tucked out of the way and, therefore, they are unlikely to be affected by the pressure of the water. He can then cock his feet, bringing the heels together in preparation for the backward kick, when the feet reach the behind.

As he becomes more confident, he can slowly introduce the idea of drawing the feet up with the toes turned out.

Breathing

Breaststroke was originally very popular because it afforded the swimmer the opportunity to swim continuously with his face out of

the water, making it possible to swim without needing to breathe underwater.

The inhalation of air usually takes place

approximately halfway through the pull, normally when the arms have pulled level with the shoulders. Some swimmers breathe a little later, others such as Karoly Guttler, the world record holder in the men's 100 metre breaststroke, during the first third of the pull. The chin should be lifted slightly forward as well as upwards and the breath taken through the mouth. Some coaches advocate keeping the chin close to the surface but we would suggest that the breath should be comfortable and without strain. The lifting of the head can be assisted by a slight downward pressure of the forearms and hands as they begin to cut back in under the face.

After the breath has been taken, the head is returned to the water for the exhalation. When the face is placed in the water the eyes should return to their fixed position about ten yards in front on the bottom of the pool. The air is then exploded in two phases: the first taking place as the face enters the water; the second as the arms straighten in front of the head.

The swimmer should breathe once in every arm stroke. Breathing every two or three arm strokes merely leads to lack of extension and the non-conclusion of propulsive limb movements.

Some advanced aspects of breaststroke

Breaststroke is based on a system of propellers which in turn is based on an aquatic screw. The pitch of the screw and the angle at which it cuts into the water are important to the amount of propulsion that a swimmer can get from the movement. In breaststroke the image of flat surfaces moving against water is incorrect. Instead the image should be one of thinner surfaces at sloping angles. The breaststroker

should try to blade the water at any point in the stroke where it can be introduced.

The flat wing-like shape of the hand should always cut the water at right angles. The wrists and elbows are structured to allow for these fan-like movements and can easily create acceleration. While the hands fan out in this manner, the shoulder muscles contract before hand recovery and this brings about a situation

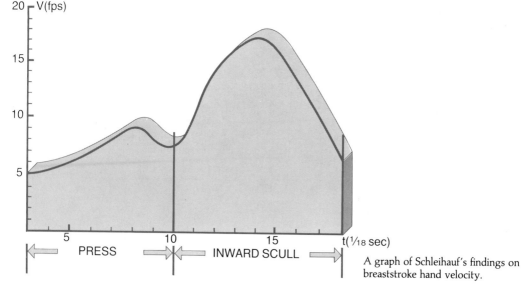

A graph of Schleihauf's findings on breaststroke hand velocity.

where there is a large amount of lift force. The body is now pulled forward with very little slipping of the hand backwards. The breast-stroke movements throughout should be into still water.

It is important to remember that the elbows are never pulled in towards the chest during the pull.

Muscles used in breaststroke

The body starts with the arms extended in front and the head in the water, with the arms together and the hands under the water to a depth of approximately 12 cm (5 ins).

The arm action is one with a continuous medial rotation. This is brought about by the deltoid muscles which cover the shoulder – these assist in keeping the elbows up on the arm pull.

With the legs, the medial collateral ligament on the inside of the knee is important in terms of stability. The quadriceps at the front of the legs and the hamstrings at the back of the legs are important muscles in the breaststroke leg kick.

The quadriceps are responsible for straightening the legs by extension whilst the hamstrings look after flexion and the bending of the knees in the recovery.

A small muscle, the peronei, is the major muscle involved in exerting the foot.

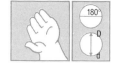

David's physique and stroke analysis[3]

The aim of a study by Lindsay MacPherson was to analyse my breaststroke technique in order to measure velocity and accelerations of the swimmer throughout the stroke which may provide indicators of stroke efficiency. The method used to analyse performance involved high-speed cinematography.

As the film was shot using an aerial view, 2 m (7½ ft) above water level, it was difficult to distinguish the hip area, where the centre of gravity is situated, due to the 'wash' created by the swimmer in motion. To overcome this problem the foremost part of the head was used for plotting, under the assumption that its movement related to the motion of the centre of gravity. This obviously caused some dis-

crepancy in the results, ie because the head is not the centre of gravity and also because the head does not experience the same forces as the hip area and therefore will not totally reflect the same movement. Ideally, an underwater camera with a liquid lens should have been used (a normal lens would refract the centre of gravity) but as this equipment was unavailable a 16 mm high-speed Bolex was used.

After a warm-up period to allow the subject to familiarize himself with the surroundings and test procedure, the subject performed some single lengths of breaststroke from a push start stroking approximately 50 per cent of full stroke rate. The camera was located approximately 3 to 5 m (10 to 15 ft) away. The swim was filmed from front, back and side views to try to build up a complete picture of stroke technique. Only the side views were analysed as these show the distance travelled per frame, which is necessary for the analysis.

The film was projected onto white paper attached to a flat-surfaced wall. From the film the two clearest side-view performances were selected for analysis. Reference points were taken from the surrounding background of the film to act as 'landmarks'. These landmarks were to keep the film in alignment in order to cut down errors and to gain as accurate results as possible. As the camera was fixed, the results are subject to motion parallax.

To analyse the velocities and accelerations, the foremost point of the subject's white cap was plotted for each frame. The analyses started when the body was in the fully extended position and finished in this position, one full-stroke cycle later.

From the plotted points a perpendicular line was drawn to intersect the graph baseline and form a 90° angle. As the subject was only swimming at 50 per cent stroke rate and was swimming with more of a glide than in a race, another analysis was calculated from his performance in the 100 metre breaststroke final during the Munich Olympic Games, hopefully to achieve results at race speed. The same plotting procedure was used for both analyses.

At each frame a diagrammatic progression of the stroke technique was recorded. This gave a pictorial account of the analysis which allows references to be made from the results

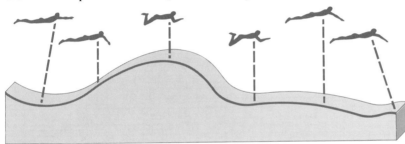

The diagrammatic interpretation on the left shows the complete stroke cycle.

Direction of travel

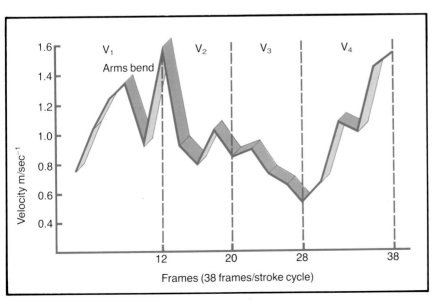

The graph on the left shows four reference points for velocity which are expressed in terms of V.

and the stroke diagrams. This makes it easier to make inferences about the velocity and acceleration throughout the stroke.

To calculate velocity and acceleration from the results, a programme was run through a computer. This was compiled with the assistance of Mr M. Lindsey of Dunfermline College of Physical Education. The velocity graphs were very detailed and to cut down the findings the second set of analysed results was scaled down from single frames to double frames (Analysis 2). This gave a much clearer result of velocity.

The results of both analyses taken from the cinefilm prepared in the pool show remarkable similarities for both acceleration and velocity. The graph shows reference points for velocity plotted from Analysis 2 for every second frame. These results of one full-stroke cycle were divided into four sections: V1 the arm pull, V2 recovery of the arms, V3 recovery of legs and arm glide, V4 leg kick.

There are two clear sections which are producing propulsion, V1 the arm pull and V4 the leg kick. These two sections show similar maximum velocities. The two phases which produce minimum velocities are V2 and V3, the arm recovery and leg recovery. The lowest velocity was recorded at the end of the leg recovery (commonly known as the 'non-propulsive phase').

During the first phase (V1) the velocity steadily increases, but at the fourth frame there is a sudden decrease in velocity. The subject bends his elbows during this part of the pull. This elbow bend could have caused him to lose 'hold' of the water. As the graph increases steeply after this it can be assumed that he has regained his 'fix' on the water. The subject also produces forces which cause his shoulders to rise up to 50 cm (18 ins) out of normal body waterline. This means his frontal resistance is reduced by elevating the body out of the water line and his pull will continue to provide propulsion. However, at V2 there is a sharp decrease in velocity. At this point in the arm action the subject's arms pause then his shoulders drop back into the water. This could account for the decrease of velocity accompanied by the fact that the arms are no longer

providing propulsion.

V3 shows a steady decrease in velocity. There is no source of propulsion so the body steadily loses velocity. The legs are also recovering at this point. This means the legs will begin to bend and present frontal area to the oncoming water. This will cause resistance which will retard the forward motion of the body. It is at the end of this phase that the lowest velocity is recorded. This is at the point when the legs have reached their maximum recovery.

V4 shows a steady increase in velocity gained from the leg-kick propulsive phase. The length of time to kick is the same length of time taken to pull.

As the subject is only stroking at 50 per cent maximum speed, there may be a longer gliding phase in the stroke which will reflect in V1. The arms do not usually pull until the body slows down enough for them to pull faster than the velocity of the body in motion (Counsilman, 1968). If the arms start to pull before the body has slowed down enough, the arm action will cause resistance rather than propulsion to the motion of the body. Because of this fact the velocity (shown during the arm action) may reflect some effects gained from the leg kick.

The graph for acceleration shows fast–slow swimming. The whole action causes great variations in accelerations throughout the stroke. As there are so many negative accelerations, it would be almost impossible to identify the cause of each.

These results were compared with those gained from the Olympic film. As this was in the 100 metre breaststroke event the subject may have been using a shorter stroke than he would normally use to do this. Counsilman suggested cutting out the glide phase. The stroke viewed from the side, however, does not give a complete picture of the technique used. It only shows lateral and horizontal movements of the stroke and does not indicate the width of any body movement. To build up a three-dimensional picture of the technique the stroke has to be viewed from all angles.

David would normally be identified with a longer-stroking 200 metre type of technique rather than a shorter 100 metre stroke.

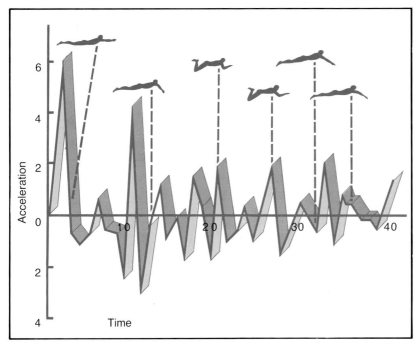

The illustration on the left relates the stroke cycle to the acceleration and velocity aspects of David's stroke cycle.

The findings on David's stroke were summarized as follows:

Using human judgment, an overall stroke action can be built up from the film. With this buildup image a comparison can be made between the subject's stroke technique and the recommended technique of top-class coaches from Britain, Australia and the U.S.A.

1 The subject has a good glide position at the beginning of the stroke cycle.

2 The subject has very flexible ankles and demonstrates the point well.

3 The great flexibility in the ankle joints allows maximum surface area of feet and foreleg to be utilized in the kick.

4 The subject's feet are approximately 45° apart.

5 The subject's body drops 45 cm (18 ins) into the water to add body weight, impetus and power to the kick.

6 The subject exhibits an acceleration towards the end of the leg recovery.

7 The subject kicks in the conventional backward kick but finishes his kick with his legs rather low which causes drag forces.

8 The subject also has his arms about 30 cm (12 ins) apart at the end of the glide (in the Olympic 100 metre final). This cuts out some of the sideways push at the beginning of the arm action and allows an earlier catch point.

9 The subject catches the water with very wide arms about 60 cm (2 ft) apart, his push is directed in a slightly curved pathway initially with a straight but later with a bent elbow pull.

10 The subject keeps his arms in front of the shoulder line. The subject, however, produces a lift of 45 cm (18 ins) out of the water due to the arm action. The subject pulls very deep in the water.

11 Due to his longer levers he pulls deeper and wider than normal.

12 Although the subject's arm and leg actions are wide, he has great power to execute these wide actions, which are performed at a slower rate than some other swimmers.

13 The subject performs his breathing but it results in a very high body position.

For those budding young breaststrokers, the measurements of David's physique carried out by the College of Health and Physical Education, University of South Carolina, during the National Independent Colleges Swimming Meet in the U.S.A. in March 1976, the Olympic winning year, were as follows:

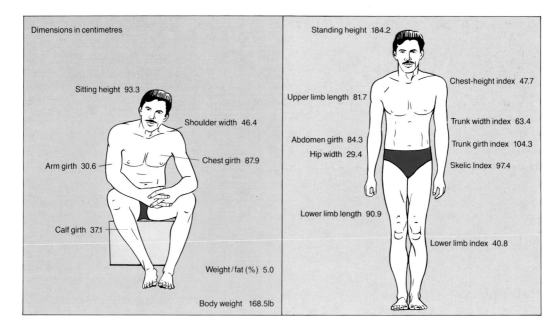

Dimensions in centimetres

Sitting height 93.3

Shoulder width 46.4

Arm girth 30.6

Chest girth 87.9

Calf girth 37.1

Weight/fat (%) 5.0

Body weight 168.5lb

Standing height 184.2

Chest-height index 47.7

Upper limb length 81.7

Trunk width index 63.4

Abdomen girth 84.3

Hip width 29.4

Trunk girth index 104.3

Skelic Index 97.4

Lower limb length 90.9

Lower limb index 40.8

The conclusions were that David's shoulders are wider than average but the chest girth was only 4.3 per cent greater than abdominal girth. The length of his lower limbs (90.9) is great and when related to his sitting height provides a skelic index of 97.4 per cent.

This index was well above average for a breaststroker and other swimmers. David had much longer legs in relation to his trunk and thinner but much longer arms than the average for a group of 47 top college swimmers tested at the same time. The comment was made: 'Wilkie gives the impression of an elongated symmetrical airfoil with a blunt leading edge.'

A closer look at my physique. My stroke suited my particular body type.

References
1 Terry Gathercole transcript at A.S.C.A. Clinic, Las Vegas, U.S.A., in 1974
2 *Howard Firby on Swimming*, Howard Firby, Pelham Books 1975
3 Cinematographical Biomechanical Analysis of David Wilkie's Breaststroke by Lindsay MacPherson in B.S.C.A. Magazine

8 Butterfly

Butterfly can be regarded as the sister stroke to frontcrawl, although the relationship stops there. Despite its frontcrawl double arm and leg movements, it appears that butterfly has developed as an entirely separate discipline without any regard for the mechanical concepts adopted in its sister stroke.

Butterfly is the most graceful of the four strokes and this grace can often be accompanied by great power, but it requires a considerable endurance capacity to be able to swim the 200 metres event and considerable strength to be able to swim the 100 metres.

Unlike frontcrawl, there are dead spots in the stroke where one of the limbs is not being used for propulsion. Frontcrawl is continuously propulsive.

Most modern butterfly swimmers try to lie as flat as possible on the surface whilst making undulating, caterpillar-like movements. Youngsters find butterfly difficult because the dual arm movements require the upper body to have a fair degree of strength. They often make the mistake of trying to crash the hands through the surface of the water in a vigorous movement. The fingers should be sensitive and the entry soft and capable of searching for a good catch position.

General body position

The guiding factor with regard to the body position is the head. A good butterfly swimmer will try to let the weight of his head be carried by the water rather than to use his neck muscles.

When the head is in the water the swimmer wants to be looking along the bottom of the pool approximately 5 m (6 yds) in front of the perpendicular position his head would create if he looked straight down. In this instance the heels should be about 3 cm ($1\frac{1}{4}$ ins) below the surface and the hips about half a metre (20 ins) underneath. The shoulders would be wrapped on and over the surface.

When the head is lifted the swimmer should try to limit the breathing movement so that the chin rests on the surface. This will result in the shoulders dropping a centimetre ($\frac{1}{2}$ in.) underneath, the hips remaining at half a metre under and the feet being about half a metre down.

The position of the body is also affected by a series of rotations at both the hips and the shoulders which we will explain later.

If the body is allowed to undulate too much the result can be a breaking effect on the stroke. Undulation refers to the up and down movements which are employed by the body in total in order to get the propulsive muscles into the correct position. Overexaggeration of this undulation can destroy the flat body position for which all swimmers should aim. The butterfly should consist of a small range of up and down movement driven by great power. Lifting the ankles so that feet break the surface and the lower leg is upright will have a retardatory influence.

If one ignores the arms, you can imagine the swimmer's body as travelling down a narrow cylindrical tube (see diagram overleaf). Movements that are too large will result in the

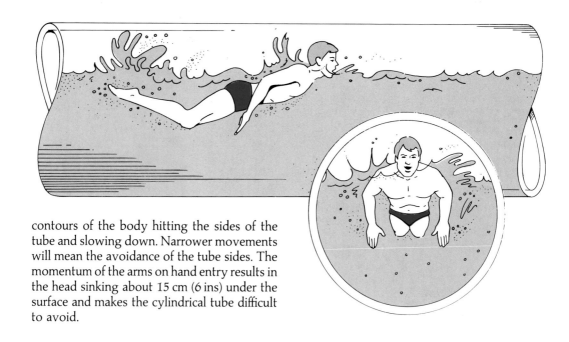

contours of the body hitting the sides of the tube and slowing down. Narrower movements will mean the avoidance of the tube sides. The momentum of the arms on hand entry results in the head sinking about 15 cm (6 ins) under the surface and makes the cylindrical tube difficult to avoid.

Arm action

The general movements of the arms are in tandem with a circumlatory movement taking place at the shoulders so that the arms are swung in a circular pattern at the shoulder sockets. The shape of the pull itself has been likened to that of an hourglass or keyhole because of the direction of the hand movements.

The hands enter the water just inside the shoulder line on each side. On entry the palms face outward at about 45° to the water's surface. The fingers should slide in first with the hands cocked so that the thumbs enter first and the little fingers last. The hands should be extended so that the elbows are extended at an angle of 180°. The aim should be to try to gain maximum extension in order to increase the potential length of the lever involved, brought about by the water pressing on the arms as they move water back. This is achieved by your hands and hips driving forward and down. When the arms have been extended to their maximum the hands start to pull in a curved pattern.

The swimmer should start by pressing at the fingertips and then with the whole of the hand and forearm. His aim should be to pull back towards his stomach. The first move is to push slightly down in making the backward movement towards the stomach. In all swimmers the shoulder structure lacks the strength for the water to be held by the hands. The water forces the hands in a circular path with the extent of the circle being approximately a metre (3 ft) from the central axis. Throughout this movement, the slightly cocked position of the two hands remains.

The catch

The point where the hands catch hold of the water is normally the point where the hands start their circular path outwards. This point is generally about half a metre (20 ins) under the surface. The hands here are usually in contact with less disturbed water and this continues as they move outwards.

The swimmer should aim to keep the elbows peaked above the hands in order that the forearms can apply pulling power as well. The catch continues with the hands being pulled in from a position where the elbow forms a right angle with the hands at their maximum point outside the shoulder line, about 20 cm (8 ins) outside. The swimmer achieves the inward movement by pulling the hands together strongly in front of the stomach. The elbows tend to fix in order to manage this, the forearm and hands pulling around the elbow which acts as a pivot.

The push

The press backwards takes place when the hands have been drawn slightly in front of and underneath the stomach. The hands never come completely together. Each hand creates its own column of disturbed water. There is little advantage in two columns of disturbed water acting on one another.

The middle fingers of each hand should at this point face diagonally in to one another. The elbows have bent to such a degree under the stomach that they almost come to a right angle again. This enables the swimmer to get greater power into the movement, particularly the push backwards which now starts. The hands are now turned so that the fingers face down towards the bottom and the shoulders forwards and upwards. The swimmer should drive his hips down towards his hands in order to create the feeling of pushing them under the body as they pull back towards the feet.

The hands pull back to maximum extension with each hand continuing its backward movement so as to be in line with each of the upper legs. The palms do not push straight back as in frontcrawl but with the little finger leading out of the water. The hands now lift out of the water about 20 cm beyond the hips (towards the feet). The hands should now face upwards and this is achieved by the swimmer keeping the elbows rotated.

The release

The hands are now released from the water in a final whisking movement. As the hands leave the water the palm should remain uppermost with the little fingers leading the movement. The hands should clear the water before recovery to the front position.

Swimmers who have difficulty in getting their hands to clear the surface at this point could try a number of methods to overcome this problem. The easiest method is to attempt to explode the remaining breath in the lungs before releasing the hands. The second method is to lower the head by looking immediately down at the bottom of the pool which brings the hip region, and consequently the hands, into a higher position for recovery. And finally, by ensuring that the palms of the hands don't face down towards the surface of the water.

The arms are lifted clear of the water ready for the recovery.

The head is lowered and the shoulders rotate as the arms recover.

The recovery continues and June begins to breathe out.

The recovery

The hands now make a semi-circular loop from their exit position beyond the hips to the entry position at maximum extension in front of the head. The hands should remain within 20 cm (8 ins) of the surface throughout. The whole movement should be assisted by the swimmer rolling the shoulders. This means that the shoulders bear part of the burden of recovery by rotation and will lighten the workload of the arms at a time when there needs to be a degree of relaxation.

Again the recovery can be aided by dropping the head a little further under the water.

The palms of the hands should face outwards during the recovery with the little finger uppermost. This discourages the elbows from dropping and catching the surface.

When the hands recover to a position where they are in line and in front of the shoulders prior to entry, they should be rotated so that the palms face down and the thumbs enter slightly first. If the elbows are not fully extended on entry, and it is advisable not to achieve this position too early, then the hands should enter in an elbows-up position with the fingers being driven into the water about 25 cm (10 ins) in front of the head.

The leg action

Loose ankles and supple legs are important to the butterfly kick. As with all the up and down kicks in swimming, a swimmer with hyperextension of the knee joint has a distinct advantage. A large range of up and down movement is needed and this can be increased with this type of physical makeup.

Intrinsically, the feet are down in the water when the hips are up and vice versa. The parameters of the kick are full extension of the legs at an angle of approximately 30° to the surface and the bending of the knees to an angle of 45°.

The kick should normally take place either before or towards the end of the pull but not during it. The rhythm of butterfly is such that the stroke usually has one major and one minor kick per complete arm cycle. Many swimmers kick when the arms are first entering and kick again when their arms are being released from the water for the recovery. The major or harder kick is usually made on hand exit with the second kick partly used for balance at the start of the arm pull and, therefore, the strength of this kick tends to be dependent on this factor amongst others. A highly skilled swimmer makes a relatively major kick at the start of the pull with a major beat at the end. In addition, the swimmer who can make two major kicks is very rare indeed.

The kick emanates from the hips and consists of a foot-shaking movement. The knees bend to an angle of about 120° in order to prepare the feet to be driven downwards. The water presses on the calves and soles of the feet during this movement and it's important that while the ankles relax, the rest of the leg structure continues to partly contract in order to provide some propulsion and partly to overcome the force of the water acting on it.

The feet are plantar flexed and therefore the toes pointed. As the knees are bent, the heels shouldn't break the surface but should remain about 4 cm (1½ ins) underneath at their peak. This movement is facilitated by a slight drop of the hips. The toes are in a state of slight relaxation so that the weight of the feet is borne by the water during the recovery phase. The feet are now driven down towards the bottom of the pool by kicking hard at the toes and the result is an extension of the whole leg at the diagonal to the upper part of the body. The hips rise as the toes are pointed at the end of the kick down.

The knees are bent and the feet drawn up to the surface. The bending of the knees would normally take place as the arms, which are recovering over the water, swing back in line with the shoulders during their forward trajectory. This would bring the feet into position to kick down as the hands enter the water in front of the head. The knees bend for a second time during the pull underwater. This bending movement usually takes place as the hands pull back and become positioned immediately under the head. This positions the feet for the second downward kick as the hands are coming out of the water.

The second kick should be employed by the swimmer in order to come up for breath. A solid downward kick helps the lift of the head. However, there is an important difference between kicking to come up to breathe and coming up to breathe in order to kick! The former ploy should always be adopted but we suspect that many young swimmers always go for the latter because of insufficient strength and flexibility. The second kick which takes place during the latter part of the pull helps to balance the lifting of the arms, which moves the hips downwards and keeps the body moving in a forward direction.

When only the leg movements are swum, butterfly legs are the fastest of all leg actions. The isolated kick is almost as continuously propulsive as the frontcrawl leg action and has double the power because of the use of both legs at the same time. The leg kick can be described as fishtail-like. When swimming slowly a major kick is made at the start of the stroke with a minor one at the end. This tends to reverse itself at speed.

Breathing

Both the explosive and trickle methods can be used in butterfly in the same way as in other strokes. The optimum time for taking a breath is when the arms have finished their underwater pull. At this point the legs have kicked downwards and forced the upper body higher in the water.

The swimmer should now merely lift the head by extending the neck region. The aim should be to lift the chin so that it is both comfortable and lies close to the surface of the water. It should be lifted forward rather than just upwards during the stroke. The inhalation now takes place.

When the swimmer has taken in air he drops the chin so that the hairline rests on the surface. This will assist in trying to reduce the range of head movement and the subsequent effect on the rest of the body. Swimmers who have difficulty in either getting their hips or feet up, or in getting their arms clear of the water, will need to drop the head lower by looking vertically downwards. The air is exhaled through the mouth (which in turn leads to it being exhaled through the nose) at any time when the face is under the water. Most good swimmers will breathe out when the arms reach the end of the pull. The explosive exhalation assists the hands in their release from the water. In addition, the retention of air in the lungs throughout the first phase of the pull helps the rib cage and upper body to ride higher and so reduce resistance.

Other swimmers do, however, breathe out as the catch takes place and again as the hands are about to leave the water.

Occasionally, there are swimmers who find that their personal timing system is such that they need to take a breath earlier in the stroke, usually when the arms are still halfway through the recovery. This type of breathing tends to be less fluent and tends to create a situation in which the spine, body line and lumbar region are in a state of extension and hyperextension. Generally the tone of the stroke should be one in which the body is flexed and slightly curled in order to aid the rotatory movements of the hips and shoulders. Nevertheless there have been a number of top swimmers who have swum this way — the American Olympic medallist Fred Schmidt immediately springs to mind.

Timing

As far as butterfly is concerned, most find the learning and mastering of the arm pull and leg kick are relatively easy. The really difficult part is coordinating the two so that the swimmer gets the idea of kicking twice to every arm cycle.

The timing can be developed in the early years by giving the young swimmer plenty of kicking with the emphasis on movement throughout the body, with the exception of the shoulders which should be kept still. The kicking is best completed with the arms extended in front, without a float, breathing every two or three kicks. The body can be immersed to a depth of about half a metre. Kicking along the surface will not give the body the feeling of equal pressure on both sides as it will from time to time break the surface. Kicking whilst immersed is closer to the full stroke situation where water surrounds the hips and legs and the pressure of water on the body is more equal.

A downward kick takes place forcing the hips to rotate upwards.

The hands start to pull from a position wide of the shoulders.

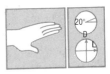

The elbows are kept high as June starts to pull the hands towards the stomach.

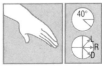

The knees begin to bend as the swimmer lifts her head to breathe.

As the hands pull under the body, the knees are bent still more and the head lifts.

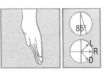

There are various exercises that one can set to help a swimmer overcome the feeling of kicking and pulling at the same time. Possibly the best way at an early stage is to get the swimmer to place his hands well out in front of him. He will be kicking along the surface on this occasion. The swimmer makes four kicks with his hands in front. At the end of the fourth kick the arms are recovered and then pulled through the water and a further kick made. The timing is therefore: one, two, three, four, pull, five. The fifth kick should be emphasized and not forgotten, and should be made at the end of the pull. The four previous kicks give the swimmer time to set himself up.

One of the kicks is then deleted making it three kicks, a pull and then a further kick. A further kick is then deleted so that the practice become two kicks, a pull and a kick. Finally the practice is reduced to a kick, a pull and a kick, the correct rhythm for the stroke. This would need to be thoroughly practised with young swimmers who are experiencing difficulties with the double-beat kick.

There are individual differences from swimmer to swimmer as far as timing is concerned but every individual has a different breathing timing which helps to keep the body up and improve the general timing of the stroke. Some swimmers breathe every two strokes, others on each arm cycle. A third method is to breathe at the end of the second arm pull and then at the end of a single arm pull, and to alternate in that manner. Most swimmers use this as a flattening-out process. At one time a greater number of butterfly swimmers breathed to the side than at the present time.

If one were to consider the shoulders and upper body in isolation, a good swimmer, whatever the timing, should be able to assume literally the same position during the recovery whether a breath is being taken or not. The hallmark of a good swimmer can be seen in a situation where a swimmer both lifts his head up to breathe and also breathes with the shoulders in the same position. This keeps the overall body position constant and the muscular system functioning efficiently.

The shoulders should always be kept close to the surface while the hips do the undulating and driving. The ability to retain this position is determined by the swimmer's personal hip flexibility rather than shoulder mobility.

The rules

The amateur rules require that the total stroke be kept perfectly on the chest with little lateral deviation. The rules mean that there should be no body tilt to one side.

The arm action also should be simultaneous and symmetrical. The arms should mirror one another. In addition, the recovery of the arms must be made over the water, which distinguishes the stroke from breaststroke.

The legs should be driven up and down as opposed to kicking to the side. There shouldn't be any outward movement of the legs – again, a distinction from breaststroke. The legs should be, as with the arms, simultaneous, but the rules have been relaxed in recent years so that the legs no longer need be symmetrical.

These rules are extended to the butterfly turn where the shoulders should be level in the horizontal plane, but they vary from country to country where the hands touch simultaneously in the horizontal plane either above or below the water.

Muscular analysis

There is relatively little flexion or extension of the shoulders during the recovery or pull-through phase of the stroke. The recovery is produced by adduction and external rotation of the region. The hands are brought forward by external rotation of the humeri, unless the arms are kept quite flat and close to the surface where there is a greater rotation of the shoulders.

Unlike frontcrawl, the hands can't pull straight on the centre line because the adductors and internal rotatory muscles of the upper body are in a weak pulling position. This is overcome by body roll in the frontcrawl, but in butterfly it is only overcome by the arms moving in a semi-circular path under the body.

The muscles employed for these movements are very similar to those used for very similar movements in the frontcrawl. The power of the pull underwater is developed by internal rotation of the humerus. The pectoralis major and minor, the latissimus dorsi and the subscapularis muscles are responsible for this. During the push phase the latissimus, pectorals and the teres major continue the movement. The shoulder blades, or scapula, rotate downwards as a result of the actions of the rhomboids and pectoralis minor. This helps to bring about the movement down to the end of the pull. The elbows are held up higher than the hand with some flexion of the elbow which comes about as a result of firm movements by the biceps, brachialis, brachioradius and pronator teres. The pronator teres and the pulmaris longus work to keep the wrist in its slightly prone position. The final push is, however, achieved with the wrist and fingers flexed at the metacarpophalangeal joints. Five groups of flexor muscles help to bring this about. The fingers and thumb are adducted by the palma interossei, the oppens digita quinti, the adductor pollicis and the oppenens pollicis.

The leg movements merely duplicate the frontcrawl leg movements already described, except that the larger quadriceps muscle has twice the strength of movement at any one propulsive phase because of the use of two limbs instead of one.

9 Individual Medley

Individual medley, particularly the 400 metres, is considered to be the sternest aquatic test. It requires the all-round ability of the decathlete in track and field, although the similarity stops there: the decathlon is broken up over two days with as much as an hour's rest between the ten disciplines; the individual medley is fused together and requires stamina over a four- or five-minute period at the maximum.

It's often said that the individual medley favours breaststrokers because it is the slowest of the four disciplines and therefore easier to make up more headway. However, it's also important to have a good backstroke and for the whole swim to be evenly balanced. Whether the event is 200 metres or 400 metres, the last leg of frontcrawl should be of equal speed to the butterfly on the first leg in order that the swim is balanced and energy used in an optimum manner.

The origins of individual medley stretch back over this century, although there were various military events where both Greek and Roman soldiers were required to complete an omnibus of various sports including swimming. L. de B. Handley, the well-known American swimming coach, can remember competing for his swimming club, Knickerbocker and N. Y. Athletic Clubs, in an event in September 1901 which was simply known as The Medley[1]. The event included walking, running, horseriding, cycling, rowing and swimming, a quarter of a mile each. Handley set a world record of 15:42 in this event, which was more of a pentathlon than a medley.

The first recorded individual medley champion was a woman. It was Hilda James of Liverpool who won the first individual medley in the 1922 U.S. Championships. At this time the medley comprised backstroke, breaststroke and frontcrawl. The men didn't in fact compete in a medley but swam in another event called the pentathlon in 1923 when Johnny Weissmuller tied with Stubby Kruger, both of Illinois Athletic Club. The event was 100 yards backstroke, breaststroke, 500 yards any style, 100 yards of any stroke other than backstroke or breaststroke, plus 50 yards lifesaving. The pentathlon lasted for four years in the U.S. Championships and was then gradually replaced by the medley with Kruger also winning the first U.S. 300 yard individual medley championship.

Experiments with butterfly were carried out throughout the 1930s in the U.S.A., but it was not accepted by F.I.N.A. as a separate stroke until 1953. Johnny Weissmuller can also remember experimenting with the dolphin kick as early as 1923[1]. So it was not until after 1953 that the individual medley grew into a fully fledged international swimming event.

The first long course (50-metre pool) world record holder was Australia's Frank O'Neill in March 1953, with Dick Roth of Santa Clara, U.S.A., the first Olympic Champion in Tokyo in 1964. The first women's individual medley Olympic Champion, Donna De Varona of Santa Clara, was world record holder over 100 metres in three of the four strokes. Nowadays this is only likely to happen in two events at the very most, such is the degree of specialization in the sport, but De Varona's feat indicates that the medley swimmer has to be very close to the top or at the top in all the disciplines in order to win Olympic titles.

Cadence

Cadence, which can be identified as the measured arm movements in the medley, and pace are two important linked features. There is, of course, a substantial difference between the endurance-based 400 metres and the 200 metres which requires a quicker turnover.

As a general rule, the butterfly leg, which comes first, should be stretched out with the swimmer aiming to eat up as much ground as possible whilst still remaining as relaxed as possible. The turns are important here, but we shall look at these later on. The swimmer should aim to take the wall on the butterfly turn at long reach with the head going down.

Tactically, a competitor should try to set himself up for ground-gaining legs in the backstroke and breaststroke. Keeping up with the leaders without using up too much energy is important. Try never to look at your opponents, particularly at this early stage in the event.

The rhythm of the backstroke is not substantially different from that of the butterfly. The alternate arms of the backstroke roughly double the rate of the turnover on the butterfly leg. The legs now need to be worked harder with a strong attempt to really work the first 10 m of the leg or each length in order to get the body high. It's important that the breathing is kept up and that the swimmer exhales as much carbon dioxide as possible.

Again, the turn should be taken at long reach. Immediately after the push off on the breaststroke the swimmer should ensure that he brings his body in line with the surface before going into the length. There is now a temptation to race through the arm pulls and to try to adopt the same rhythm of the previous two strokes. This just won't work – feel the full scull out of the arms and complete the movement back in. Try to make the kick as effective as possible. Finish each kick before going into the next stroke. Again, try not to look round to see where your opponents are positioned.

If you are aware of where your competitors are then try to either catch them up if you're behind or pull away if you're in front. The breaststroke is an important leg from this point of view.

The rhythm of the frontcrawl is once again quite different. The swimmer is now confronted with a situation at the turn where there isn't a tremendous amount of momentum off the wall due to a tiring body. Mentally it's easy to sag here. Try to get out of this by swimming the first ten strokes with a very quick turnover of the arms. This breaks down the image that the mind has of the turnover to be used in the forthcoming leg. It also breaks up the neuro-muscular message of the previous length.

The frontcrawl length should see the swimmer really letting go. Don't panic as you get towards the end if you know you're not in front. Try to hold onto your technique and finish with the last three strokes with the face in the water.

Pace

The ability to pace an individual medley is partly determined by the swimmer's inbuilt personal timing system. At different times, writers have laid out a series of what they would consider to be ideal target splits. We have tried to follow this through basing our tables on figures of the most successful Olympic Champions. There is, of course, great room for personal variation according to one's own particular strengths and weaknesses but Table 1 overleaf provides an insight into medley trends since the 1968 Olympics.

Table 1 gives the split times of the Olympic event winners between 1968 and 1980 and the times of one of the leading British competitors, in the same races. Listed beneath each time is the percentage amount of overall time recorded that this split represented.

Table 1: Analysis of Olympic medley splits

Olympic medley winners with the competitive proportions that each leg took them in relation to the overall time.

1968
400 metres

Men	Charles Hickcox	1:02.40	2:15.90	3:44.60	4:48.40
		21.63	25.48	30.75	22.12
Women	Claudia Kolb	1:08.20	2:27.90	3:57.90	5:08.50
		22.10	25.83	29.17	22.88

1972
200 metres

Men	Gunner Larrson	28.00	1:01.70	1:38.07	2:07.17
		22.01	25.21	29.09	22.08
Women	Shane Gould	31.07	1:08.46	1:51.07	2:23.07
		21.71	26.13	29.78	22.36
G.B.	Shelagh Ratcliffe	32.97	1:11.66	1:56.28	2:31.04
		21.82	25.61	29.54	22.74

400 metres

Men	Gunnar Larrson	1:03.41	2:14.07	3:32.17	4:31.98
		23.32	25.97	28.71	21.99
G.B.	Barry Prime	1:04.55	2:18.42	3:48.31	4:57.77
		21.67	24.80	30.18	23.32
Women	Gail Neall	1:08.64	2:25.33	3:55.51	5:02.97
		22.65	25.31	29.76	22.22
G.B.	Sue Richardson	1:09.72	2:32.02	4:04.82	5:19.53
		21.81	25.75	29.04	23.38

1976
400 metres

Men	Rod Strachan	1:00.61	2:05.92	3:32.92	4:23.68
		22.98	24.76	29.58	22.64
G.B.	Alan McClatchey	1:01.38	2:10.95	3:33.35	4:34.31
		22.37	25.36	30.03	22.22
Women	Ulrike Tauber	1:03.73	2:15.29	3:38.00	4:42.77
		22.53	25.30	29.24	22.90
G.B.	Sue Richardson	1:07.60	2:27.80	3:55.36	5:06.39
		22.06	26.17	28.57	23.18

1980
400 metres

Men	Alexander Sidorenko	59.18	2:04.59	3:20.81	4:22.89
		22.51	24.88	28.99	23.61
G.B.	Simon Gray	59.67	2:07.99	3:28.45	4:29.43
		22.14	25.35	29.86	22.63
Women	Petrea Schneider	1:01.72	2:12.22	3:32.19	4:36.29
		22.33	25.51	28.94	23.20
G.B.	Sharron Davies	1:04.86	2:17.60	3:42.97	4:46.83
		22.61	25.38	29.74	22.26

116

The results show constant trends in medley swimming have changed little since it was first introduced as an Olympic event. In both men's and women's swimming, whether it be 200 or 400 metres, the butterfly leg represented between 21.63 and 23.31 per cent, the latter percentage representing a time which was 0.4 seconds slower than any of the others.

The backstroke legs can be identified as a range of 24.76 and 26.17 per cent; the breaststroke range was 28.71 and 30.75 per cent; while the freestyle leg can be seen as being between 21.99 and 23.61 per cent. In no way can these figures be considered to be fully representative but they contain a number of Olympic title wins over both distances and in no case is there a differential of more than 2.5 per cent.

It follows that in a race situation the breaststroke has always occupied a larger proportion of the time and it therefore follows that someone who is strong on this particular leg has a longer period in relation to his own swim in which to make headway. The butterfly and freestyle percentages, which are almost the same, demonstrate the idea of balancing the medley so that the swimmer achieves the same time in both. As a general observation, it's very hard to grasp the feeling of slowing down the

butterfly in order to avoid the buildup of an oxygen debt too early in the race.

In a race situation energy is normally supplied by anaerobic sources for the first two minutes. After that period the oxygen requirement increases and aerobic respiration comes into being. In a medley the butterfly and some of the backstroke in the 400 metres and nearly the whole race in the 200 metres are swum anaerobically. It's impossible to determine the degree to which these percentages are affected by the buildup of lactic acid and the respiratory change which results, as opposed to the mere hazards of changing strokes.

The closest means of comparison would be by examining the Olympic 400 metre freestyle winners, as we have in Table 2.

In relation to the overall race performance, the average first 100 metres is equal to between 23.58 and 24.76 per cent, some 2 per cent more than that of the Olympic 400 m medley swimmers. The 2 per cent difference probably comes about because of the deliberate holding back of top medley swimmers in anticipation of the changing strokes producing a quicker rate of fatigue.

The second 100 metres shows a variance of 25.18 to 25.53 per cent, which is very close to the back leg of the medley (24.76 to 26.17); the

Table 2: Comparison of 400 m freestyle splits

		100 m	200 m	300 m	400 m
Men	1968	1:00.60	2:03.80	3:07.40	4:09.00
		24.33	25.38	25.54	24.73
Women	1968	1:04.10	2:13.60	3:22.50	4:31.80
		23.58	25.57	25.34	25.49
Women	1972	1:01.50	2:07.04	3:13.55	4:19.04
		23.74	25.30	25.67	25.28
Men	1976	56.73	1:55.95	2:54.62	3:51.93
		24.45	25.53	25.29	24.71
Women	1976	1:01.19	2:04.68	3:08.32	4:09.89
		24.48	25.40	25.46	24.71
Men	1980	57.28	1:55.55	2:53.64	3:51.31
		24.76	25.19	25.11	24.93
Women	1980	1:01.12	2:03.77	3:06.54	4:08.76
		24.56	25.18	15.23	25.01

Olympic 400 metres freestyle winners with the competitive proportions that each 100 metres took them in relation to the overall time.

third varies between 25.11 and 25.67 per cent against the medley range of 28.71 and 30.75 which is to be expected; whilst the final 100 metres shows 24.71 to 25.28 compared to the medley freestyle leg of between 21.99 and 23.61.

It would therefore seem that most medley swimmers would expect to emphasize the last leg even more than a 400 metre freestyler would expect to emphasize his last 100 metres.

Suggested target pace

Based on the assumption that the Olympic winners as a whole have ideal pace for this particular event, we have recorded the following averages of the Olympic Champions (not G.B. swimmers):

First Leg	Second Leg	Third Leg	Fourth Leg
22.37	25.43	29.40	22.67

We realize that swimmers have different strengths at certain stages of a medley race but Table 3 will provide a guide for those who are trying to develop pace in their training at a younger age.

There has been an increased capacity on the part of top swimmers in recent years to handle both the changes of stroke and cadence involved. Table 4 indicates the ever-closing gap

Table 3: Suggested breakdown of target times

400 metres target times

5:30	1:13.84	1:23.98	1:37.35	1:14.81
5:15	1:10.46	1:20.16	1:32.92	1:14.10
5:00	1:07.11	1:16.35	1:28.05	1:08.01
4:45	1:03.75	1:12.53	1:24.07	1:04.60
4:30	1:03.99	1:08.71	1:19.65	1:01.20

200 metres target times

2:45	36.91	41.99	48.67	37.40
2:35	34.67	39.44	45.72	35.13
2:30	33.55	38.17	44.25	34.00
2:20	31.31	35.63	41.30	31.73
2:15	30.19	34.35	39.82	30.60
2:10	29.08	33.08	38.35	29.47

between the individual events and the four disciplines put together on an increased basis, particularly on the part of women.

For young swimmers the stroke changes need to be practical in training by swimming different combinations of strokes in training. The swimmer needs to get used to having his head in for fly, upside down for back, face in for breast and then turned sideways for the frontcrawl.

Reference
1 *All About Individual Medley*, Deryk Snelling

Table 4: Progress of medley in relation to individual strokes

		Total of Olympic winning times of four individual events over 100 metres	Individual medley winning time	Differential
Women	1972	4:21.29	No event	
Men	1972	3:47.00	4:31.98	44.98
Women	1976	4:08.77	4:42.77	36.00
Men	1976	3:42.94	4:23.68	40.74
Women	1980	4:06.29	4:36.29	30.00
Men	1980	3:44.94	4:22.89	37.95
Women	1984	4:07.61	4:39.24	31.63
Men	1984	3:40.32	4:17.41	37.09
Women	1988	4:02.77	4:37.76	25.01
Men	1988	3:38.72	4:14.75	36.03
Women	1992	4:01.94	4:36.54	25.40
Men	1992	3:37.82	4:14.23	36.41

10 Turns and Starts

The muscles used during starting and turning are quite different from the muscles used during the course of a swimming race between the walls. A swimmer with great leg strength and a fair degree of mobility should be able to perform the starting and turning movements more efficiently than most. However, timing and reflexes play an important part.

The importance of starting, turning, finishing and good relay takeovers cannot be stressed enough. They come at a time when the swimmer's body is in contact with a solid object, even if only for an instant, and there are great gains to be made during that instant by the most efficient use of the wall. Many swimmers tend to treat the turns in particular as a separate item to the race itself. This attitude is wrong. It should be an integral part of the total race situation. The turns can mean the fraction of a second between winning and losing.

The turns

Frontcrawl

The A.S.A. law states that in freestyle turning and finishing the competitor may touch the wall with any part of his body. There is, therefore, no requirement to touch with the hand or arms.

Various turns have been used over the years including a grab turn, a spin turn which involved the swimmer remaining on his stomach but turning through 180°, and a back flip which meant the swimmer approaching the wall, revolving onto his back, with his outstretched hand then assisting him to make a backward somersault. This brought him onto his front again as he pushed off.

Gradually these have been superseded by the universally quicker tumble, or somersault, turn and we will concentrate on the description of this as the other turns do not play a role in modern competitive swimming.

The tumble turn was known originally as the somersault turn because it involved the body in a full circle forwards, but gradually the word tumble came to be used because the turn gave the feeling of tumbling downhill as one went into the turn. It was first used at the N.C.A.A. Championships in the U.S.A. in 1936 by swimmers coached by David Armbruster. Nowadays, swimmers tend to turn with either straight or bent legs.

The swimmer should aim to maintain the rhythm of his stroke right up to the wall. There should be no break. His final stroke should start about one-and-a-half arms lengths away from the wall. If we imagine he is turning with his right hand having made his last stroke at this point.

His aim should be to keep his head down as he makes the final pull. He should pull sharply backwards with his right hand in a circular movement towards his stomach. As he starts to make his pull he should drop his chin onto his chest and tuck his knees up to his torso. The rotatory movement can be fractionally aided by flipping his left hand, positioned by the hips

119

at the end of its pull, up and out of the water.

As the chin drops down to the chest, the whole body follows the head, which is the controlling force, through a somersault-like circle of 360°. Bringing the body through a complete circle of 360° can be disadvantageous in positioning the feet and getting in a quick pushoff. It's better to drop the chin so that it finishes in a line with the left shoulder (or vice versa), which should be facing diagonally backwards as the right hand begins its pull. This brings the body at a slight angle (as in the photograph) before the pushoff. The feet should point diagonally upwards at 45° on impact with the wall.

When the swimmer has somersaulted forwards and over he should feel for the wall with his feet. The aim should be to get a good first-time pushoff from the wall without a pause to set himself up. On impact with the feet, the body begins to open out and extend. The swimmer's arms are drawn up to a pushoff position above the head in preparation for extension at the elbows. The swimmer now

The left hand makes its final pull prior to the turn.

The left hand completes its pull and the chin drops down.

The hips now pike whilst the upper body curls up. Note that the legs are now parallel with the surface.

Whilst the eyes face upwards, the knees bend and the body rotates through 360°.

As the hands are drawn up above the head, the feet feel for the wall.

June starts to push off from the wall and the knees and elbows straighten.

The neck rotates so that the head starts to face down, turning the body the right way round.

pushes hard from the wall with his feet by straightening at the knees and pushing back hard. He achieves this by gradually squeezing the wall with his toes.

He now has the task of turning his body off his back into a frontcrawl swimming position. He manages this as he pushes away about threequarters of a metre under the water. He merely turns his head to face the bottom of the pool so that the body rotates around its long axis whilst extended during the pushoff.

As the knees straighten the elbows do likewise. The face stays under the water throughout until the body comes back to the surface before commencement of swimming. A good breath before the turn is important and the swimmer should try to 'bounce' off the wall so that he doesn't get a mental impression of using the turn as a rest during the swim.

Clearly a tumble turn is very rarely made in a race situation where the swimmer is fresh. It's a good idea to practise the turn time and time again until the body is tired rather than to practise it once, take a long rest and then to try once again.

A number of swimmers have difficulty in whipping the feet over. The feet should be clear of the water, the swimmer aiming to throw his heels to the wall. The ability to tuck up and rotate can be assisted by a standing practice in the shallow end of the pool. The swimmer is merely asked to jump up, somersault over and stand up again. Done on a group basis with the aim being not to finish last, this can be fun and helpful.

Other swimmers find it difficult to avoid spinning round on the surface of the water. A partner standing in the middle of the pool can be of use here. The performer tucks his chin in and pulls hard with both hands backwards behind the hips. His partner merely grabs his costume near his behind and helps him round and over.

Some swimmers prefer to turn from further away and to turn with their legs only slightly bent. This can help the tall swimmer but the somersault movement can be slow because the body is more opened out and the pushoff not so strong, the knees having already been partially extended.

Teaching the young swimmer

The tumble turn can be difficult for young swimmers to learn and can be learnt in stages by breaking the turn down so that it takes into account both timing and mode of movement.

Start by getting the young swimmer to push off from the wall so that he is travelling at speed. A certain amount of speed will aid the total movement. Then the swimmer should pull backwards with both hands as far as the thighs in a similar manner to a breaststroke arm pull. The head should be dropped at the chin as the pull backwards is made. Once the head has dropped, the hips should pike as they come parallel with the surface.

The hands continue to pull backwards and upwards as the hips rotate in the opposite direction. When the body is positioned vertically upside down with the legs straight, the young swimmer can pull up and the body go down headfirst as though making a surface dive. The swimmer should use this as a mean of practising lifting the legs with the hands.

The same movement can be made on the next practice but the swimmer can let the legs go right over whilst still straight. The legs will produce a light splash behind. Progressively the swimmer can produce a splash in this manner. The next stage is for the swimmer to let the legs just give way at the knees so that now the calves and not the whole of the legs should hit the surface.

This brings the swimmer to the position where he is on his back and, in a young inexperienced swimmer, not sure where he is. His awareness can be improved by bringing the movement up to the wall and getting the swimmer to reach for the wall with the heels.

During this period, the youngster can practise and determine if he prefers to pull his legs over with two hands or one. In the case of the one-arm movement, the other arm pulls normally from the frontal position whilst the controlling arm completes its pull at the hips and turns palm down, beginning to press. The two-arm movement requires that the pulling arm pauses at the hips until the other arm has completed its pull through to the hips. The two arms then scoop in unison.

Pike and tuck

The tumble turn may be identified as two different types of turn: the pike and the tuck. The pike can be seen as a turn in which the swimmer makes one large bend of the hips throughout the movement, while in the tuck turn, the knees are bent much more to increase rotatory speed and to bring the whipping action of the feet into play much quicker.

Arguments as to which is the faster of the two turns have varied. Tests carried out by Schiessel[1] found the pike the faster because it was faster into the wall than the tuck. Although slower in movement off the wall, his overall results showed the turn to be faster.

By comparison, Ward[2] found that the tuck turn was better for beginners simply because of the ease with which it could be developed. He also found that the tuck was significantly faster in all aspects. For instance, he recorded that the average of a group used for study purposes showed the time taken for getting the feet up to the wall was on average 0.121 second faster and 0.89 second faster coming away from the wall to the pushoff.

Backstroke

The backstroke laws state that during the turn shoulders may be turned over the vertical to the breast, after which a continuous single-arm pull or a continuous double-arm pull may be used to initiate the turn. Once the body has left the position on the back there will be no kick or arm pull that is independent of continuous action. The swimmer must have returned to a position on the back upon leaving the wall.

The rules also recommend that flagged ropes should be suspended across the pool 1.8 m above the surface from fixed stands positioned 5 m from each end wall of the pool.

Having established the parameters as far as regulations are concerned, one can see that the rules are complicated, in fact too complicated for the young swimmer. In much the same way, the young swimmer finds the basic backstroke turning technique the most difficult technique to grasp. There are three types of backstroke turn used in the world today, although one is employed to a much greater extent than the others. We will describe all three.

Old backstroke turn

The swimmer should try to ensure that he maintains speed right into the wall rather than slowing down to make the turn. A lot of practice during the warmup prior to a race is important here. A good swimmer should be able to count the number of strokes from a position where his nose is perpendicular to the backstroke flags until his hand touches the wall. He should be able to make these strokes without turning his head off the water to look for the wall.

The last arm stroke to the wall should be taken at long reach with the elbow extended. Again, it's important for a top backstroker to be able to turn on either hand. Let's take the case of the righthand turner as an exemplification. With the normal backstroke pull the hand would be turned so that the palm faces outwards. The last stroke is made so that the palm faces upwards. The hand is driven well back on the wall with the fingers giving a little as they make contact with the wall. The fingers are now in a position where they can help with weight bearing. The arm bends slowly but surely at the elbow. This has the dual function of keeping up the body momentum as it travels towards the wall and it also helps to stabilize the fixing action of the hand on the water. The hand now acts as a sucker on the wall whilst the elbow remains facing upwards.

When the elbow has completed its bend to a point where it is at a right angle, the swimmer's head should start to drop back in order to bring the centre of gravity close to the point of rotation. The swimmer merely positions his eyes back over his forehead and towards the wall. As the head is dropped and the hips rotate upwards the knees are bent up to the stomach. The feet remain naturally curled at the toes during this movement.

Using the grip of the hand, which has now dropped to about threequarters of a metre under the surface, the swimmer now aims to direct the path of his feet to a position close to where his hand was previously positioned on the wall. Although the upper body has dropped back low into the water, the lower section from the hips downwards simply spins laterally whilst remaining in a horizontal plane. During the course of this movement, drag is decreased by lifting the feet clear of the water and the feet are directed towards the wall with a whipping movement.

When the feet make contact with the wall the rest of the body will have spun to a position where it should be in a flexed situation but the whole of the body in alignment for the direction in which the swimmer will be travelling. Prior to the pushoff from the wall the head is brought to face upwards, the arms are bent and the hands drawn up so that the hands, with palms upwards, are positioned adjacent to the ears. It's a good idea to pause until the hips

have dropped slightly on the wall. The pushoff can then be made from a deeper position where there will be more still water. The feet now merely squeeze the wall, the knees playing a somewhat obsequious role in that they straighten as the feet squeeze. At the same time the elbow begins to straighten and the arms stretch to add length to the pushoff. The glide is made with the arms around the ears.

A large breath has to be taken immediately prior to the head dropping back in the water as plenty of oxygen is necessary for the long movement. The majority of the exhalation takes place to coincide with the glide. The swimmer can now extend the glide to a maximum of 15 metres, by which time the hand must have broken the surface. He can achieve this either by a series of upside-down dolphin kicks or by alternate backstroke kicking.

The backstroke somersault: the head drops well back, as the hands reach for the wall.

The knees now bend as the fingers make contact with the wall.

The elbow begins to give as the body drives towards the wall.

As the left arm helps to control the movement, the right arm anchors the body as it rotates horizontally.

The feet now search for a solid pushoff base on the wall while the hands are drawn up above the head.

Notice that the general position prior to the pushoff is lower on the wall than in the spin turn.

The body now finishes in a straight line on its way back to the surface.

Spin turn

A more horizontal variation of the backstroke somersault turn was developed in the 1970s with the outstanding exponent being the 1976 Olympic Champion John Naber.

The turn follows the same mode as the normal somersault turn but is executed with the body much flatter on the surface. Leonard Barbiere (U.S.S.R.) used the turn successfully in winning the European 200 metres in 1962 in Leipzig.

When the hand is placed on the wall the chin remains tucked into the chest so that the head is kept on top of the water. The result is that the hips are flexed instead of extended. They are positioned just under the surface of the water. The swimmer needs to kick hard for the

125

wall because the chin-forward movement tends to prevent the natural drive to the wall.

The feet are flipped down towards the pushoff wall with more vigour than in the normal somersault turn. The overall advantages of this particular turn are that it is considered to be easier to get quickly into the stroke; the water is under the shoulders and not over them and into the armpits which creates extra resistance.

The backstroke spin turn shows the hand going out to the wall, with the palm uppermost. The chin remains tucked in at the chest.

The knees are bent and the hand remains in contact with the wall until the feet are planted on the wall.

The body now extends with a flatter pushoff, closer to the surface than other backstroke turns.

Backstroke tumble turn

The third turn is a rolling type of tumble turn. The rules are such that one doesn't need to be on one's back in the period between when the hand touches the wall and when the feet push off from it.

With the roll over turn the swimmer rolls over so that the lead hand towards the wall is recovered diagonally across the body towards the opposite shoulder. At the point of maximum extension, the swimmer rolls on to his front, as with a tumble turn in frontcrawl. The swimmer now makes a tumble-like somersault finishing on his back.

The turn has become very popular in recent years now that FINA and the ASA have changed the rules to make judging and swimming easier by employing this type of backstroke turn.

The roll over: the swimmer is seen approaching the wall in a normal backstroke position.

Now the body rotates through 180° at the hips as the right arm is directed towards the wall.

By now, the swimmer is facing downwards and the body on its front.

The body now buckles and curls up as the swimmer begins to lift his feet over the water.

A normal freestyle somersault now takes place with the body curling up.

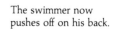
The swimmer now pushes off on his back.

Teaching the turn to the young swimmer

The total movement is complex and it's therefore important to realize that a young swimmer who is upside down in the water will have difficulty interpreting all of the movements. The turn should be built up slowly stage by stage. Start by rehearsing the spinning movement against a wall whilst lying flat on the back on the pool side.

Next ask the swimmer to position himself in the centre of the pool. He should now merely lie on his back in the water with his knees bent up to his stomach. Using sculling, or figure of eight movements, with his hands by his sides, the swimmer should spin through 180°. The knees need to remain bent throughout. This should give the swimmer the correct feeling in terms of direction.

When he feels confident, the next stage is to make exactly the same movement against a pool wall. The planting of the hand on the pool wall is next added and the turn steadily built up in the normal manner.

Butterfly and breaststroke

There is a great similarity between the turns for butterfly and breaststroke, mostly because they are both made with two hands. The breaststroke turn rules state that a simultaneous but uneven touch is permitted. The butterfly rules say that when touching at the turn and finish a swimmer shall touch the end of the course with both hands simultaneously on the same level and with the shoulders horizontal.

In both cases the swimmer should aim to approach the wall with the head down and the arms at long reach. When the hands, which are stretched out adjacent to one another, make contact with the wall the elbows start to bend and the body is 'sucked in' towards the wall. There is, of course, great speed on the butterfly approach, which makes the turning movements easier.

If the turn is to be made to the left the swimmer should now withdraw the left hand from the wall as the legs are drawn up at the knees. The head remains down or close to the surface as the feet are drawn up to the wall for the pushoff. The traditional pushoff now takes place. The swimmer should avoid lifting the head to look at the other end prior to the pushoff and should aim to look at the surface of the water immediately in front of the wall as he is leaving it.

The left hand remains in the water to steady and balance the body whilst the right hand is thrown, in a bent-arm movement in a circular fashion, over the water until it's in a position to join the left hand ready for the pushoff.

In the case of breaststroke, the pushoff should be slightly deeper to accommodate the underwater pull. The fingers, therefore, should be directed diagonally towards the bottom of the wall at the other end of the pool.

Butterfly turn

June reaches for the wall at full stretch.

The hands fix on the wall firmly and the knees begin to bend as the rest of the body moves towards the wall.

The left hand has now dropped down to stabilise the body as the feet are drawn up to the wall.

The body continues to pivot at the wall.

By now the feet have been drawn up to the wall and the right arm is pulled over the water.

The two hands have now been drawn up in front of the head.

The pushoff now takes place with the eyes fixed in front of the swimmer.

Butterfly turn: the swimmer attempts to make the last stroke one complete one and long reach.

One hand holds the wall, the other is placed by the side in the water as the feet are drawn up to the wall.

The hands fix on the wall, the elbow bends and the head and torso continue to move towards the wall.

The left arm is thrown above the head to join the right arm as the swimmer looks back and then finally forwards.

Breaststroke turn

The swimmer approaches the wall with two arms outstretched.

The elbow bends and the left elbow is drawn slightly in towards the wall.

The forearm is now in parallel with the vertical end wall and the feet brought up under the body.

With the right arm used as a balancing agent, the legs come right underneath and are moved up towards the wall.

The feet are now planted on the wall and the head now returns to the water.

The arms are placed in front of the head ready for the pushoff.

Individual medley

Butterfly to backstroke turn

The swimmer needs to remain on his stomach until he has touched the wall with both hands. He can't turn onto his back until the touch has been made at the end of the butterfly leg.

He should approach the wall with the chin kept low and close to the surface. Here again, he should reach for the wall going downwards at maximum extension. When he makes contact, the arms give a little at the elbows as the body buckles and the elbows give in order to let the head come closer to the wall. When the head gets to a position where it's only about 12 cm (5 ins) from the wall, the knees are brought up under the body so as to be close to the stomach.

The swimmer now thrusts the back of his head into the water by looking up above. His shoulders should remain square on to the turning wall throughout. The hands are drawn up above the head in the manner already described for the backstroke turn. The pushoff is then made as in the backstroke pushoff.

It is very easy to literally bounce off the wall on this turn and to push the head back too far prior to the pushoff. This should be avoided by keeping the eyes firmly fixed above.

An overview of the butterfly to backstroke turn in a race situation would see the swimmer attempting to conserve energy bearing in mind the fact that he still has some 150 or 300 metres to go in a race. Swimmers who are weak on butterfly and backstroke will try not to overuse their leg kick during these two sections and will, therefore, probably push off less hard on the turn.

Many top individual swimmers swim the butterfly leg mainly on arms with the legs just balancing the body. These swimmers will be able to push harder from the wall on going into the backstroke leg.

A swimmer will need to practise his medley turns regularly in order that the strength of his pushoff will fall within the requirements of his own race strategy.

Again the swimmer reaches for the wall with the arms extended.

Note how the elbows give but the rest of the body continues to drive.

As with the breaststroke turn, the chin is drawn up and one hand leaves the wall slightly before the other.

The head is now thrown back so that the eyes look up and both arms now start to move up above the head.

The hands come together and the elbows and knees begin to straighten.

The swimmer aims to turn the face during the pushoff to look up bringing the body fully on to its back.

Backstroke to breaststroke

Here again, the swimmer must remain on his back until he has touched the wall. He can then push off on his front for the breaststroke leg. There are a number of turns which can be employed here: the most spectacular but tiring is the back somersault.

The swimmer approaches the wall on his back, puts out one of his hands and then drops his head back by looking back over his forehead at the wall behind his head and forearm, then forms a lever with which he can pull his body back and over through a 360° circle.

When the hand makes contact with the wall, the knees bend up to the stomach and the body curls up to assist the total body rotation. Obviously, the more the body is drawn in around the centre of gravity the faster the movement. Swimmers who have difficulty with the movement may find it easier to put both hands up and to pull themselves round.

When the feet hit the wall after the rotation, the toes need to feel for the impact. The legs

will probably have dropped to about half a metre under before the pushoff. The pushoff should be deep enough to accommodate the underwater pull on the breaststroke leg. Frequently the buttocks are positioned a little too close to the wall to get the heels up correctly for the pushoff. This is generally overcome by practice more than by a technical correction.

Often swimmers find the amount of air required to make the whole movement plus the underwater pull is too tiring. They therefore either drop the underwater pushoff or make a grab turn. Here the swimmer approaches the wall on his back, touches the wall and then pushes off on his front. This is more often known as an open turn.

As this turn is completed, the swimmer is about to go into the most crucial part of the medley race. It is therefore important that he gets the pitch of his pushoff absolutely right for him personally to get the most from his underwater pull. A glide which is too deep will mean time lost on this pull.

The right hand goes out towards the wall.

The hand approaches the wall with the palm facing upwards. The legs have stopped kicking and start to bend at the knees.

Using the right hand as a lever, the body twists backwards through 360°, the eyes have looked directly back behind.

The feet reach for the wall as the head and upper body unfold with the face down.

The body is not quite level prior to pushoff but the body is adjusted by aligning the head as the push off takes place.

The movement finishes off with a good, long pushoff. The position of the body is quite deep in preparation for an underwater pull.

Again, the swimmer reaches for the wall.

As his hand makes contact with the wall, the elbow bends but the legs keep driving.

The elbow bends right up to the wall as the head is lifted off the water.

The feet are tucked up, bent at the knees and drawn under the body.

The feet come right under the body and the left hand starts a forward movement prior to the pushoff.

The head is now turned to look sideways and the right arm brought over the water to a point in front of the head.

The pushoff begins from side on.

The body is now brought on to the stomach by the face looking down to the bottom of the pool.

Breaststroke to freestyle

The laws require that the swimmer touches with two hands simultaneously before passing onto the freestyle leg. The turn is made in exactly the same manner as the breaststroke turn, the only difference being that the pushoff is made so as to be a little shallower than a normal breaststroke turn because of the absence of an underwater pull.

When the feet have made contact with the wall, the fingers are directed towards the vertical wall at the other end by placing them in the water parallel but some 15 cm under the surface. The head and the rest of the body are positioned in exactly the same manner in relation to the rest of the body.

The swimmer reaches for the wall and as he does so, he inclines the body at the angle he needs for the movement.

The chin continues to move towards the wall, and the right hand is dropped down into the water.

The feet are rolled under the body and the body is now tilted away from the wall by the movement of the head which is still looking back by moving over the centre of gravity.

Both arms are drawn up with the left arm following the right arm forward.

The push off now takes place and the body is levelled up.

The finish

The finish is the most important part of the race. As the conclusive stroke, races are won and lost on both the mental attitude and the physical application of this stroke.

The finish should always be made at long reach with the head down. If the swimmer has sufficient breath then he should try to make the last three or four strokes with the head to the front and face in.

The rhythm of the stroke should not be shortened substantially but some shortening will take place in the last two or three strokes as the swimmer summons his remaining power with as much speed as possible.

Always aim to swim through the wall rather than just to it. This type of mental approach helps to overcome the decelerating feeling in the last strokes in a race.

The start

The rules

In all races the referee indicates that the event is about to start by a series of short blasts on his whistle. When he feels that both competitors and officials are ready, he then gives one longer blast and the swimmers take up positions on the back of the starting block or a short pace back from the starting line or in the water.

When the order 'Take your marks' is made by the starter, the competitors must immediately take up a starting position with at least one foot at the front of the starting platforms. The swimmers remain stationary until the final signal to go is given. This may be related by klaxon, gun, whistle or the word 'Go'.

The starter will call the swimmers back at the first false start and remind them of not starting before the starting signal. After the first false start, any swimmer starting before the starting signal has been given will be disqualified.

The rules for each stroke

In freestyle races the competitor may start with a plunge or jump, or in the water holding the rail on the side of the bath. A breaststroke start only differs in that when the swimmer starts in the water he must face the course and hold the rail or side with both hands. The butterfly

follows the same pattern as the breaststroke.

The backstroke is obviously completely different in that the swimmer has to line up in the water facing the starting end with hands on the end rail or starting grips. The feet and toes need to be under the water and the toes are not allowed to be wrapped over the lip of the gutter. Standing is prohibited.

Techniques of the start

Starting dive

Clearly, any racing start in the water will lack the transfer of momentum built into a diving start. A start from pushoff or from the wall would normally be used by a young swimmer in the early racing stages.

The most effective method of starting known to us at the present time is the racing dive. The racing dive or start has changed from time to time since the war in order to create situations where the angle of entry or angle of glide are at their most effective, or to a position where the swimmer can make better use of his own limbs in order to drive his body into the water.

We have seen the Australians in the 1950s with their orthodox dive with the hands behind the back but clasped. We have seen the hands moved to the front for the start. We have seen the circular arm-swinging start, the track

start and the grab start which first really came to prominence in the 1972 Olympics with the Americans. There have been many offshoots. A start with a kick halfway through the air movement became popular towards the end of the 1970s. At one time it was fashionable for dives to be quite deep and then on other occasions for them to be flat along the surface.

The basic start

Diving has been known to man certainly since Roman times and probably well before that. It was therefore easy to see its development as an extension of the racing situation.

On the command 'Take your marks', the swimmer steps forward and wraps his toes over the end of the starting block or pool side. He positions his feet so as to be about 20 cm (8 ins) apart, with the knees facing forwards and bent to an angle of about 140°. He should also lean slightly forwards so that his centre of gravity (about 5 cm (2 ins) above his belly button) is placed perpendicular to the feet. The shoulders are curled and the back flexed. The hands and arms are held behind so that the palms face up towards the roof and the arms are almost straight. The hands are positioned adjacent to the bent hips. The position of the head is controlled by the eyes which look about 10 m (30 ft) in front on the surface of the water.

On the word 'Go', the swimmer swings his

Basic start

hands forwards in line with the shoulders. The feet start to push and squeeze away from the wall. As they do this the knees automatically extend. During this period the swimmer should aim to keep his head down and to ensure that power is transferred forwards by the arms and legs. As the centre of gravity moves forwards, the swimmer may adjust his centre of balance by making one forward movement with his arms which would bring his arms level with a forward point in line with his shoulders and level with his nose. The arms are then pulled back almost to start point and then thrown out and forward again.

When the arms are thrown to a fully extended position, the elbows lock and the fingers stretch forward. The head is lowered between the arms and the ears protected by the insides of the upper arms. The head should not be kept up as this will increase resistance. The hands should attempt to make a hole for the head. The hands and arms should cut through the surface so as to drive the body in parallel with the surface about 1 m (3 ft) down.

The swimmer should start swimming either by kicking and then pulling or by pulling and kicking simultaneously when the glide from the dive has slowed down to swimming speed.

The position of the hands at the start preparatory position can change from individual to individual. Some swimmers reason that the forwards–backwards–forwards move-

ment of the arms which takes place when the hands start from behind can be reduced to backwards–forwards if the hands start from a point in front of the body. They, therefore, position their hands diagonally in front of the shoulders. A good armswing in the standard racing dive produces a reasonably strong transfer of momentum – more than the grab start but less than in the swing start. The period of applying the force is greater than in the latter but less than the former. Too much backward rotation can take place and the backward–forward rotational balance can only be balanced by stopping the armswing at approximately 45° to the surface. In diving terms, the application of force is over a reasonably lengthy period of time.

Try to avoid following through too strongly with the arms as they are being thrown forwards. If the armswing is carried too far upwards there will be too much backward rotation and the swimmer has to pike in order to prevent his feet hitting the water first. This pike will increase resistance at the entry point and lead the body to go in at too sharp an angle. Those swimmers with weak legs may find the conventional racing dive or the swing start to their advantage as it can lead to an addition of all the forces involved in the movement and bring other stronger limbs into play. In effect the body should leave the starting block in an almost horizontal plane. It

has been estimated that the angle of the chest to the starting platform should be about 40°

The track start

Many ideas in swimming have been both borrowed from and lent to athletics. The track start is a typical example of this. As yet, it has to become widely used but a number of good swimmers have used it. The swimmer starts with the body crouching and the arms shoulder-width apart. The hands are placed over the front of the side or starting block so that the palms face backwards.

One leg should be placed in front of the other so that the rear leg which is bent at the knees is positioned about 20 cm (8 ins) behind the front leg. Overall, the start now combines aspects of the grab start and the track start. The head should be relaxed at the neck, which releases tension on the spine.

At the 'Take your marks' command, the swimmer lifts the hips so that they are higher than the shoulders. The legs don't quite straighten. The centre of gravity moves slightly forward so that the weight is on the front and not the back leg. The swimmer should now breathe in, ready to explode air on the gun. Obviously, the lower the centre of gravity the more the body can move forward without tipping into the pool. There is too the advantage of starting nearer the point of entry.

When the gun goes the swimmer aims to drive himself out horizontally at 45° as strongly as possible. He bends his arms at the elbows and pulls himself down towards the water by levering on the starting block with his hands.

The arms are then thrown horizontally and the head follows the movement so as to be positioned slightly above the arms before entry to prevent the body dropping too fast and then between the arms when entering. The trunk is bent at first as the body is pulled down on the starting block and then it extends as the body straightens out. Again, as the trunk is bent more the knees bend even more and the ankles are plantar flexed which sets the body up for a powerful outward thrust.

The swimmer explodes his air as the body extends completely. The rear leg is brought up so as to be adjacent with the foreleg. The body drops under the surface slightly on entry until the swimmer's head directs the body back to the surface ready for swimming.

The track start is particularly suitable for swimmers with strong leg extensors who lack the actions required to be able to move quickly on either a grab or standard start. Psychologically there is a backward feel to the total movement before the body goes forward at a time when on the start signal most other starts appear to go directly forward. It is possibly for this reason that many swimmers fail to opt for the track start.

Track start

The grab start

The grab start has often been considered to be the fastest start of all and the effectiveness of this style of starting was brought to worldwide attention by Mark Spitz in Munich in 1972. Mark demonstrated that a swimmer doesn't need to be extremely large to make maximum use of this start. In terms of the time of flight and the amount of time before entering the water, the grab start would appear to be the fastest start. However, it lacks the power of the conventional start and this reduces its effectiveness somewhat.

At the preparatory position the hands can be placed either outside the toes, which are wrapped over the edge of the starting block, or inside the toes. This depends on individual comfort, but stability can be determined as a result. The body is bent so that the hands can reach down and wrap over the starting block and result in the legs being bent to about 120°. The weight is balanced on the balls of the feet. This preparatory position should be more stable than the conventional start as the centre of gravity is lower. The bodyweight can be moved forward with more control.

As with the track start, the swimmer flexes the elbows at the initial movement and then straightens the arms so as to extend the

shoulders. At the same time the swimmer pulls himself forward so that the greater proportion of his bodyweight is in front of the original base of support. This comes about by leaning forward and then by pulling with the arms.

The time taken to actually enter the water can be short here because, like the track start, the centre of gravity is relatively low and this is increased by the short radius of rotation.

The shoulders start to flex and the stomach and spine extend. The body moves in an upward curve until the lower legs are parallel with the surface of the water. The extension of the body helps to add strength to the forward movement. There is a strong force during transfer of momentum as the arms are flexed forward at the shoulder. As the arms rotate forwards the body rotates backwards. The balance between these two forces and the relationship between the moment arms will determine the most effective angle of flight through the air. There is, in effect, a very short period of time for the movement.

The body should go into the water as streamlined as possible and the angle of entry should, therefore, be between 10° and 15°. Forward rotation should continue during flight until the body is in the right entry position. On entry, the movements should be the same as the track start prior to swimming.

Pike or kick start

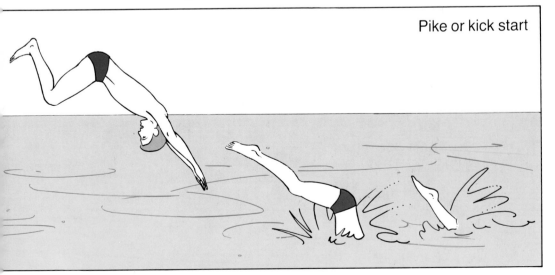

The pike or kick start

The grab or conventional start can be varied by a piking movement in order to get a better angle of entry.

The swimmer rotates the upper body upwards to a much greater extent than in the normal grab start – to such an extent that the upper body is higher than the hips and lower body which are still parallel with the surface of the water. When the dive has reached its maximum height (about 1 m (4 ft) above the surface) the swimmer drops his head and pikes at the hips. The heels are drawn up to the behind and a kick backwards is made by bending the knees and projecting the feet outwards so as to extend at the knees and be in line with the dropping upper body.

The angle of entry as the elbows straighten should be about 30°. The swimmer falls from a greater height and is therefore able to travel further under the water before resistance starts to slow his body down.

The swing start

The swing start ideally suits the swimmer with strong arms and upper body. The swimmer positions his feet approximately six inches (15 cm) apart on the starting block with his body bent at the hips and the arms either

hanging loose in front or diagonally behind the hips, as described in other start stances.

The arms are then circled in a long arc from their start point in a backwards direction. Unlike other dives, the arms are kept straight with the hands swung towards the roof above and circled right round so as to circle past the hips. They are then projected together in front of the face so as to lead the body into the water.

During the first part of the swing backwards, the head is lifted to accommodate a rocking back on to the heels and a slight straightening of the legs. This allows the arms to circle more easily and allows this movement to take place over the centre of gravity whilst the body is almost upright.

As the arms sweep forward in a downward and forward circle past a point just beneath the hips, the feet push from the wall and the knees are bent to facilitate this. The body has tipped slightly forward off the wall by this time and the tremendous momentum generated by the arm movements is now transferred forward. The feet push, the head drops down and the arms are directed outwards in the same manner from now on as the normal standing start.

The swing takes longer than other dives but is capable of driving the body further from the wall and, therefore, in some swimmers, has the potential to be quicker.

Standard backstroke start

Standard backstroke start

The swimmer holds the rail, gutter or starting block so as to face backwards. The shoulders rest on the water surface with the elbows bent. The arms are, therefore, partly supporting the body position. The eyes are fixed on the starting position and the feet, whilst the legs bent at the knees, rest on the vertical pool wall so as to be about ten centimetres apart, with the toes curled ready to push.

When the starter gives the 'Take your mark' command, the swimmer lifts his chest closer to the starting block by bending his elbows. This has the effect of lifting most of his body out of the water. The swimmer's chin is now within ten centimetres of the starting block.

When the starting gun sounds, the swimmer forces his head both back and slightly upwards. He needs to inhale air prior to this. The swimmer's first move is to push down and inward with his arms against the starting block. This enables him to propel his shoulders and upper body back and away from the starting block. The head and shoulders rotate backwards as the swimmer releases his hands.

The feet squeeze the wall and push hard, forcing the knees to straighten. At the same time, the arms swing rapidly forward in front of the head by moving in a flat, horizontal pattern, whilst the hands are kept both close to the surface and facing upwards. This movement has been aided by an arching of the back. He prevents too much arching with the aid

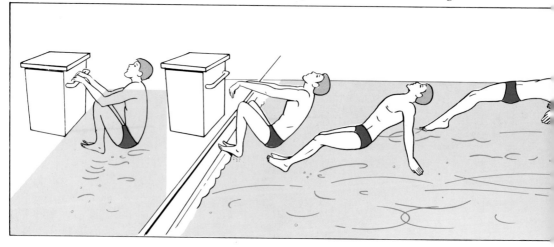

of the external oblique muscles in the abdomen.

At this point, he points and extends the toes and the arms continue their swing outwards. As the feet finally leave the wall, the arms have moved to a position where they are diagonally out in front of the shoulders, halfway through

The Naber variation

The 1976 Olympic Champion John Naber started from the same position but drove his body through a much higher parabola. The their path to a point where the arms are together in front of the head. The swimmer has to break the surface of the water with one part of his body after 15 metres to conform to the rules.

deeper trajectory, means a potential for a longer glide and greater distance.

The Matthes variation

The 1968 and 1972 Olympic Champion Roland Matthes adopted a much flatter trajectory and brought his hands to a point two centimetres in front of the head. The hands are then projected forward in a straight line during the last part of the push by the feet.

References
1 'An Analysis of Competitive Freestyle Swimming Turns', unpublished Masters Thesis by M. Schiessel, 1966
2 'A Cinematographical Comparison of Two Turns' by T. Ward, *Swimming Technique* Spring 1976

Backstroke start adopted by Matthes

11 Training for Swimming

Aims of training

Most swimming coaches in Britain plan their season from mid-September to mid-August of the following year. Eleven months of swimming involves a lot of planning. It's therefore important that in the first instance coaches decide what they are aiming for and then sit down with their swimming squads and explain both their aims and how they are going to achieve them.

The standard aims of swimming training should be:

1 To improve the technical ability of the individual swimmer.
2 To develop endurance by improving the condition of the heart and/or
3 To improve strength by developing the musculature.
4 To increase the efficiency of the body in carrying oxygen by increasing the number of red blood cells.

These four aims can be achieved in different ways.

Technical ability

This can be developed by:
(a) stroke drills (overemphasis and repeating the segment of technique which needs correction)
(b) single-length stroke correction for whole groups
(c) set distance focusing on one stroke point
(d) use of hand paddles
(e) correction by going through stroke movements on pool side or in front of a mirror, or with the aid of video facilities.
(f) use of a flume

Developing endurance

This is normally achieved by:
(a) long swims, eg 2 to 3,000 m
(b) short rest repeats, eg 10×400 m with 10 sec rest
(c) timed distance swims. Swimmers aim to swim as many lengths as possible in a set time. They might, for instance, aim to swim 200 m in $2\frac{1}{2}$ minutes, taking 15 sec rest with a whistle blown on the start and stop
(d) controlled interval swims. The swimmer swims a number of repetitions with the combined time of the swim and rest remaining constant. For example, a swimmer might swim 20×100 m freestyle leaving every $1\frac{1}{2}$ minutes.

Endurance swims are normally made aerobically, ie the swims do not incur an oxygen debt.

Improving strength

This is brought about by strengthening work on land where maximal loads are moved over short distances. Strength is normally associated with the capacity to sprint.

This is, in turn, associated with quality repetitions and long rest repeats, often with the rest lasting as long as the repetition itself. These repetitions are of a higher quality than controlled interval repetitions with times as close as possible to personal bests.

This type of training can deplete the nervous system and other body functions and is, therefore, not to be recommended more than once a week.

Increasing body efficiency

This comes about through all types of distance training whether it be through very long straight swims of 2,000 to 4,000 metres without breaks, running or circuit training.

The aim is to increase the capillary function in order that oxygen can reach the muscles that need it more quickly and easily. The pusle rate remains steady on the distance swims with a pulse rate of about 150 beats per minute.

Associated aspects

A good coach will keep a log of everything completed. There are not that many young swimmers who will do this and it's therefore important that the coach makes the effort for future reference.

Although each session should be planned at the start of each month according to the oncoming race programme, there needs to be a degree of flexibility. If swimmers are jaded or tired, or alternatively swimming really well, the coach needs to be able to ad lib in order to get the best out of the swimmers.

Training sessions should also account for individuals. This is more difficult for large squads with swimmers swimming a number of different strokes and different distances. However, coaches should try to include at least two types of programme with the training sessions: one for sprinters and one for middle- and long-distance swimmers.

The training session should always start with a swim of less than optimum effort, often regarded as a warmup. The session should conclude with a loosen-down swim roughly equivalent to the length and intensity of the warmup.

Variety is an important function within the training sessions. Swimmers should be encouraged to use the clock regularly to measure performance. They should also be encouraged to take pulse counts over ten or fifteen seconds when interval training rests are longer than this. In the case of men this can be done by simply placing the hand over the heart; in the case of women by pressing the middle and index finger over the carotid artery in the neck.

Pulse counting won't tell the swimmer how strong each heart beat is nor will it measure the amount of peripheral resistance, but it will indicate the amount of work the heart is being called on to perform.

The coach must be dedicated, confident and able to motivate his swimmers. Motivation could be a chapter in itself because there is so much involved. The important ingredient in motivation is the level of reality as far as each individual is concerned. The coach should set the swimmer goals which the swimmer recognizes are obtainable both in training and in racing or credibility will be lost. The goal of each swimmer should be to attain the highest possible standards of which he is capable.

Training terminology

We have listed below some of the regularly used training methods not related under the 'Aims of Training':

Interval training – the rest period is the considered aspect here. It's a general term which refers to steadier controlled swimming with the same, short rest. The swim remains constant.

Interval or repetition work – this is faster interval swimming over short distances with longer rests.

Tempo work – swims made at near race pace where the racing distance is broken into a number of regular distances.

These three can be developed through the following training methods:

1 Descending or reducing swims. Here the swimmers are asked to make a number of repeats, finishing with a time as close as possible to their personal best, eg a swimmer who has a personal best of 59 seconds for

the 100 m might swim 10×100 m aiming for 70, 68, 67, 66, 65, 64, 63, 62, 61 and 60.

2 Regressive repeats. Obviously the opposite to descending swims, these tend to be used less because they are often considered to be psychologically less beneficial to the swimmer.

3 Broken swims. Here the repeat distance is broken up by a short rest for partial recovery. These swims can be an important mental lift to the swimmer in the phase before competition because performances close to race personal bests can be achieved through this in an easier manner, eg a 400 m swimmer might swim 4×400 m over $5\frac{1}{2}$ minutes with a 10-sec break at each 100 m.

4 Alternating repeats. Two distances or strokes can be alternated to produce variety with a similar effect, eg the swimmer might cover 10×100 m as a descending repeat, leaving every $1\frac{1}{2}$ minutes, alternating with 10×200 m aiming to hold a time on his second choice stroke every $2\frac{1}{2}$ minutes.

5 Mixed swims. As their name suggests, the coach is normally aiming to break the monotony of swimming here by introducing another stroke over another distance, eg 20×200 m – 1st choice might be as follows 8×200 m – No. 1 off $2\frac{1}{2}$ mins followed by 400 m – No. 2 followed by 8×200 m again followed by 400 m – No. 3 finally followed by 4×200 m – No. 1 but descending.

Planning the season

Unlike many sports, swimming is essentially non-contact and injury-free. This makes planning a year very much easier because you know what the interruptions are likely to be.

You should aim for one major peak during the year and one minor peak. The major peak should come at the height of the long-course season in August and the minor peak at the end of December. The distances to be covered should also be planned as an annual training programme. A top 400 m swimmer at national level with a time of 4:10 might use the plan below.

The structure of the 100 m sprinter's season would be for shorter overall mileage and a great emphasis on daily strength training on land. Whereas the mileage covered by 200 m swimmers on backstroke, breaststroke and butterfly may well be close to that of the 400 m freestyler, the 100 m sprinters on all four strokes would work as in table (1) whilst the 1500 m, 800 m and 400 m individual medley swimmers would aim to cover distance as in table (2) opposite. The 200 m stroke specialists would also need to maintain a fair degree of strength training.

Month	Distance to be covered per day (m)	No. of sessions	Time spent (hours)	Race times (aim)
Sept	2,500	1	1	4:25
Oct	10,000	2	3	4:22
Nov	15,000	2	4	4:20
Dec	12,000 1st peak	2	4	4:10
Jan	15,000	2	4	4:12
Feb	15,000	2	4	4:12
Mar	15,000	2	4	4:12
Apr	15,000	2	4	4:12
May	15,000	2	4	4:11
June	15,000	2	4	4:11
July	18,000	2	$4\frac{1}{2}$	4:11
Aug	4,000 2nd peak	1	$1\frac{1}{2}$	4:02

A typical annual plan for a national level 400 metre swimmer in Britain.

(1) Month	Distance to be covered per day (m)		No. of sessions	Time spent (hours)
Sept	2,500		1	1
Oct	10,000		2	$2\frac{1}{2}$
Nov	12,000		2	3
Dec	4,000	1st peak	1	1
Jan	12,000		2	$3\frac{1}{2}$
Feb	12,000		2	$3\frac{1}{2}$
Mar	12,000		2	$3\frac{1}{2}$
Apr	12,000		2	$3\frac{1}{2}$
May	12,000		2	$3\frac{1}{2}$
June	12,000		2	$3\frac{1}{2}$
July	16,000		2	4
Aug	3,000	2nd peak	2	$1\frac{1}{2}$

A potential annual plan for sprinters based on two peaks to the season.

(2) Month	Distance to be covered per day (m)		No. of sessions	Time spent (hours)
Sept	4,000		1	1
Oct	15,000		2	$2\frac{1}{2}$
Nov	20,000		2	$3\frac{1}{2}$
Dec	14,000	1st peak	2	3
Jan	18,000		2	$4\frac{1}{2}$
Feb	20,000		2	$4\frac{1}{2}$
Mar	20,000		2	$4\frac{1}{2}$
Apr	20,000		2	$4\frac{1}{2}$
May	20,000		2	$4\frac{1}{2}$
June	20,000		2	$4\frac{1}{2}$
July	20,000		2	$4\frac{1}{2}$
Aug	8,000	2nd peak	2	$2\frac{1}{2}$

This shows the same table for middle distance swimmers.

The training distances can only be maintained by a predominance of full stroke employed by sprinters. In all cases, please note they are examples only of possible distance covered and are therefore not ideal for all individuals – only recommendations. Many coaches, for instance, would not increase training loads in the penultimate month before the long-course championships.

Once you have planned your mileage by the month you then determine the content of each month.

Training session content during these months should include these elements:

Sept–Jan Long-distance swims, aiming to build up capillary development, in terms of size and number. Long and middle-distance repeats with short rests work on developing the size of the heart and its ability to recover, plus an increase in the size of the adrenal glands and spleen. This is often known as the preparation period.

Feb–March Continue with the middle-distance repeats with short rests.

May–June This can be mixed with higher tempo swims (or speed play) and some work over longer distances. This would be considered to be mid-season, or pre-competitive period.

April, July, Aug The competitive period. The move from short-interval endurance work to speed and longer interval workouts has now taken place. Rests are increased and distances shortened working on power and speed. The ability to work with oxygen debt is increased during this period.

Stroke practices

The major types of practices are:

1 Arms only on all four strokes with legs crossed at angles or hanging loose
2 Arms only on all four strokes with a pull buoy (polystyrene leg support) or float between the legs
3 Arms only on all four with a rubber band around ankles
4 Arms only with a diver's weight belt around the hips
5 Legs only with hands out in front, arms straight, on free, back and fly
6 Legs only with hands by sides, on all four
7 Legs only with kick board, on free, fly and breast
8 Legs only underwater (about a foot down), on free, breast and fly
9 Legs only backstroke with arms above head at an angle of 90° with the head
10 Legs only backstroke with arms above head and on water
11 Full strokes with diver's weight belt
12 Legs only with one arm above head, the other down by the side and the body on one side, on free
13 As in 12 on butterfly
14 As in 12 on backstroke
15 Legs only on free, back and fly with flippers on
16 Full, leg and arm practices in tee-shirts
17 Bilateral frontcrawl
18 Breathing holding and hypoxic training on frontcrawl and fly
19 Legs only on all strokes wearing tennis shoes

These practices can be supplemented by stroke drills or subdivided into drills to develop technical refinements or to make stroke corrections. Below is a table of stroke drills and their results.

Practice	Stroke	Effect
Pull, breathe, kick, kick, kick. The three kicks are made with the head in	Breaststroke	The swimmer gets used to making the pull whilst under more pressure for breath, as in a race
Arms by sides, lift the heels up to touch the outstretched fingertips	Breaststroke	The swimmer gets used to lifting the heels closer to the behind and surface
Make underwater pull following pushoff – allow it to slow down and try to lengthen the pushoff by making the pull to gauge constant speed	Breaststroke	The swimmer can develop correct underwater pull timing
Underwater recovery without kick. Aim to keep hands near to body	Breaststroke	Encourage swimmer to reduce resistance created by elbows and arms on underwater recovery
Kick with finger stretch. The hands are brought straight back to head without a pull. They pause until heels are brought to behind. They are brought to behind. They then merely stretch forward on kick. Hands stay together throughout	Breaststroke	Develops synchronization of pull and kick
Kick with two or three floats piled on top of one another	Breaststroke	Places greater stress on ankle region. Develops ankle flexibility and strength

Practice	Stroke	Effect
Kick with hands together behind and head out. The elbows should be held tight together in small of back	Breaststroke	As above
Pull, breathe, kick, and count one, two — often known as glide breaststroke	Breaststroke	Encourages swimmer to kick into next pull
Catch up freestyle. One arm enters the water and pauses whilst the other arm catches up and is pulled when the second arm comes into a frontal parallel position. This is then repeated on the other arm	Frontcrawl	This practice ensures that the swimmer settles into the catch correctly before beginning the pull
Monkey swimming. Normal frontcrawl is swum but every time an arm is recovered the fingertips touch the armpit of the same arm prior to the fingers stretching forward to enter the water	Frontcrawl	This gets the swimmer used to bending the elbows and keeping them higher than the hand during the last phase of the recovery
Normal frontcrawl is swum with the upper surface of the fingertips scraping the surface as the hands recover and move to the hand entry	Frontcrawl	The swimmer gets used to keeping the hands close to the surface during the recovery
Frontcrawl with a long, over-exaggerated push-through towards feet. Aim to straighten arm at end of pull	Frontcrawl	This results in the swimmer pushing right through and an extra long recovery
A set swim on breathing, eg a six-length swim: the 1st length, normal breathing; the 2nd, normal; the 3rd, every 3 strokes; the 4th every 4; the 5th every 5 and the 6th every 6	Frontcrawl	Breath retention development
Single-arm frontcrawl. The arm not in use remains outstretched in front at the entry position. Breathe normally	Frontcrawl	Aids concentration on correct entry position and pull
Water polo crawl with head out of water but with a long push-through at the end of the stroke	Frontcrawl	Gives the legs a feel for kicking in sprint position and keeping the upper body high as in sprinting
Final phase of pull. The swimmer kicks normally whilst the hands are lifted to a position where they are in parallel with the shoulders. A double final phase of the pull is then made to the hips	Backstroke	The two arms working together makes the pull bend correctly at the elbow. This discourages pulling with the arms straight
Left arm, right arm, both arms — one following the other with a normal leg kick	Backstroke	The swimmer can concentrate on entering the hands in the right position

Practice	Stroke	Effect
Single-arm backstroke	Backstroke	This follows the same pattern as single-arm frontcrawl
Double-arm backstroke	Backstroke	This encourages both the first and second phases of the pull to be made correctly
Single arm working on shoulder lift. One arm is kept permanently by the side whilst the other is recovered with an exaggerated lift of the shoulder	Backstroke	Develops shoulder roll and good recovery position
Backstroke swum with a pause as the pulling arms when two extra kicks are made. The pull then takes place	Backstroke	Gives the swimmer time to find the correct hand entry position and in timing the catch
Rising with hunched shoulders – seahorse effect. The swimmer exaggerates his shoulder and upper body lift during the inhalation. He then pulls very wide and shoots his arms through on the recovery. The whole movement is accompanied by dolphin kick	Breaststroke	The swimmer learns to adopt a more powerfully based early body position
Breaststroke kick on back	Breaststroke	Feet get used to rotatory action
One pull followed by three kicks	Breaststroke	Works on getting the heels up in the kick
Single arm – left arm, kick, right arm, kick, both hands, kick	Breaststroke	Concentrates swimmer on correct hand position
As above with 3 left arm pulls, followed by 3 right arm and then one on both hands	Breaststroke	As above
Four full strokes with a dolphin kick; four strokes with a breaststroke kick	Breaststroke	The swimmer can work on following the hand recovery through with shoulder and hip rotation
Three full strokes followed by three kicks underwater. These two are then alternated	Breaststroke	The swimmer gets greater pressure on the ankles during the kicking and develops greater resistance
Single-arm butterfly on either left or right with the other arm out in front. The breath is taken to the side	Butterfly	This helps the swimmer to work on his hand entry position
Left arm, kick, right arm, kick, both arms, kick	Butterfly	As above

Practice	Stroke	Effect
Dolphin kick with hands clasped behind back. The swimmer works on over-exaggeration with the undulating kick	Butterfly	Develops the use of hips and upper legs
Dive butterfly. The arms are recovered in a normal manner and three or four kicks are made under the water with the arms stretched out in front	Butterfly	The swimmer gets used to kicking with the legs completely surrounded by water
Swimming with shoulder brushing ear	Frontcrawl	Develops flexibility
Entering the hands with a slight pre-entry hesitation	Frontcrawl	Improves hand entry and strengthens kick
Swim the stroke with a clenched fist	Frontcrawl/or backcrawl	The swimmer gets a feel for pulling with the wrist and forearm
One arm only with that arm's shoulder against a lane rope or wall	Frontcrawl	Because the arm is limited by the wall or lane rope, the elbow must be kept up and the hand entered in line with the shoulder
Swim full stroke balancing a plastic cup of water on the forehead	Backstroke	The swimmer learns to keep the head still
Butterfly kick with or without a float with one leg only	Butterfly	Develops the action of one leg
Full stroke swum with head up	Butterfly	Increases resistance and strengthens kick
Full stroke with hands aiming to touch together in front immediately prior to entering	Butterfly	This drill develops flexibility and encourages the swimmer to lengthen his stroke
Breaststroke leg kick swum with one leg on kickboard	Breaststroke	This is useful for isolating faults in one leg
Breaststroke leg kick, hands in front. Egg beater kick: one leg kicks first, the other afterwards	Breaststroke	This develops strength in the legs
Breaststroke full stroke. Pull starting as two-hand scull, becoming larger into a normal pull	Breaststroke	The correct pull develops through the correct wrist movement
One arm pulling with the non-pulling arm behind the back. The heels are then lifted to the behind	Breaststroke	This strengthens the leg action and works on body position

Practice	Stroke	Effect
One arm pulling with the non-pulling arm behind the back. The heels are then lifted to touch that hand. From time to time the arms are changed round	Breaststroke	This strengthens the leg action and works on body position

It's very easy to become bogged down in training sessions by a stroke drill mania particularly in the preparation period. Nothing improves a stroke like swimming that stroke itself. The moment a technique is broken into its component parts, the weakness may be improved but the totality of the stroke could suffer. There are other water skills or fun drills that can be used to break up sessions:

1 Combining the arm action with the leg action of another stroke
2 One-length sprints with walk back to the start
3 Two swimmers kicking against one another. The two face one another, place their hands on each other's shoulders and start kicking from a position where a line on the bottom of the pool lies between them when they lay out flat
4 Towing a partner whilst swimming arms only — the partner may or may not kick according to the coach's requirements
5 Locomotive swims, ie one length fast, one slow, two fast, two slow and so on up to a pre-determined level. The swimmer can then reduce again in the same manner
6 Swimmers pulling against each other. This is achieved by using a rubber ring. They would both have their toes linked into the tube on either side
7 Handicapped (timed) races and swims
8 All types of team races

The relationship between training and racing

Race situations involve the employment of two types of energy systems, anaerobic and aerobic.

Anaerobic, or developing what is commonly known as an 'oxygen debt'. Hard swimming at speed in this way has only a limited period. The energy used for this is ATP (or adenosine triphosphate). But this type of energy can only last for ten seconds at high speed. However, this period can be extended by using creatine phosphate to resynthesize adenosive triphosphate.

A second anaerobic system. Results in ATP being derived from the breakdown of muscle glycogen, commonly called glucose. Glycogen can be converted to pyruvic acid which in turn can be converted to adenosive diophosphate (ADP) and then to ATP. Here there is a lactic acid buildup with pyruvic acid being changed to lactic acid and the duration and intensity of the swim are therefore dependent on the buildup of lactic acid. The swim should however last up to two minutes. Here again an oxygen debt, which has to be repaid, is built up.

Aerobic swimming. Swimming can be carried out with the muscles having a steady supply of oxygen and oxygenated blood. The oxygen coming through to the muscles is in sufficiently large supply to be able to oxidize and resynthesize lactic acid which develops with exercise into glycogen.

Oxygen is continuously supplied and lactic acid constantly converted to glycogen.

The implications of these systems for training

The swimmer's individual training programme must therefore be tailored to meet the type of energy system that a swimmer will use in a race. Training with a short rest tends to be anaerobic and with a longer rest aerobic.

On the other hand, a swimmer who is racing often uses at least two of the three systems described. Training should, therefore, be of a broader spectrum. A swimmer who swims with maximum effort uses approximately the following systems in a ratio to one another:

Swimming for	10 sec	1 min	2 min	4 min	18 min
Anaerobic respiration	85%	65%	50%	30%	10%
Aerobic respiration	15%	35%	50%	70%	90%

Hypoxic training

This type of training is now regularly used to increase the swimmer's cardiovascular efficiency, ie the efficiency with which the body can deliver oxygen to the muscles and other vital organs. When the average person inhales, only 16 per cent of the oxygen in the lungs is used.

If the swimmer can learn to use up more of the available reservoir of oxygen then there is less chance of oxygen debt development early on. Hypoxia is the state that the body develops through lack of oxygen. Hypoxic training forces the body to work under stress without ample oxygen, the result being a greater number of red blood cells for gathering more oxygen from the lungs.

The body must build up steadily and hypoxic training will only take place under stress with little oxygen intake, eg 4 × 400 m − 10 sec rest − breathing every fifth stroke. The end result should also be an increase in the size of the capillaries carrying blood with those not in use or partially closed coming into use.

Race preparation

The taper

The period when a swimmer is beginning to rest up and sharpen up for an important competition is crucial. A swimmer who rests too often will become unfit; it's therefore important to limit peaking in a major way to one or two efforts a year.

During the taper period the swimmer should be aiming to:

1 Rest more in order to let the body recover from periods of hard training
2 Swim less far in training and to devote less time to training
3 Sleep longer
4 Sprint more in order to sharpen up and cover less distance work
5 Work on starts and turns, ready for the race situation
6 Prepare himself mentally for the race

Swimmers like to approach their taper differently. Some like a long taper, others only two or three days. Trial and error will determine what suits each individual. Other swimmers like to actually increase their training loads by up to 40 per cent in the month prior to competition only to return to their previous training loads in the week before competition. The swimmer develops a tapering feeling whilst keeping the training load high.

At the end of it all the swimmer should be physically relaxed but mentally keyed up. Generally the shorter the distance to be raced the longer the taper. Lack of taper will lead to reducing speed, and speed is something a sprinter must have.

A sprinter needs a lot of rest at the end. Age also plays an important part because a younger swimmer will be training over less far and will therefore need less rest before competition. Coaches must also consider how many races a swimmer has during a competition. If he has a whole number of swims his taper will be less than someone who needs to be brought to a fine edge on the day of competition.

Training requirements must also be more specific during the taper. Weight training may be reduced, straight swims replaced by broken and descending swims. These need to be supplemented by easy swimming, kicking and pulling over 200 and 400 m, interspersed with sharpening work from a pushoff over 50s and 25s. Loosening down to reduce stiffness at the end of each session is important.

There is no one definite approach to tapering, and dialogue between the coach and swimmer is important. The coach needs to know both how the swimmer feels and how he feels relative to previous tapers.

The race day

The day of an important race is one of the foremost features of a swimmer's life. We have listed below some dos and don'ts.

Do ensure that:

1 You rest in and get sufficient sleep. The more sleep you get before midnight the better
2 You eat a meal which contains mainly carbohydrates but little protein and definitely no fats. A fatty breakfast or a lunch with meat will take a long time to digest and may be of little use to the body for energy
3 An easy stroll with some light flexibility work a couple of hours before the event will help
4 At the gala have a good warmup (at least twenty minutes of early swimming)
5 Then wrap up well in a tracksuit, shoes and sweater, aiming to keep the body really warm
6 Keep an eye on the programme so that you report when you are called up
7 At this point, try not to be distracted by either idle or competitive chatter
8 When you are sitting on the poolside seats in the race prior to yours, concentrate on the race. Swim the race through in your mind and that will generate adrenalin at just the right time. To swim the race through half an hour earlier will generate adrenalin too early

Don't:

1 Over-extend yourself physically or mentally on the day of the race
2 Take your tracksuit off too early
3 Neglect to dry well down and wrap up after the warmup
4 Over-use the 25 m and particularly 50 m sprint in the warmup as they can become debilitating
5 Report late for the race or leave your goggles or costume adjustments until just before you race

The warmup should contain the following major ingredients:

1 Long easy swims on first choice stroke
2 Some sharpening sprints
3 Work on starts and turns – get used to walls. Get used to the number of strokes from the wall in the case of the backstroke turns and finishes.
4 Some kicking at moderate tempo
5 Some higher tempo *fartleck* work getting the feel of the pull and adjusting to the correct racing position in the water
6 Try to make your warmup as close to the race as possible. Physiologically, the benefits of the warmup are greatly reduced if made one and half hours or more before the race
7 A hot shower for five minutes and stretching exercises in the range to be used in the race will help

Part of the object of the warmup should be to raise the pulse rate and open up the blood vessels in the muscles to be used in the race. These muscles should be encouraged to become warmer, but making the body and the surface skin warmer will direct blood flow and encourage the blood to be used for cooling other areas rather than for warming the muscles.

Establishing pace in training

The middle- or long-distance swimmer who knows or can control his own pace has a great advantage. Negative splitting in 400 m, 800 m and 1500 m racing has become important. The negative refers to the swimmer's capacity to swim the second half of the race faster than the first.

Physiologically, even-pace swimming is

vital. The 400 m swimmer with a time of 4:05 who clocks 59.0; 62.5; 62.5; 61.0 is taking less out of his body early on and is more likely to achieve his time target than the swimmer who clocks 56.0; 63.0; 63.0; 63.0. The swimmer who achieves a negative split might aim for 60.5; 62.0; 61.5; 60.0. His stronger finish might be psychologically important.

This built-in human pace clock should be developed from the early part of the season. This can be developed by repetition swimming in which the swimmer swims in a chain with other swimmers of similar speed. The controlled repetitions should be regular both in speed and in terms of rest. The swimmer can be encouraged to aim for certain regular times in which the second part of the swim is faster than the first. Sprinters can learn pace in this way through reducing swims.

A swimmer can also train over race sets in which he is training over his race distance broken up into components. Pace towards the race period can be maintained by broken swims in which again the swimmer aims for specific times.

Some swimmers may find it hard emotionally to go out steadily, coming back faster. They should be encouraged to temper their early pace but they may never lose that early edge. The coach has to recognize this and to get the swimmer to try to control his pace a little more in order that his early energy expenditure doesn't result in the squaring of effort being invoked too early.

In a one-to-one situation the coach can teach pace in the autumn by walking up and down the poolside with the swimmer whilst watching the pace clock, or by using signals with a float or towels to the swimmer in the water which indicate whether or not he is on a previously agreed target.

All the year round skeleton training table

	Water work	Dryland work	Mental training
Sept–Nov Conditioning phase in early season preparation	1 Short-rest freestyle swims over 400s and 800s 2 Stroke drills and coaching discussions on technique 3 Use of video & playback 4 Use IM over 400s and 800s as basic conditioner 5 Some early resistance training with equipment	1 Circuit training and some distance running for condition 2 Heavy weights and use of 3/4 days per week based on pyramid lifting 3 Stretching and flexibility to counteract stiffness from lifting weights for strength gains 4 Testing and measuring of lung capacity, blood lactate count, pulse at rest etc	1 Goal orientate whole season 2 Retrospective look at mistakes in previous year as well as good points 3 Establish positive approach to winter's training – set out rationale for programme 4 Talk about target times for various stages of season
Mid Nov–Dec Short-course competitive season	1 Quality stepped up; rests between repetitions a little longer 2 More repetitions over 100 to 400	To continue as in step-up period	1 Use times performed by competitors as spur to individuals 2 Use splits of opposing teams to

Water work	Dryland work	Mental training
range, eg 10 × 200 with 20 sec rest		motivate faster team swims
3 More reducing swims and specific No. 1 swims		3 Use team swims as springboard for better individual performances
4 More reducing sets, eg 4 × 200 off 2:45, 4 × 200 off 2:30, 4 × 200 off 2:15		4 Talk about race aims and splits required
5 Increase of negative splits for MD and LD swimmers		5 Study race performances to date
6 Target swims over 200s and 100s		6 Determine which races are important and which races can be dropped from programme
7 Harder and shorter kicking for speed over 50s		

	Water work	Dryland work	Mental training
Jan–Mar Step-up phase Overloading training	1 Reintroducing short-rest work. Work on freestyle & first choice – distances increase to 800s and 1,000s	1 Heavy weights continued but increased in size – 3/4 days per week	1 Educate swimmers and parents in approach to winter's training
	2 Straight swims ontechnique on 2,000s and 3,000s, some on IM variations	2 Use of swim bench and mini gym	2 Talk about discipline in training approach and approach to times of sessions etc
	3 C/M – 20 × 200, 15 × 400 8 × 800 – No. 1 stroke	3 Stretching continues	3 Educate swimmer to understand that times he is achieving will be affected by stages of training
	4 Stroke drills give way to kicking hard on singles and pulling over distances	4 Scientific tests to control and gain information on swimmer's flexibility	4 Establish healthy living principles away from pool for athletes
	5 Kicking with plimsolls, flippers		
	6 Pulling with rubber bands, diver's weight belts and tee-shirts, hand paddles		
	7 High variety of training combinations here		

	Water work	Dryland work	Mental training
	8 Use of video and blackboard continues 9 Pulse counts taken whilst swimmer uses clock 10 One-to-one stroke coaching for swimmer once per week		

	Water work	Dryland work	Mental training
Mar–Aug Long-course and season's peak	1 Dive, 50s & 25s 2 High quality sets – long rest 3 Continue broken swims 4 Continue descending C/M series with longer rests 5 Kick quality 50s with long rest 6 Some·longer swims to train some endurance – length of these gradually reduced	1 Legs – emphasis on power lifting. Weights only 2 per week 2 Step up flexibility to everyday 3 Keep weights going with less pressure 4 Some swim bench work concentrating on technique of pull	1 Key championships racing approach into how to beat opponents 2 Orientate swimmer's mind to the natural results of his hard training, ie winning 3 Should expect to win etc – look at overall progressive programme of wins through the season's pinnacle 4 Ascertain whether goals so far have been attained – can they continue to be attained or how can they be attained? 5 Talk about enjoyment of achieving year's targets, winning, being successful etc (ie be positive)

12 Land Conditioning

Land conditioning has become an integral part of the swimming training programme. Endurance, flexibility and power can all be developed by work on land. Land conditioning, however, should be seen as a means of supplementing work carried out in water in order to develop these three – it should not be a substitute. Often, though, training on land can greatly assist those swimmers who have less water time available to them than they need.

The hallmark of a good land programme is specificity. The closer one can get to the stroke itself, the better. There is a great biomechanical difference between some types of weight training and the strokes themselves. The swimmer has to also recreate the neurological stress experienced in a race situation.

Flexibility

Flexibility is a vital aspect of swimming that can be more easily developed on land than in water. Many British swimmers are too stiff, and daily training should be supplemented by half-an-hour's stretching at home. Stretching and loosening should always precede sessions in the water. Ten or fifteen minutes on the poolside is to be advocated.

Mobilizing exercises make the swimmer work in the extreme outer range of movement. The stretching should be progressive, the aim being to increase the range of movement in the relevant areas of the swimming strokes. A more carefully controlled application of power should come about during the strokes. Swimming shouldn't be carried out with jerky movements; they should be smooth and fish-like in their slipping and sliding movements. Mobility exercises can help develop this and should themselves not be jerky or too hurried. Soreness can be slowly eased.

Below are some of the most useful exercises that one can carry out.

4 Stand with feet apart, squat with knees at right angles to hips (a), knees are then pressed apart by elbows (b), back straight, head up (c). Hold that position (d).

a

The legs

1 Kneel on floor, turn feet out sideways, lean back. The back can also be arched and head on the floor as an alternative.

2 Ground hurdle: one leg stretched out in front, other leg bent to side with lower leg at right angles to thigh, lower the head placing chest towards knee.

3 Whilst sitting on floor with feet extended and body erect, make toes point and soles stretch

down then invert and evert feet. Keep heels on ground and turn toes in and out.

c   d

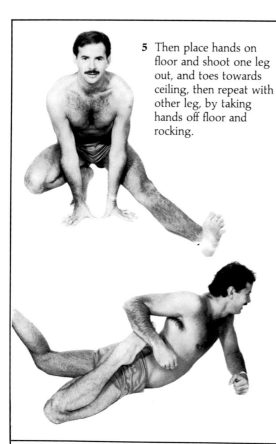

5 Then place hands on floor and shoot one leg out, and toes towards ceiling, then repeat with other leg, by taking hands off floor and rocking.

6 Kneel on floor, throw hands in semi-circular movement over head, rock back with behind over heels onto balls of toes.

7 Body lies on stomach, right arm reaches back and holds right foot in crook of arm, squeeze towards behind, change sides.

Shoulder joint

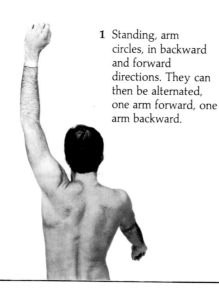

1 Standing, arm circles, in backward and forward directions. They can then be alternated, one arm forward, one arm backward.

2 Kneel on ground, circle arms backwards immediately over line of shoulders, slow, attempt to scrape shoulder blades together.

3 Stand, with elbow bent, one hand should be dropped back onto upper back.

4 Interlock fingers, kneel on floor, hold hands, behind, push arms over to touch floor behind head.

5 From kneeling position, place hands behind head and cross with elbows in air, push hands down behind back and then change, cross hands position over.

6 With use of partner: kneel, hands behind head, partner to press elbows together behind head, no force to be used.

7 Whilst kneeling: place one arm behind head on centre of spine, pull elbow with other hand so as to press hand further down back, change hands.

8 Now place the arm over shoulder and onto back, the elbow is behind head, the other arm is bent at elbow which is positioned near the hips, the two hands reach for one another behind back.

9 Place both hands behind back on spine, back of hands should touch one another, keep shoulders back, try to push hands up.

10 Interlock fingers above head, hands should be extended above, push up, hands face upwards.

Trunk

1 Hold ankles whilst standing, bend head down to touch knees, then grasp the ankle, bend back and turn head to touch that knee, then change left.

2 Lie on back with hands and arms out in line with shoulders, roll over lifting feet to touch the ground beyond the line of the hands.

168

3 Lie on stomach, hold ankles from behind, arch back, rock backwards and forwards.

4 Sit on floor, legs apart, feet at 90° to one another, keep back of legs straight and flat on floor, arch back until nose touches one knee and with hands touch feet. Then move to opposite leg. Then get forehead to touch floor whilst each hand is wrapped over corresponding feet.

5 Press up into crab, lie on back, push up and back until toes and hands are fully stretched, hold for 5 seconds and repeat.

6 Kneel on floor, place hands on floor, head back, arch back and push hips forward, try to hold for 10 seconds. Repeat.

7 Press up with lower body flat on floor, push with hands, aim to bend and lift head upwards.

8 Start with feet and legs outstretched, arch feet in together, stretch forward and hold feet, place soles of feet so as to face into one another, pull feet in under crutch, straighten back and breathe in, then breathe out and drop body at same time so as to have head on feet.

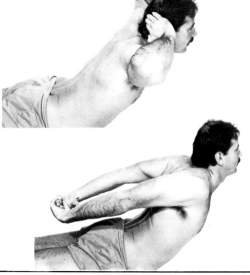

9 Lie flat on floor, hands behind head, bend back and arch head upwards, hold and then follow this by placing both arms straight back, as head is lifted reach with hands to touch one another. This can then be repeated with arms together, outstretched in front.

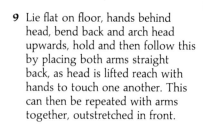

10 Start by standing upright with the legs apart and the elbows bent by the sides. Arch the back as far as possible whilst still standing. Twist the body about the hips, so that the right shoulder rotates first towards the ground until it reaches as far as it can without the body losing balance. Then repeat with the left shoulder.

11 Start in a sitting position with the shoulders in line with the rest of the back. The hands need to be held over the feet. The soles of the feet face one another with the knees out. The posture of the track now alters from one of extension to one of flexion with the back curled and the chin brought as closely to the feet as possible and then held for five seconds before straightening the back again.

12 Move from a cross legged seated position to one where, for instance, the left leg lies with its outside surface to the ground. Now twist the body, look back immediately behind and place the upper left arm behind the right knee. You can now alter this by twisting the head back to the front and by placing the left arm in line with the right leg so as to hold the ankle. Bend the right arm at the elbow so as to place the outside surface of the hand as high as possible.

Feet

1 Flex your feet towards your legs, curl your toes downward forcibly, extend the foot slowly.

2 Sit on floor, force feet downwards and then up, then turn your feet outwards.

Flexibility exercises for swimming can be seen in two forms: static, where the joint is held briefly in a position that stretches the muscle to its greatest possible extent; and ballistic, where the tissue is moved with such force that the momentum continues beyond the normal range of that joint. Static is the safer of the two because it doesn't produce sudden stress on joints and muscles.

Strength and power

The swimming world has yet to devise a universally used system of developing strength and power in the water. In the absence of this, top swimmers will continue to build strength on land. As related earlier, strength is the capacity of a muscle to exert force against a resistance. Power refers to the speed with which this movement takes place.

Strength can be developed through:

Isometric contractions or muscular contractions against static objects. There was a period when this type of exercise was in vogue. However, the muscular movements in swimming do not fit in with this pattern because the only time the body's muscular structure is moving against a static object is when the body is leaving the poolside. Throughout the contraction, the external length of the muscle remains the same.

Intermediary contractions. Here a weight is moved continuously but held at a number of stages.

Isotonic contractions. A weight is moved quickly through a complete range; the muscles or muscle groups involved contract to move the weight which again moves continuously. This type of contraction is often seen through weight training particularly 'pyramid' weights. The muscles shorten against a constant resistance as the contraction goes through a full range of motion.

Isokinetic contractions. A weight is moved through a specific range of muscle. The weight is a centrifugal brake exerciser. Consequently, as more force is applied the resistance increases proportionally. The muscles used therefore work at maximum capacity through the complete range of movement.

At the end of the pull and push, the level of force drops to nil and because of the recoil spring in the unit, the limb can be recovered as in swimming back to the start of the pull. The movements are made at a slightly slower speed than that of swimming speed.

The land conditioning programme of swimmers at this moment in time normally contains a mix of 'free' weights, or isotonic contractions, and isokinetic weights. If weights with barbells are used, a pyramid system of repetitions should be used in order to develop strength, ie 1×10; 1×6; 1×3; 1×2; and 1×1.

Remember to take basic precautions when using the barbell. Breathe naturally throughout exercise. Attempt to keep the back straight and your knees out when lifting the barbell from the ground.

Here are some of the exercises we recommend in a 'free' weight training programme.

For breaststroke

1 Bench press. Lie on back on bench, lower barbell from outstretched position above head to chest and press up again.
2 Toe raise. Barbell is placed on back, press on toes and lift heels.
3 Squats and jump squats. Place barbell on back, keep back straight and head up. Bend knees to 45° and then straighten your legs. This straightening movement can be replaced by a jump. A foam support under the barbell will help to protect the vertebrae.
4 Pull back. Keep the body upright, hold the barbell behind the buttocks, try to force the hands back as far as possible.
5 Clean (squat style). Lift the barbell from the ground to the thighs, then, keeping the chin forward, lift the weight to the chest by dropping your centre of gravity under the weight and rotating the weight at the elbows.
6 Pull over. From flat or inclined benches: lie on back arms outstretched, keeping arms straight, pull barbell over in a semi-circle and down to thighs, then return it.

For backstroke

1 Squats. For starts and turns.
2 Pull over. As with breaststroke.
3 Bench press. With hand grip outside shoulder line.
4 Press out from neck. Use dumb-bells and lie over a bench on your back with your head over the edge of the bench, start with the dumb-bells close to each side of the neck, push the arms straight out backwards to arms length. Hold for a second and then pull back to start.

For butterfly and freestyle

1 Squats with bar at front of chest.
2 Pull back. As in breaststroke.
3 Bench press. With both feet and head raised at different times.
4 Pull over with bench inclined. This can be performed with dumb-bells.
5 Bent over rowing. Bend body forward at hips, pull the weight from a position when the arms are straight, bend the elbows and pull the weight to the chin.

6 Elbow extensors. This exercise is more effective from a kneeling position than standing: keep the elbows still and flex the elbows so as to curl up the lower arms, the barbell is then lowered and the elbows kept up.

7 Arm rotators. Lie on back and bend elbows so as to be in parallel with shoulders. Lift the barbell from the ground in an arc-like movement until the weight is above the head, rotate upper arms.

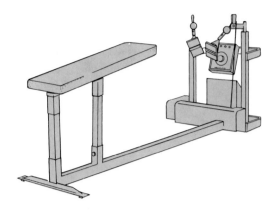

Development of specific strength

Isometric exercise has made a more than useful addition to the swimmer's land programme in the last ten years.

The swim bench (see drawing) is the most commonly used device today. The swimmer can lie on the bench and pull the handles either together or alternately. He can work at swimming speed with the hand paddles and the resistance can be adjusted to suit his needs. Such strength training improves the contractile nature of muscle proteins and improves energy capacities.

The biolimetric swim bench ensures the maximum tension of a muscle or group of muscles at all joint angles over the full range of movement during the shortening of the muscle. Each of the muscles involved in the movement is progressively overloaded and a greater number of motor units brought into play than in other systems.

The mini gym (also see drawing) can be used to strengthen both the arm action or from above as a latissimus machine. A leg press can help the leg extensors or a further machine can

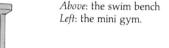

Above: the swim bench
Left: the mini gym.

help the extension of the lower leg in the last phase of all except the breaststroke kick. A butterfly rotator cuff model mimmicks the butterfly arm movement where the arms rotate at the elbows in order to catch hold of the water.

Endurance

Stamina is best developed in the pool. Some out-of-season cross-country running will not harm your early season conditioning. However, running, football, rugby and other winter sports do tend to harden the muscles and make them less supple and should really only be employed during the early off season.

Endurance for swimming, as with endurance for so many other sports, is best developed by swimming itself. We would recommend swimming if pool time is available. In the event of large amounts of pool time not being available, circuit training or cross-country running will help.

174

13 Associated Aspects of Swimming

Under this very broad title of Associated Aspects, we hope to consider some of the adaptations in his lifestyle the serious swimmer will have to make if he wants to reach the very top. We will be covering many of the problems that older swimmers have to face, as well as some problems which confront the younger ones.

Nutrition by Peggy Wellington

Diet is essential to a swimmer's success and a well-planned nutrition programme should be a fundamental element of any training regime.

Carbohydrate – the fuel

The most important dietary consideration for all swimmers is that of energy. Carbohydrate is the main fuel used by the muscle during hard, intensive swimming. Fat is also used as a fuel when swimmers are working aerobically (ie with oxygen). Therefore, during lower intensity, longer duration workouts, fat will contribute to a significant proportion of the fuel for muscle metabolism. As exercise becomes more intense there is a greater reliance upon carbohydrate for energy and when a swimmer is working anaerobically (ie without oxygen) only carbohydrate and not fat will be utilised.

A major factor that may cause an individual to feel exhausted during training is the depletion of carbohydrate (glycogen) energy stores. During a workout a swimmer will draw on energy from glycogen stores in the muscles and liver. These stores are small and will deplete to low levels during long, hard sessions. The symptoms? Swimmers may feel that they 'run out of steam', feel tired and weak with wobbly legs and arms as their times become noticeably slower. In contrast, the body fat stores are virtually unlimited so that even the leanest swimmers will not run out of fat!

Table 1: A graph to show glycogen depletion during training

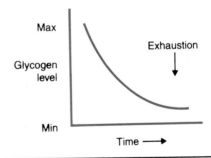

To avoid exhaustion swimmers should be encouraged to start every day with fully stocked glycogen stores. Successive days of training will drain these stores, even if a one-off session does not, so it is essential for athletes to pay attention to what they are eating.

To boost energy levels between training sessions and to ensure that glycogen stores are topped up, swimmers should consume a carbohydrate-rich diet, since the amount of

175

glycogen that is stored is related to how much carbohydrate is eaten.

American researchers[1] discovered that swimmers on a low-carbohydrate regime were forced to swim slower during hard training than their counterparts on higher carbohydrate diets. The slower swimmers had lower glycogen values which led the investigators to conclude that some swimmers may experience chronic muscular fatigue as a result of their failure to ingest sufficient carbohydrate to match the energy demands of heavy training.

Scientists recommend[2,3] that about 60% of our calories should come from carbohydrate with the rest of our energy from protein (15%) and fat (25%). Swimmers often eat less carbohydrate than this recommendation[4,5] and as a result their diets are usually higher in fat as well.

To achieve a carbohydrate-rich diet swimmers must focus on meals and snacks that contain plenty of this nutrient. Carbohydrate as sugars (simple carbohydrate) and starches (complex carbohydrate) is found in a large number of foods. It is important that a *wide variety* of these foods are selected to ensure that plenty of vitamins, minerals and fibre are consumed as well.

Table 2 summarises some ideal meal choices.

Table 2: 'Energy boosters' (for carbohydrate)

- Bread / rolls / pitta bread / french stick
- Rice and pasta / noodles
- Pizza (with thick base)
- Potatoes (*limit chips/roast potatoes and eat plenty of jacket/mashed and boiled varieties*)/ potato cakes
- Beans / peas / lentils / sweetcorn and root vegetables
- Couscous / polenta / sweet potatoes / yams / cassava
- Breakfast cereals / oats / porridge
- Fresh / tinned fruits
- Low-fat yogurts / low-fat milk puddings (rice pudding / custard / semolina)

NB You should also eat plenty of vegetables, although these are generally low in carbohydrate.

Individuals should identify whether they really fill up with high carbohydrate foods or whether they 'overload' with lots of high fat alternatives instead! The idea is to boost carbohydrate intake and not fat.

Snacks

Snacking is an important part of a swimmer's nutrition programme and will help to restore energy levels quickly. Variety is the key to successful snacking and these snacks should not replace balanced meals. The secret is to alternate a favourite biscuits / cake / chocolate or crisp snack with other choices to maintain a healthy sports diet.

Table 3: Snacks ideas

- Toast / breakfast cereals / sandwiches
- Crumpets / muffins / bagels / tea-cakes / scones / currant buns
- Scotch pancakes / malt loaf
- Fresh fruit / dried fruit (*raisins/currants/dried apricots/banana chips/dates*)
- Bread sticks / rice cakes / Pop Tarts / Rusks
- Commercial energy bars / plain popcorn

Muscle glycogen is restocked more rapidly if carbohydrate is consumed immediately after training. The refuelling process should be continued throughout the day by ingesting carbohydrate on a regular basis.

Eating before early-morning training can pose problems for some individuals. If food or a light snack cannot be tolerated at this time then experts recommend that a drink is used to set swimmers up for the following session. The important thing is to refuel properly *after* the workout with a hearty, high-carbohydrate breakfast.

Whilst swimmers should focus on their intake of carbohydrate, it is important to remember that a well balanced diet will also contain a mixture of protein, fat, vitamins and minerals as well.

Fat facts

It has been well established that a high-fat diet has been linked to a number of illnesses. So why do we need fat? Fat provides a concentrated source of energy which is used during certain types of swim training. One gram of fat provides 9 calories compared to 4 calories per gram from protein and carbohydrate. Fat also provides a protective layer around internal organs and plays an important role in the insulation of the body. So, contrary to popular belief, fat is an important nutrient.

Although fat provides a swimmer with energy when training aerobically there is no need to 'fat load' in anticipation for a long, hard workout! Fat intake should be kept relatively low to accommodate the swimmer's extra requirement for carbohydrate. For many swimmers this represents a decrease in their current fat intake.

Common favourites amongst swimmers are chips, roast potatoes, pies, pasties, sausage rolls, fatty meat, creamy/oily sauces, fried foods, and certain snacks. All these foods are relatively high in fat and if eaten in large quantities may contribute to a high-fat diet.

The secret to achieving a moderate intake of fat is to check that the majority of meals and snacks are not ladened with fat. This does not mean that all the food eaten should be very low in fat but that, over the period of a day, total fat intake is not excessive. Practically, this means that the occasional indulgence in curry sauce and chips, kebabs or fried breakfast will not do a swimmer any harm!

If an individual establishes that they focus on fatty foods then steps should be taken to replace some of the fatty foods with carbohydrate-rich alternatives to bring the diet in line with the current recommendations.

Conversely, a no-fat diet is not to be recommended either. Despite recent trends in the dieting industry to encourage drastic, very low intakes of fat (sometimes as low as 10% of energy or less), this practice may actually be harmful. Whilst a low/moderate fat diet is desirable for both health and performance reasons, a small amount of dietary fat is essential for health.

Protein facts

The body requires protein, or more precisely amino acids (the building blocks of protein), for the growth and maintenance of new tissues. Contrary to popular belief, tucking into huge quantities of protein will not magically build huge muscles! To increase muscle mass a swimmer must combine a lot of hard training (particularly weight training) with a well-balanced, high-carbohydrate diet.

Although swimmers have elevated protein requirements compared to non-active individuals,[2] this increase is almost always covered by a 'normal' food intake. If a swimmer is eating enough food to cover his/her energy needs then they will probably be consuming enough protein as well. By including a mixture of foods from Table 4 a swimmer will ensure that they are well stocked up.

Table 4: Dietary sources of protein

Animal	Vegetable
Meat	Pulses (peas/beans/lentils)
Fish	Nuts
Poultry	Bread/pasta/rice
Eggs	Breakfast & other cereals
Cheese	Tofu/TVP mince
Milk & Yogurts	Quorn/soya-based products

Vegetarians

The foods in the vegetable column tend to lack one or more of the essential amino acids (conversely animal proteins contain these amino acids in the correct ratio) so a variety of different sources of protein must be eaten over a day to avoid a shortfall. Many top swimmers are vegetarian. These individuals have a high energy intake and as a result will be routinely ingesting more food and therefore more protein than non-active counterparts. Swimmers should be able to get all the protein they need from foods without relying on costly supplements, even vegetarians.

Vitamins and minerals

Vitamins and minerals are substances that are required in tiny amounts to perform many functions essential to life. The key to ensuring that adequate levels of vitamins and minerals are obtained is to consume a variety of different foods. If food intake is restricted or lacks variety then problems may arise. However, most swimmers increase their food intake whilst training and this will automatically be associated with an increase in vitamins, minerals and other nutrients, provided that sensible food choices are being made.

The nutrition conscious swimmer will:

- Eat plenty of cereals and grains such as rice/pasta/bread/breakfast cereal, including lots of the wholegrain varieties of these foods as well.
- Eat plenty of fruits and vegetables. Experts recommend that at least five portions (combined) are eaten per day.
- Stock up with pulses (peas/beans/lentils), sweetcorn, potatoes and other similar, high-carbohydrate foods.
- Regularly eat low-fat dairy produce (milk/yogurts/cheese) or soya products.
- Regularly eat lean cuts of meat, poultry and fish or vegetarian replacements for these foods (see Table 4).
- Occasionally consume nuts, seeds, pure vegetable oils and oily fish supplying fat-soluble vitamins and essential fatty acids.

If a swimmer is worried about obtaining enough vitamins and minerals from the diet then study the guidelines above. If there is still concern then seek the advice of a GP or a qualified nutritionist/dietician before investing in a supplement. If a supplement is recommended then use it to support positive nutritional changes and not as an excuse for poor eating habits. It's worth remembering that there is no magical pill, powder or potion that will transform a swimmer into the next Mark Spitz or Matt Biondi!

Fluid

Training and competing in the hot and humid environment of a pool can lead to dehydration.[3] It has been well documented that dehydration will impair an athlete's performance.[6] Drinking is a good habit to adopt if performance is to be maintained.

Thirst is a very poor indicator of the need to drink. By the time a swimmer is thirsty they may already be dehydrated. The trick is to drink a little and often, starting before training, by maintaining an adequate fluid intake through the day. It's easy to neglect drinking habits at this time and to arrive at a workout already dehydrated.

Experts recommend that drinks are consumed before, during and after each workout. A quick and easy method to check an individual's fluid status is to monitor the urine. If a swimmer is producing copious quantities of pale coloured urine then they are well hydrated. If urine is dark, concentrated and smelly then fluid should be taken on board as a matter of urgency.

It's important to remember that no one drink is ideal for every swimmer. In fact requirements vary from individual to individual and are influenced by all sorts of factors, such as the environment, length of session, cost and availability of the drink.

Years ago the scientists suggested that drinking water was the best way to replace the fluid lost. However, recent research has revealed that some sports drinks may be even more effective fluid replacers. Drinks which are formulated to contain a small quantity of carbohydrate and sodium help to ensure fast rehydration.[6] The carbohydrate also provides additional energy which is an advantage for those swimmers who run out of steam during long, hard workouts. The sports drinks which are currently popular amongst swimmers include Isostar, Go, Gatorade and Lucozade Sport.

Competition nutrition

Nutritional planning for competition is an extremely important part of any event preparation. Unfortunately it is the aspect that many swimmers neglect. The competition diet should be an extension of the training plan, with the swimmer aiming to maintain glycogen stores and hydration at all times.

The pre-event meal should boost energy reserves, top up fluid levels, stave off hunger and provide swimmers with a psychological boost. Foods ingested during this period should be high in carbohydrate and low in fat, since high-fat foods digest more slowly. They should also be low in fibre and bulk if individuals are prone to pre-event nerves and accompanying diarrhoea.

The timing and size of this meal will depend on the start time of the heats. As a general rule, swimmers should leave 3–4 hours to digest a large meal and 1–2 hours for a lighter version. This timing is, however, dependent on individual preferences.

Table 5: Pre-event favourites

- Breakfast cereal and low-fat milk/porridge with syrup and raisins
- Toast (scraping of fat) with honey/jam/banana or jam sandwiches
- Muffins/crumpets with jam/honey/pancakes and syrup
- Beans on toast/bagels/toasted tea-cakes/currant buns
- Pasta/rice/noodles with tomato-based sauce
- Jacket potato with low-fat filling

The length of time between races as well as individual preferences will determine food selection over a competition day(s). Typically, if there is less than one hour between races, choices are limited to drinks rather than food. If there is longer, and the competitor is sure that they are able to tolerate food, then carbohydrate-rich meals or snacks may be preferred. The length of time between heats and finals is often long enough to consume a meal or a series of snacks.

A carefully chosen sports diet will help swimmers to support consistent and hard training. This will ultimately help them to swim faster. The message to all swimmers is follow the recommendations in this chapter and you will be nutritionally well prepared to take on all your rivals! Use food as your trump card and play it before your next race!

For further information about nutrition and swimming write to the Amateur Swimming Association of Great Britain, Harold Fern House, Derby Square, Loughborough, Leicestershire, LE11 0AL UK, requesting the series of practical nutrition leaflets by Peggy Wellington.

References
1 Costill, D. *et al* (1988), *Effects of repeated days of intensified training on muscle glycogen and swimming performance*, Med. Sci. Sports. Exerc. 20: 249–254
2 Devlin, J. T. & C. Williams (1991), *Food Nutrition and Sports Performance* (Proceedings of an International Scientific Consensus), J. Sp. Sci. Vol. 9, Special Issue, Summer
3 Troup, J. P. *et al* (1994), 'Physiology and Nutrition For Competitive Swimming'. In: Lamb, D. R. *et al* (eds) (1994) *Physiology and Nutrition for Competitive Sport, Perspectives in Exercise Science and Sports Medicine*, Vol. 7, 99–129
4 Hawley, J. A. & M. M. Williams (1991), *Dietary Intakes of Age-Group Swimmers*, Br. J. Sp. Med, 25 (3), 154–158
5 Wellington, P. (1989), *Nutrition Knowledge, Awareness and Dietary Practices – A study of swimmers and coaches*, Unpublished Masters Thesis
6 Maughan, R. J. (1994), *Fluid and Electrolyte Loss and Replacement in Exercise*, Coaching Focus, No. 25, Spring

---

Injuries and infections

In this day and age such is the rigour of swimming training that the body is constantly exposed to injuries or infections which come about as a matter of course in regular training. We intend to look closely at the most regular of these in order to clarify what happens.

Infections of the ear

The most common and recurring ear infection in swimmers is *otitis external*. It comes about because of excess water being left in the ear. If, for instance, the ear isn't dried properly, the moisture will slowly work its way out but in doing so will leave debris in the external auditory canal. Moist warm conditions are ideal for this infection to develop.

However, further swimming on an ear with this debris in it will cause it to be attacked by bacteria or fungus which use the debris as food. The canal becomes swollen, creating more debris and producing pus.

For a swimmer who is training regularly, a visit to the doctor should solve the problem. Doctor's views differ greatly but it is not felt that a swimmer needs to stay out of the water in order to treat this problem. Treatment consists of cleaning and keeping the ear dry. Alternatively, it can be treated prophylactically by using acetic acid which has the same effect before infection can set in. Alternatively, a cotton wool wick of cortisporin Otic suspension can be used or, as a final resort, antibiotics.

To avoid getting ear trouble, never get soap or shampoo in the ear after training or run water directly into the ear in a shower after training. Dry the ear thoroughly and take your time doing so. Swimmers wear ear plugs but they tend to irritate the ear in a person who is prone to ear infections.

Swimming in excess in open water *may* cause a thickness of bone in the middle ear. This is known as *exostosis*. Baby oil or olive oil may help to create a shield here.

Middle-ear infections tend to occur where the swimmer has a nose or sinus infection. Hard noseblowing may force pus up the eustachian tube into the middle ear. When the tube is shut the blocked ear can develop fluid behind the ear drum, called serous otis media. Yawning and gentle inflation will help the fluid to drain away, but this is best treated by a doctor.

Eye troubles

Many eye problems have been eliminated with the introduction of the modern lightweight goggle. We would recommend the wearing of goggles for any swimmer who has a regular problem and feels the necessity to rub the eyes continually after training.

The conjunctiva of the eye is frequently the most irritated area and comes about when the PH or acid–alkaline base of the water is very much greater or smaller than 7.4. At 7.4 the state of the water is close to that of the eye. It tends to get worse in warmer water or in brighter lights. Swimmers who have difficulty wearing goggles may like to take an eyecup of salt in water solution before training as a preventative, or eye drops at the end of the session.

The two-session-a-day swimmers may find that even rinsing the eyes in a bowl of ordinary water may help to prevent the eyes being reactivated on entering the water a second time.

The part of the eye is the cornea where rubbing can cause a red eye. The cornea fills with water and can produce this swelling. The cornea actually loses some of its cells on the surface and the eye becomes even more sensitive to smoke, light and reading when studying after training. Most people who have conjunctivitis cannot pass on the infection. However, it is better not to wear someone else's goggles if you can help it because adeno virus type 3, the only transmittable eye infection in swimming pools known to us, can be passed on in this way.

Tendonitus and other should problems

Pain in the *shoulder tendons* is a common problem in swimming. It comes about through

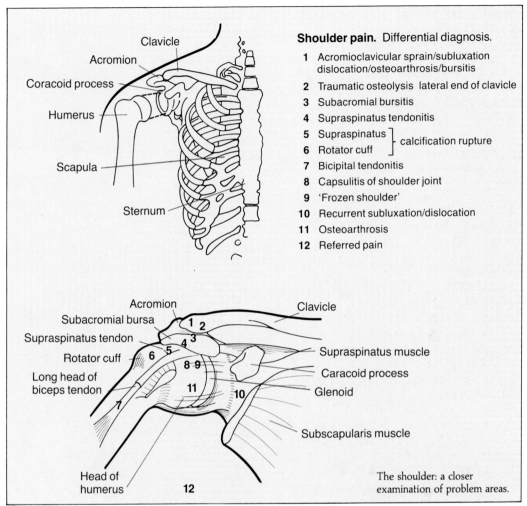

Shoulder pain. Differential diagnosis.

1. Acromioclavicular sprain/subluxation dislocation/osteoarthrosis/bursitis
2. Traumatic osteolysis lateral end of clavicle
3. Subacromial bursitis
4. Supraspinatus tendonitis
5. Supraspinatus ⎤
6. Rotator cuff ⎦ calcification rupture
7. Bicipital tendonitis
8. Capsulitis of shoulder joint
9. 'Frozen shoulder'
10. Recurrent subluxation/dislocation
11. Osteoarthrosis
12. Referred pain

The shoulder: a closer examination of problem areas.

continual overuse of the shoulders, mostly in butterfly and frontcrawl, and also to a much lesser extent in backstroke.

It starts as discomfort on top of the shoulders and slowly becomes more painful. It can become extremely painful to lift the arms sideways from the normal standing position. If the back of the hand is placed against a light resistance the pain becomes acute and it becomes even more difficult to lift the arms to a fully stretched position above the head.

The regular pattern of movement by the rotator cuff muscles, particularly in a young swimmer, can produce tenderness on the major tendons of the shoulder. If the swimmer gets pain after the training session or during it, the coach may have to either reduce the yardage covered or the strokes swum to reduce the pain. Often the pain is common to one stroke and a change of strokes helps greatly. A change of arm position or hand entry, such as a higher arm recovery, may well do the trick.

Ice packs can be applied to the area after training and these kept in place for approximately 20 minutes. This can be helpful but is often inconvenient.

For swimmers who have *acute pain* the whole time rest is the only answer – a few sessions on the kickboard may help here. If it continues over a period, steroid injections into the surrounding suprispinatus and biceps tendons should be considered by the doctor.

Backstroker's shoulder occurs when the arm is in full abduction and external rotation, for

181

instance going into the turn. During the turn, the head of the humerus or shoulder joint can be seen to be almost jumping out of its socket. This can be a difficult pain to overcome as it occurs about the subscapularis. Early identification on the part of the coach can help to alter the turning or backstroke extension techniques in an individual where this occurs. In chronic cases it can even end in an operation.

Both tendonitus and backstroker's shoulder occur because the area damaged is not strong enough or flexible enough to stand the strains of training. Land conditioning will help here. Most strains of this nature will become more obvious towards the end of a training session.

The difference between strains and fatigue

Coaches may find it difficult to differentiate between the above injuries and the normal stresses and strains which occur during training. This is a matter of monitoring on the part of the coach because early symptoms of tendonitus are similar to normal strains. Soreness should subside after a couple of days; if it doesn't the coach knows that he must observe further. *Bursitus* can also occur at the shoulder where, instead of the long head of biceps being under strain the sub-acromaxial bursa comes under pressure.

Where tendonitus has occurred and the swimmer has had to rest for a period, the coach will need to build the stroke up again slowly, checking that the stroke isn't changed to accommodate further risks of injury. If this happens, it may lead to other areas of strain and create further areas of weakness. Light weights to rebuild muscles which have lost strength and light, progressive stretching exercises on land are the hallmarks of sensible rehabilitation on the part of the coach.

Breaststroker's knee

Breaststroker's knee must be the most commonly talked about ailment in the swimmer's anatomy. It tends to occur in situations where a breaststroker is swimming too much of that stroke – generally over 50 per cent of their

training sessions. It can become so bad that it can lead to operations on the knee and eventual retirement from the stroke.

Breaststroker's knee comes about because of strain to the tibial collateral ligament which crosses the knee joint spanning the adductor muscles and inserting in the tibia bone, some 4 to 5 cm (1¾ to 2 ins) under the knee joint. There are one or two other causes of breaststroker's knee.

It can also be caused by overstretching on the deep capsule in the knee joint. This can lead to excessive external rotation of the knee on the femur, which leads to a breaking down of articular cartilage. As the knee moves from flexion to extension, there is a considerable amount of strain on the tibial collateral ligament. This may be increased by the external rotation of the tibia, ankle and knee.

Breaststroker's knee can be recognized by a tender pain at the origin of the ligament. It can also be demonstrated by lifting the knee whilst standing and for pain to be felt whilst the knee is rotated about 30°.

Here again, ice applied to the tender area for about 20 minutes can provide relief. Ultrasound may be applied to the area for about 5 to 10 minutes over a period of about ten days. An injection of cortisone acetate suspended in water should be made into the ligament area itself. Cortisone injections can once again be made as a final resort but these must be carried out disparagingly and ruptured tendons have occurred in areas where injections have been made injudiciously. Continuous pain can only really be relieved by giving the swimmer and that particular movement up to two months rest.

Unfortunately, breaststroker's knee is ever more likely to come about in breaststrokers who have an even greater degree of valgus stress at the knee joint. Complete rupture of the ligament as a result of breaststroke kicking is unknown. The main problem overall is that the breaststroke leg action comprises a number of quite complex and unnatural movements. These really start when the feet are turned outwards which twists the tibia outwards at the knee. The quadriceps or muscles on the front of the leg extend, which stretches the knee and drives the body forward. The knees tend to be held together (the valgus movement) in order to catch water on the inside of the tibia.

Knee problems in other strokes

Knee problems can occur in the other four strokes. These tend to be forgotten and are often referred to as breaststroker's knee simply because in this day and age of multistroke racing and training it is difficult to classify one from another in each individual. The coach therefore tends to go for the easier, general term.

There is certainly a fair requirement on the knee joint as far as range of movement is concerned. The angle of movement can vary from 45° during flexion to 200° when hyperextended or propelling at the knee. As the knee flexes and extends, the patella or knee glides in a groove at the front of the femur. During flexion pressure of the patella on the femur increases dramatically.

The large quadriceps muscles and the cartilage around the patella take the strain when this occurs. If the patella fails to glide properly, it can lead to even greater increases of pressure on the cartilage. A high-riding patella, ie a situation where the patella comes out of its groove, can create problems for the swimmer. During hyperextension the patella can come out of its groove and there can also be resulting pain in the back of the knee joint. Situations where there has been a dislocation of the patella due to it being driven into the femur can create grating or clicking problems in much the same way as the other two cases.

The feeling of the knee locking or buckling is also fairly common in freestylers or backstrokers. The upward/downward movement of the legs won't relieve the pain which comes about, even when very easy swimming takes place. These pains are known as *chondramalacie patectal* or softening of the cartilage. They can take months to slowly recover and are therefore even more of a problem than breaststroker's knee. Rehabilitation consists of building up the quadriceps through progressive weights and stretching exercises, but these should never involve the knee being flexed by more than 40°.

Long before rehabilitation takes place the average medic will probably recommend aspirin for its anti-inflammatory properties and as a pain reliever. Once again, a twenty-minute ice massage may be of use. In more advanced cases the leg may be placed in a plaster cast to rest or re-align the patella. A small operation may produce an even better effect.

One other knee problem which can cause problems to swimmers and is very painful is *patella tendonitus*. It can come about at the pushoff or turn or after it and is normally caused by the pressure of extension on the knee joint. It should be treated in much the same way as the above problems.

Massage

Massage is the breaking down of tissue and is generally administered by a coach. It was first used on a large scale on poolsides in the 1960s and has since been used as an excellent medium for a coach to communicate with his swimmer – at a time when the two are emotionally close before a race, and when a coach can relate race tactics.

In terms of physiology, massage has negligible effect. Most swimming coaches use it as a means of warming an area in order to loosen and prepare it for a race situation. Only deep massage will relieve a muscle knot. Because coaches massage mostly large muscle groups they do not rub deeply enough to loosen them.

Massage tends to make the skin red as the rubbing brings blood to the surface of the skin, where it is not really required in a race situation. The blood needs to be brought into the muscle. The muscles during massage remain uncontracted and are acted upon. It isn't until a muscle is contracted that the required chemicals are released in order to open the blood vessels in the muscles ready for action.

Ergogenic acids

In international swimming, doping and drugs have increasingly occupied the public's mind. The problem first came to light after the 1972 Olympic 400 metres freestyle which was won by the young American Rick Demont. Demont was stripped of his gold medal after failing a dope test. Demont always protested his innocence and claimed that he took the drug ephedrine (which you can buy over the counter in the U.S.A.) to control his asthma.

In 1978 the Soviet backstroker Victor Kutznesov had his bronze medal in the World Championships 100 metres backstroke taken away from him after he failed an anabolic steroid test. He was only 17 years of age.

Renate Vogel, the former East German world breaststroke champion, defected to the west and it has since been reported that she was taking pain-killing injections because of trouble with her wrists and ankles. These troubles were believed to be as a result of cortisone, a drug which affected her vital organs to such an extent that she was unable to race.

The use of drugs in sport looks like being with us for some time, or at least until science develops an even better alternative for the body. We are now involved in a scientific race in which some swimmers are merely representing the most advanced laboratory in international competition. It is therefore as well to be aware of potential pitfalls.

Dope tests are constructed so that swimmers are banned if traces of a substance are found in urine. It is hoped that new regulations will set quantitative levels in urine as being pharmacological and not ergogenic. For instance, it is possible for someone who buys ephedrine for a cold and sprays or inhales the substance to be banned.

Caffeine has been of interest since tests were first introduced by the I.O.C. at the 1984 Olympics. It stimulates the central nervous system, dilates coronary arteries and speeds up the heart rate and force of contraction. It also has the effect of freeing fatty acids in order to burn them for energy which means that carbohydrates can be saved.

Caffeine is now on the list of prohibited substances but the quantity of caffeine obtained from coffee is minimal and would require about 30 cups to be drunk prior to a race.

The most well known drugs in sport these days are anabolic steroids. They can be taken either as an injection or in tablet form. Sprinters tend to use this drug because they feel it will make them stronger and faster. Steroids virtually extend another body hormone, testosterone, which again increases muscle mass. Middle-distance athletes have also been known to use them because they aid recovery by stimulating red blood cell formation. This, in turn, aids the capacity of the blood to carry oxygen quickly.

Most difficulties over the years have come from swimmers at international level who are innocently taking banned substances in respiratory decongestants or using eye drops which contain sympathomimetics, for relief of conjuctivitis.

Amphetamines are also dangerous; they accelerate the nervous system.

Below is a list of substances banned by the world governing body F.I.N.A.

Psychomotor stimulant drugs		
amphetamine	diethylpropion	methylamphetamine
benzphetamine	dimethylamphetamine	methylphenidate
chlophentermine	ethylamphetamine	norpseudoephedrine
cocaine	fencamfamin	pemoline
	meclofenoxate	phendimetrazine

phenmetrazine
phentermine
pipragol
prolintane
and related compounds

Sympathomimetic amines
chlorprenaline
ephedrine
etafedrine
isoetharine
methoxyphenamine
methylephedrine
and related compounds

Miscellaneous central
nervous system
stimulants
amiphenazole
bemigride
caffeine
cropropamide
crotethamide

doxapram
ethamivan
leptazol
nikethamide
picrotoxine
strychnine
and related compounds

Narcotic analgesics
anileridine
codeine
dextromoramide
dihydrocodeine
dipipanone
ethylmorphine
heroin
hydrocodone
hydromorphone
levorphanol
methadone
oxocodone
oxomorphone

pentazocine
pininodine
thebacon
trimeperidine
and related compounds

Anabolic steriods
clostebol
dehydrochlormethylteste-
terone
fluoxymesterone
mesterolone
metenolone
methandienone
methyltestosterone
nandrolone
norethandrolone
oxymesterone
oxymetholone
stanozolol
testosterone
and related compounds

Stress

Stress is one of the factors in swimming which is so difficult to quantify. We can be fairly certain that the ability or inability to cope with stress will have an important influence on the performance of the individual, particularly in a young swimmer.

Stress should not, however, just be associated with the race situation; it can also play an important role in training. Most of the time a swimmer can handle the training loads which he is asked to undergo. This is known as the process of adaptation: as the body adapts, so it is prepared for the potential of even greater strains being placed on it in race situations. The body always has the *potential* to adapt because its major systems are inherently designed that way. Occasionally, though, the individual cannot cope with the training loads with which he is presented and this is known as 'failing adaptation'.

How can a coach identify failing adaptation in an individual undergoing rigorous training?

Physiologically this can be difficult without regular testing. The pituitary gland produces adrenocortotrophic hormone (ATCH) which, in turn, stimulates the adrenal gland to secrete adrenocorticoids and catecholamines. These chemicals increase the metabolic rate, blood pressure and the blood sugar level. By this means the body attempts to allow for stress. However, even this chemical can become depleted if the body fails to adapt.

A coach may observe lethargy in training, a sharp increase in the swimmer's training times and a slow recovery rate in terms of pulse counts after a training repetition. A coach's ability to assist a swimmer in overcoming this stage in training, without affecting his annual training pattern to any great extent, is important. He may change the training stroke, decrease the distances swum, increase repetition resting time, intersperse heavy training with easy swimming, or ask for repetition swims at less than all-out effort.

The coach must have a good understanding both of the physical and mental signs of stress, which can be cumulative. The stress can be physical or psychological or combinations of both.

It is also worth noting that an individual's response to stress may alter from one occasion to another. Inadequate diet, lack of sleep, the pressures of home expectations or those of coaches or friends, illness, financial or family problems or fear of failure may be just a few of the contributing facets other than training itself.

Again from a coach's point of view it's important to be able to differentiate between stress and staleness. Staleness can normally bring on boredom and be counteracted by varying the training. Some level of remotivation may be necessary to overcome staleness. Motivation is not a factor with stress, although a coach may need to explain training schedule alterations, race tactic alterations and goal changes to swimmers who may suffer some anxiety and stress if he does not.

When a swimmer reaches the stage of extreme irritability, swollen glands, skin rashes, lose of appetite, then the coach should recognise these as signs of stress and act accordingly. It can be a diffcult time for the coach. If he pushes a swimmer too hard, the swimmer will go into this post-adaptive phase. If he holds back, he may be preventing that swimmer from undergoing training which ultimately is going to do him a lot of good.

Hans Seyle defined stress as: 'the state manifested by a specific syndrome which consists of all the non-specifically induced changes within a biologic system'. Seyle in the 1950s was the first person to identify the 'general adaptation syndrome'. He saw this as being in three stages: the alarm reaction, the stage of resistance and, finally, the stage of exhaustion. The coach should attempt to push the swimmer well into the second phase without fear. The body can readily adapt to all sorts of pressures, such as heat, cold, burning, poisoning etc, and in much the same way it can cope with extremes of exercise.

The body seems to have a limited supply of adaptation energy and this varies from person to person in quantity. If a coach steadily increases training loads, all swimmers should be able to cope on a day-to-day basis, unless pushed to the extremes. Forbes Carlile[3] identified that swimmers can suffer from nervous depletion where a swimmer who seems to have adapted well fails to improve his time on his first stroke. He suggests that specific parts of the nervous system employed have temporarily become worn out. A change of stroke in which unfatigued pathways are used will help, and these are often the reason for personal best performances on such a stroke change.

The swimmer's personal rationale will nearly always prevent him from pushing himself into stage three as identified by Seyle. Very few swimmers are that self-motivating. It is therefore up to the coach to help him reach this stage without creating a phase of failing adaptation. It is worth noting that an inflexible coach may create this situation unintentionally.

References
1 *The Stress of Life*, Hans Seyle, Longmans 1956
2 'Nutritive Aspects of Physical Fitness Work' by Thomas Cureton in *Swimming Technique* July 1969
3 *Forbes Carlile on Swimming*, Pelham Books 1968
4 *The Physiology of Exercise*, H. De Vries, Staples Press 1966
5 'Stress, Drugs and Nutrition' by M. Foskett, unpublished BED, Loughborough College 1974

14 Advanced Scientific Aspects

Our scientific knowledge of swimming has increased to such an extent in the last twenty years that there is now very considerable documentation of a full range of theories. In this chapter we will examine the aspects which have a considerable influence on the way in which we swim and the way we may well swim in the future.

Propulsive force

In Chapter 3 we talked about the effect of Bernoulli's principle in relation to swimming. There are three forces that have an influence: lift, drag and the resultant propulsive force. As lift force is always perpendicular to drag, the resultant propulsive force is often somewhere between the two:

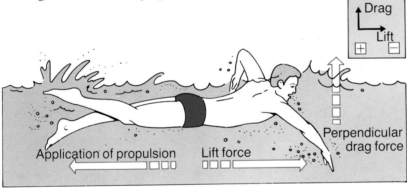

Head high

Drag
Lift
⊞   ⊟

Normal head position

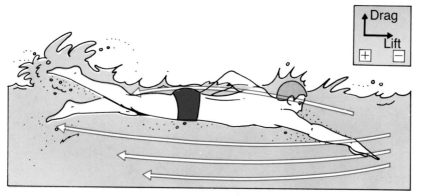

Drag
Lift
⊞   ⊟

Head low

Diagrammatically the best result is:

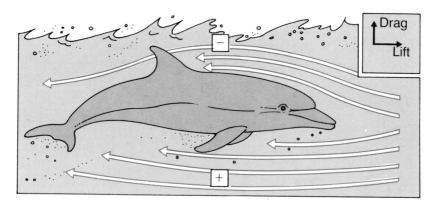

Drag
Lift

If we look at the hands and the feet, the pressure differential alters according to the position at which the limb cuts through the water. The lifting effect comes about because the water travelling over the upper surface of the hand accelerates while the water under-neath is losing speed. The differential in pressure between the two surfaces sees the upper surface losing pressure and the lower (palm) increasing it. The result is a lifting effect.

The word lift tends to be a little deceiving. The lift can take place in any direction. The angle and pitch in which both the hands and feet move therefore has a direct bearing on the resultant lift and the effectiveness of total propulsive power.

The hand and arm are lifted forward.[1] This force has to be harnessed in order to propel the body forward. This is achieved by a resistance brought about simply because of their downward movement, aided by a stabilization at the shoulder joint. The hand and arm aren't free to move forward, the lift force is transferred to the swimmer's body, which is propelled past the arm.

If the hands are placed at the correct angle then a greater area of hand can be presented to the water. More water speed and less pressure over a greater area when presented by the hand will result in even greater lift force being created.

The stiller an area of water is, the greater the potential for creating lift force. If a hand or foot tries to pull on water that has been moved then the areas of low and high pressure will have already been created.

Feel for the water

For many years coaches have tried to define 'feel' as applied by swimmers. Some swimmers have been identified as having good feel for the water. The answer is that propulsion isn't always generated by swimmers pulling and pushing backwards but more importantly by their ability to create lift at the correct times.

This has been interpreted partly as feel. At one stage swimmers were encouraged by coaches to feather the water, but this type of lift-dominated propulsion cannot be imposed. It comes about naturally as an extension of coaches asking swimmers to push water back. The swimmers with natural feel have made lateral and vertical deviations in order to develop greater lift.

Maglischo in *Swimming Faster*[1] pointed out that lift propulsion probably plays a more important role than propulsion created by normal drag. He felt that the lift propulsion could produce more distance per stroke. A slower turnover rate results and less energy is therefore required to produce more acceleration. He also pointed out that each swimmer has to be capable of changing from the more easily identifiable drag-dominated propulsion to lift propulsion during each arm cycle. They achieve this by paddling movements during alterations to limb direction. These movements are made until the hands and feet have reached sufficient pitch and velocity in the new direction to be able to work with lift-dominated propulsion again.

The pitch of hands and feet in most swimming movements is somewhere between 20° and 50° from the vertical.

Muscle fibres and their effect on swimming

All humans have two entirely different types of muscle fibre: fast twitch, which are pale pink, and slow twitch, which are red in colour. Slow twitch have a greater ability to aid aerobic metabolism and therefore aid endurance. These fibres contract between ten and fifteen times per second. The fast twitch fibres contract very quickly – between thirty and fifty times per second – they are normally associated with power and speed due to their ability to convert energy aerobically. These fibres tire more quickly.

Most muscles contain both fast and slow twitch fibres in different proportions. Some individual muscles in the body have a greater degree of one type due to the work they carry out on a day-to-day basis. Muscles which are responsible for deportment automatically have a greater number of slow twitch fibres because they are in continuous use. Some swimmers will have a greater degree of fast twitch fibres throughout their body and vice versa. In keeping with this, muscle biopsies have shown that those people with fast twitch fibres have a tendency to be better sprinters and vice versa.

The fast twitch fibres have since been

broken down into three subsections by researchers.[2] Within these three groups, one has a better aerobic capacity than the others and is therefore more similar to slow twitch fibres in capacity.

Overall, research continues to provide conflicting evidence. It's still not known whether training will turn a sprinter with a large percentage of slow twitch fibres into an endurance swimmer and vice versa. Certainly the situation can be improved but it appears that this compensation is limited. Muscle biopsies can help to direct swimmers towards training and races over distances to which they are more ideally suited.

All muscle fibres are used for sprinting while in endurance races only slow twitch fibres, which have small more easily activated neurons, are in use. The fast twitch fibres have larger neurons which are activated less easily but are only used when force or power is required. The table beneath indicates the particular distance that would be best suited to swimmers with approximate fast or slow twitch muscle fibres distributions (see table).

Nearly all working muscle fibres are completely depleted of glycogen if two hard 2 to $2\frac{1}{2}$ hour training sessions are carried out. If this type of training is carried out, the swimmer should be eating regular meals with a

Slow twitch	Fast twitch	Distance (metres)
10%	90%	50 and 100
20%	80%	50 and 100
30%	70%	100 to 400
40%	60%	100 to 400
50%	50%	100 to 1500
60%	40%	100 to 800
70%	30%	200 to 1500
80%	20%	200 to 1500
90%	10%	200 to 1500

high carbohydrate content.

As far as coaches and swimmers are concerned, the most important question is as to whether muscle fibres can be decreased, increased or proportions of types of muscle fibre altered by training. Unfortunately, research is inconclusive. It may well be that training encourages the fibres to split so that the total number of fibres within a muscle increases.

Why is it then that many coaches give large amounts of over-distance training which is not specific to the type of muscle fibre they will be using in a race?[3] Many sprinters would indeed appear to benefit from such a paradox. The answer could be that this training provides long-term energy stores, such as fats, which will be needed for the season's racing and more importantly, training.

Types of energy used in swimming

The first source used is an immediate energy source. The immediate energy sources are utilized during swimming sprints of 50 metres or less. They can be stored and resynthesized in the active muscle mass itself. They are therefore ready to carry out explosive sprinting and are known as high-energy phosphates, being the most simplified energy systems available for muscular activity.

These energy sources are known as adenozine triphosphate (ATP) and phosphocreatine (PCr). When these high-energy sources are available for muscular activity, they can be broken down and each requires only a single enzyme to be resynthesized to their normal

high-energy states. ATP is broken down as follows:

$$ATP \rightarrow ADP + energy$$

The resulting ADP is of little physiological value unless reconverted to ATP (the only compound that can supply energy for muscular contraction). This comes about from the following two processes:

ADP + PCr→ATP + creatine
ADP + ADP→APT + adenozine monophosphate (AMP)

Enzymes are substances which help to speed up a chemical reaction without changing themselves during the reaction. The proteins used in the above two processes are enzymes and can be used again as aid-reforming ATP and PCr.

The immediate sources referred to above last for 25 to 40 seconds due to the fact that the high-energy phosphate stores last for a short period. PCr within the muscle is of limited supply, as are the enzymes themselves. In swimming, unless the reconversion to ATP and PCr continues the body energy supply becomes exhausted.[4] This means that the sprinter must train on sprints in order to get used to employing this system.

As the terminal group of phosphates removed from ATP and PCr, energy released for muscle contraction as follows:

ATP→ADP + energy

PCr→creatine + energy + phosphate

Anaerobic energy

Races between 100 and 200 m have to depend on anaerobic sources of energy to supply the ATP needed. Oxygen is not required for this process as carbohydrates can be broken down to simple sugar, glucose being the main one. This glucose is stored in the form of chains of molecules known as glycogen.

Again the glycogen reserves can be developed through training so that they can be called on as the muscles become tired. Glucose for exercise can be derived either from the blood or as glycogen in the active muscle. A series of biochemical reactions can be shortened as follows:

$$1 \text{ glucose} \xrightarrow{\text{anaerobic metabolism}}$$

2 lactic acids + ATP

Here one six-carbon glucose molecule is broken down to two three-carbon lactates as the product along with two × ATP as byproducts.

The lactates which result in the muscles can be transported away by the blood system. The buildup of acid products can affect the anaerobic metabolism of stored glycogen.

When we come to 400 metres or longer, the way in which the muscles manage to produce ATP for energy becomes more complex. The aerobic energy system works with a number of enzyme pathways combining to produce an energy yield of 36 to 169 ATP for each substance metabolized. They require oxygen for metabolism. The processes which take place in the mitochordria in the muscles are as follows:

$$\text{foodstuffs} + O_2 \xrightarrow{\text{aerobic metabolism}}$$
(carbohydrates + fats)

$$H_2O + CO_2 + ATP$$

Under anaerobic conditions, glucose which is metabolized forms a total of 2 ATP. Aerobically, the same glucose produces 36 ATP; oxygen has to be supplied uninterrupted to the mitochordria in order to provide an energy yield which is eighteen times greater. Fats also play an important role. When broken down to form CO_2 and water, they create a tremendous amount of energy. The yield from fats produces approximately 30 per cent more energy and fats are therefore important in distance races. This is known as lipid metabolism.

The influence of training

Training teaches the swimmer to utilize fat as an energy source. Aerobic training increases the number and size of the mitochordria and improves the capacity of the enzymes to speed up the ultilization of fats and glucose.

In addition, training produces an increase in the number of blood vessels within the muscle which in turn aids the delivery of oxygen and sources of energy to the muscle.

Training should be specific to develop the right energy system for a particular swimmer's event. The swimmer should devote some of his swimming training to covering his own distance at close to maximum pace.

Nuclear magnetic resonance

The Americans are now developing a new system of selection for athletes called nuclear magnetic resonance (NMR). Scientists will be able to determine chemical changes in the muscle and indicate whether a swimmer is overtraining or undertraining.

An NMR analysis technique is being developed and is based on the ratio of phosphocreative to inorganic phosphate. The ratio tells researchers how much of the muscle's potential is being used at any degree of exercise. A one-to-two ratio means that about half the metabolic capacity of the muscle is being used.

These techniques were first pioneered by the United States Olympic Committee.[5]

The influence of blood lactates

More anaerobic energy and, as a result, faster speeds over longer distances can be achieved if more lactic acid production takes place. This is determined by enzymes responsible for the anaerobic phase of glycolysis. These enzymes increase their activities with training, particularly if the training is high-intensity sprinting.

Repeat swims of between 50 and 200 m at maximum effort can produce peak blood lactate state. Swims that are longer than this would only increase the activity of these enzymes if made at maximum speeds.

As the swimmer tires, lactic acid accumulates as excess lactate, which eventually becomes so great than acidosis comes about. This state heightens to such a degree that the swimmer's performance is damaged. The swimmer now needs more oxygen in order to reduce the level of lactate accumulation. Lack of oxygen will cause pyruvate and hydrogen ions to combine and form lactic acid.

Lactate molecules also accumulate in non-working muscle fibres in instances where the blood stream cannot transport them away. The ability to remove lactate is important: it can delay the onset of muscle fatigue and, in turn, of the reduction of muscle PH(acid/alkali balance) which normally causes fatigue.

Training can delay the rate of production of blood lactate as well as increase the body's ability to remove it partly through training the body circulation in distributing blood to working muscles. Lactate removal is also increased from working muscle fibres through the enzyme lactate hydrogenage. The metabolism of lactate through hydrogenage sets off a chain reaction which brings this about.

When lactic acid is diffused into the blood stream at a greater rate than it is removed, then the 'anaerobic threshold' has been reached. It is usually expressed as a percentage of maximum oxygen consumption at a point where there is excess lactate in the blood. Again, the better-trained swimmer will have a high percentage (as much as 85 to 90 per cent in distance swimmers) whereas an untrained person might have only 40 per cent of his anaerobic threshold. There is a variation between sprinters and endurance swimmers because endurance swimmers, with a preponderance of slow twitch muscle fibres, have a greater capacity for aerobic metabolism. They therefore produce less lactate during training.

The anaerobic threshold reflects the ability of the swimmer to be able to remove lactate, to reduce lactate production in muscles and in improving VO_2 maximum. A good swimmer needs to have all three working at their optimum. Distance performers, on the whole, have a higher anaerobic threshold. Often a high anaerobic threshold can counteract a lower VO_2 maximum. This would mean that a distance performer who can retain a higher threshold with a lower VO_2 maximum can more easily avoid acidosis occurring in his muscles.

Fatigue, which is reflected in a decrease in swimming speed, comes about because the muscles are no longer being provided with the energy or ATP at the rate this is needed. Training-induced increase in aerobicity in skeletal muscle comes about with the capacity to delay the onset of fatigue.

The swimmer's response to training can be assessed by blood lactic acid levels. High levels would occur normally in 100 or 200 m races where the lactacide or anaerobic systems are at their maximum use. Slow times and high blood lactate accumulations would indicate either misuse of energy by the body in terms of technique or prior conditioning. Reductions in lactate readings set against speed is a good way of indicating positive training adaptions.

Dr Clyde Williams of the Sports Science Department at Loughborough University states that increased blood lactate concentration at a prescribed sub maximal swimming speed indicates that there is something wrong with the swimmer.[11] He suggests the follow-

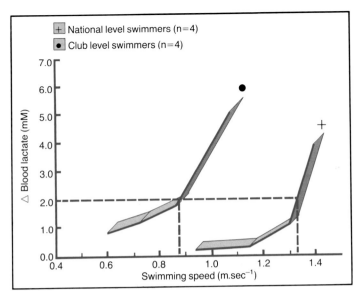

ing tests for swimmer and coach: 1) Resting – blood samples. 2) 400 yds swim (60 per cent). 3) 1 min. rest blood samples. 4) 200 yds swim (70 per cent). 5) 1 min. rest and blood samples. 6) 200 yds swim (80 per cent). 7) 1 min. rest and blood samples. 8) 200 yds swim (90 per cent). 9) Final blood sample and 200 yds.

These tests (indicated in the graphs) show a range of sub maximal swimming speeds. The swimmer's best 200 yds time to find maximum velocity (V max) instead of VO_2 max. was used. The percentages, therefore, indicate this relationship with V max. Swimming speed equivalent to a blood lactate level of 2mM is seen as V2mM and also as % V max (2mM). The swimmer's VO_2 max; maximum ventilation rate and maximum heart rate during treadmill running were also included. The graphs show the relationship between swimming speed (VM sec of % V max) and blood lactate concentrations as mean values for four recreational and four competitive swimmers.

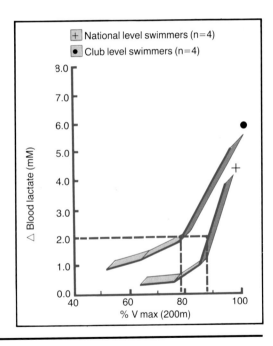

Oxygen and the blood system

Cardiac output is determined by the volume of blood that the heart ejects from one ventricle in each minute. The same volume is, of course, discharged via the pulmonary circuit. Both must be taken into account in order to determine the work carried out by the heart. At rest,

the cardiac output of the average male is about 4.0 litres. The entire volume of blood in the heart therefore circulates through the body in two minutes or less.

A person who is out of condition would need to increase the heart rate in order to maintain a higher work rate whilst swimming, whilst the conditioned swimmer would need to increase his stroke volume (or the amount of blood ejected by the ventricles). The work carried out by the heart can be measured in terms of the weight of the blood ejected multiplied by the height to which it is lifted.

The ability of a swimmer to consume oxygen plays an important part during exercise. Oxygen consumption represents the difference between the amount of oxygen exhaled and inhaled in a minute. Swimmers with better oxygen consumption generally performs better. Maximum oxygen uptake reflects this and is expressed as VO_2 maximum. VO_2 maximum is generally higher in males than females and higher in fitter swimmers. The range is normally anything between 2 and 5 litres per minute. Differences in sizes can make a difference here, and therefore VO_2 maximum can also be expressed in millilitres of oxygen consumed for each kilogram of body weight in a minute (ml/kg/min).

Heredity can limit VO_2 maximum but training will assist. Many swimmers, however, only exhale about half of the oxygen they inhale during hard training. Improvements in VO_2 maximum are therefore often made through better transport in the blood and circulatory systems and better utilization by the muscles. The transportation can be affected by the number of alveoli available (air sacs) in the lungs, the red blood cell count as they move the oxygen, and the distribution of blood flow. The blood flow and speed can be affected by peripheral resistance or the resistance of blood vessels outside the immediate cardiac system.

Once again, the ability of the muscle fibres to absorb oxygen can affect VO_2 maximum as can capillary density. Each muscle fibre has a number of capillaries (or artery extensions) for use and the ability of these to transfer blood to the muscles is vital.

The heart itself is affected by two reflex actions.[6] Mareys law states that a rise in arterial blood pressure causes slowing of the heart, an increase in heart rate and a fall in blood pressure.

Bainbridge's reflex is initiated from the aerterial side of the circulation. Here, the heart is accelerated by a rise in the pressure of venous blood entering the right atrium. The rate of the heart is automatically altered by the amount of blood it receives. In training, a greater volume of blood is moved through the capillaries of the muscles to swell the volume of venous blood, the heart fills more quickly and responds by increasing the number of beats per minute.

Oxygen consumption is improved by increases in the myoglobin content of muscle and increases in the mitochondria due to their ability to bring about oxygen absorption. Endurance training brings about an increase in the size and number of mitochondria through the action of enzymes. This partly explains the benefit of distance training to the sprinter. Aerobic glycosis tends to take place at a faster rate reducing fatigue and the need for anaerobic glycosis[1]. It has been thought that endurance training may assist in the transportation by myoglobin of oxygen to the mitochondria in the muscles. The myoglobin acts as a carrier rather like red blood cells with the oxygenated blood in the circulatory system.

The hydrodynamic effect of swimming at constant speed

Swimming at constant speed may be seen as swimming in vertical and horizontal equilibrium: the swimmer isn't accelerating and the forces acting upon him are in equilibrium. The drag forces always act in a direction directly opposite to the swimmer's velocity. If a swimmer kicks down at a certain angle, the drag force is opposite to the direction of the leg's velocity. The propulsive component will result from the effect of these two acting against one another. The vector summation of the two leg drags gives a net force forward:

The net force from the kick alter as the kick cycle changes. When both legs are horizontal, the net force is zero. At this point, the feet (as described earlier) are paddling.

The viscous drag force can be affected by:

(a) The shape of the swimmer

(b) The speed of the water travelling around it (and vice versa)

(c) The density of the swimmer

(d) The surface area of the swimmer

The mathematic relation[7] between these is as follows:

Drag in pounds $= CD\ A\ V\ 2/2$

where: CD = drag coefficient = density of fluid

V = relative velocity of liquid compared to the swimmer

A = surface area in contact

Drag coefficients are normally described by maritime engineers as a dimensioner's parameter known as Reynolds number (RE). This is defined as:

$$RE = \frac{VL}{\Psi}$$

where: V = relative velocity of liquid compared to object

L = length of object

Ψ = kinematic viscosity of liquid

As an extension, drag force on a perfectly flat human body would be:

$$\text{Skin drag force} = \frac{0.37(\Psi)\ 20\ AV^{1.8}}{(L)\ .20}$$

Average drag coefficients for swimmers can be measured as follows:

$$\text{F drag average} = \frac{2\,D\,M}{T^2}$$

where: D = distance to rest

M = swimmer's weight $\div 32.2$ ft/sec^2

The average human body surface is about 20 square feet and assuming it is all underwater, with length of 6 ft (1 m) and velocity of 6 ft per/sec, viscous drag force is approximately 2.5 lbs (1 kg). This type of drag is therefore only a small proportion of overall body drag.

Stroke rate and velocity

The mean velocity in swimming is the distance (D) moved through the water with each completed arm stroke multiplied by the product of each stroke(s) i.e. $V = S \times D$. Force is applied intermittently within each stroke cycle and is therefore varied.

Studies have shown[8,9] that velocity in top swimmers is increased by decreasing D and increasing S. They have also shown that at the maximal D the distances per stroke and stroke rates in frontcrawl and backcrawl were similar for both women and men in a studies group. However, the values of V at maximal D were slower in backstroke than in frontcrawl. Butterfly was different. The increase of V from the slowest speeds up to 80 per cent of maximal V for women and 94 per cent for men was accounted for entirely by the increased S. Throughout these ranges of V, D was constant.

In the same study, breaststroke again was quite different. Increased values of V were related to greater S and were associated with a marked reduction of D. It was found that at S per min D was 45 per cent of D used at 20 s/min in both men and women.

In frontcrawl, it was found that the fastest swimmers had the longest D at submaximal V. The study found that a given V can be swum with a faster but not slower S. As the V increases, the range of possible S decreases and maximal V occurs at a combination of D and S. This applies to all but breaststroke where swimmers were able to maintain their maximal V using a range of S up to 80/90 s/min. They concluded that a skilled swimmer can swim the frontcrawl at one m/sec with a variation – S from about 20 to 50 s/min.

Another study[10] on breaststroke velocities showed that Lina Kachushite (U.S.S.R.) achieved between 1.75 and 2.00 strokes per distance in the 1980 Olympic 200 m breaststroke finals in recording 2:29.54. Her stroke frequency of S was between 41 and 47 with a mean of 42. This resulted in a V of 1.20 and

Breaststroke

Sex	(1) Men	(2) Men	(3) Men	(4) Women
Distance	100 m (ht)	100 m (ht)	100 m	100 m
Swimmer	Fedorovsky (U.S.S.R.)	Goodhew (G.B.)	Lundquist (U.S.A.)	Caulkins (U.S.A.)
Venue	Moscow 1980	Moscow 1980	U.S. O. Trials 1980	U.S. O. Trials 1980
First 50 m	30.1 24	29.49 22	28.9 22	33.8 26
Second 50 m	33.85 26	33.99 26	33.98 32	36.6 32
Third 50 m				
Fourth 50 m				
Time	1:03.86	1:03.48	1:02.88	1:10.40

Sex	(7) Women	(8) Women	(9) Men	(10) Women
Distance	100 m	200 m	100 m (fin)	200 m (fin)
Swimmer	Geweniger (G.D.R.)	Geweniger (G.D.R.)	Goodhew (G.B.)	Varganova (U.S.S.R.)
Venue	Split 1981	Split 1981	Moscow 1980	Moscow 1980
First 50 m	33.26 25	34.17 24	29.9 21	34.3 26
Second 50 m	35.34 28	38.65 27	33.35 25	38.13 30
Third 50 m		39.33 28		38.19 30
Fourth 50 m		39.92 30		38.98 34
Time	1:08.6	2:32.41	1:03.34	2:29.60

1.30 with a mean V of 1.25. Compare this to her Soviet male counterpart Robertas Shulpa who won in 2:15.85. Like Kachushite, his D dropped steadily throughout the race from 2.00 to 1.45 whilst, again, his S increased steadily from 46 to 58 but his V remained fairly constant between 1.58 and 1.40.

Our own studies have produced results as seen in the tables.

The table demonstrates an interesting point with regard to the results. Both American swimmers maintained similar speeds to their European counterparts on the second 50 m but this was achieved with a greater number of strokes. The D in all cases was reduced as the races progressed. These results set standards for which aspiring swimmers can aim.

Some freestyle results are given in the table.

The freestyle chart above gives times for 100, 200 and 400 m and gives times for some of the world's top swimmers in their events. The velocity readings were achieved by V

$$= \frac{\text{distance}}{\text{time}}, \text{ in metres per second. When a body}$$

moves with uniform velocity, it will travel equal distances in equal intervals of time.

Freestyle

Sex	Men	Men
Distance	100 m	100 m
Swimmer	Johannson (Swe)	Woite (G.D.R.)
Venue	Moscow 1980	Moscow 1980
First 50 m	24.96 33	24.05 37
Second 50 m	26.46 37	26.15 42
Third 50 m		
Fourth 50 m		
Fifth 50 m		
Sixth 50 m		
Seventh 50 m		
Eighth 50 m		
Time	51.42	50.40

Velocity and distance per stroke

First 50 m	2.00	1.51	2.07	1.35
Second 50 m	1.88	1.35	1.91	1.19
Third 50 m				
Fourth 50 m				
Fifth 50 m				
Sixth 50 m				
Seventh 50 m				
Eighth 50 m				

<table>
<tr><td>

(5) Men
200 m
Moorhouse (G.B.)
Split 1981

30.87	23
35.3	27
1:42.0	27
	33

</td><td>

(6) Men
100 m
Kis (U.S.S.R.)
Split 1981

29.8	25
33.64	30
1:03.44	

</td></tr>
</table>

Technical data

	(1)	(2)	(3)	(4)	(5)	(6)
Distance per stroke						
First 50 m	2.08	2.27	2.27	1.92	2.17	2.00
Second 50 m	1.92	1.92	1.56	1.56	1.85	1.66
Third 50 m					1.85	
Fourth 50 m					1.51	

	(7)	(8)	(9)	(10)	(11)	(12)
Distance per stroke						
First 50 m	2.00	2.08	2.38	1.92	1.72	2.17
Second 50 m	1.78	1.85	2.00	1.66	1.47	1.78
Third 50 m		1.78		1.66		
Fourth 50 m		1.66		1.47		

<table>
<tr><td>

(11) Women
100 m
Kelly (G.B.)

Moscow 1980

33.06	29
38.34	34

1:11.4

</td><td>

(12) Women
100 m
Geweniger (G.D.R.)

Moscow 1980

33.79	23
36.43	28

1:10.22

</td></tr>
</table>

Men	Women	Women	Women	Women	Men	Men
200 m	100 m (ht)	100 m (fin)	200 m	100 m	100 m	400 m
Kopliakov	Krause	Krause	Krause	Meinike	Johannson	Salnikov
(U.S.S.R.)	(G.D.R.)	(G.D.R.)	(G.D.R.)	(G.D.R.)	(Swe)	(U.S.S.R.)
Moscow 1980	Moscow 1980	Moscow 1980	Moscow 1980	Split 1981	Split 1981	Split 1981
26.2 36	26.78 40	26.8 39	28.15 39	27.19 39	24.35 34	27.0 40
27.4 42	28.20 46	27.99 47	30.81 42	28.55 44	26.20 39	28.95 43
28.19 43			30.80 41			29.05 44
28.02 47			28.57 45			30.75 44
						29.25 45
						29.31 47
						29.69 47
						27.00 51
1:49.81	54.98	54.79	1:58.33	55.74	50.55	

1.90	1.38	1.86	1.25	1.86	1.28	1.77	1.28	1.83	1.28	2.05	1.47	1.85	1.25
1.82	1.19	1.77	1.08	1.78	1.06	1.62	1.19	1.75	1.13	1.90	1.28	1.72	1.16
1.77	1.16					1.62	1.21					1.72	1.13
1.78	1.08					1.75	1.11					1.62	1.13
												1.70	1.11
												1.70	1.06
												1.68	1.06
												1.85	0.98

Swimmers obviously travel with non-uniform velocity – velocities which normally start high and fall away. Jorge Woite achieved a velocity of 2.07 m/sec during his first 50 m, the fastest of all the results.

It's interesting to note that Vladimir Salnikov was moving at nearly the same velocity on the last 50 m of his 400 m in the 1981 European Finals as Barbara Krause in her first 50 metres in Moscow, but his stroke per distance was only 0.98 compared to a more economical but more exhausting 1.25 by Krause.

Velocity in these situations shouldn't be confused with speed. Velocity is the rate of change in distance moved with time in a specified direction or rate of change of displacement. Velocity is a vector while speed is a scalar quality. Speed is defined as the rate of change of distance moved with time. Average speed is distance divided by time, while acceleration is the rate of change of velocity with time.

In the above table, stroke frequency may be seen as the number of strokes per second. The frequency of most swimmers was close to 1.5 strokes per second. For each individual there is an optimum stroke frequency and length to achieve their best performance.

References
1 *Swimming Faster*, Ernest Maglischo
2 'Fibre Types and Metabolic Potentials of Skeletal Muscle' by P. Anderson, B. Smith, J. Henriksson and E. Nygaard in Men and Endurance Runners, Ann N.Y. Academy 1977
3 The Subcellular Basis for Competitive Swimming' by D. Ediston and W. McCafferty in *Swimming Technique* Jan 1974
4 'Energy Systems Used During Swimming', H. Bonner, in *Swimming Technique* Nov 1980
5 'American Science Takes Up Sport' in *New Scientist* 2 Aug 1984
6 *Basic Physiology and Anatomy*, Norman Taylor and Margaret McPhedron, Edward Arnold
7 'Hydrodynamics in Swimming', Paul Abramson, in *Swimming Technique* Oct 1973
8 American Coll. of Sports Medicine and Science in Sports, Vol. H No. 3 1979
9 'Relationships of Stroke Rate' by Albert Craig and David Predergast in *Swimming Technique* May 1980
10 'A View of Breaststroke Technique and Training in the G.D.R.,' by Prof Dr H. P. Pfeifer
11 'Energy Metabolism during Swimming', Clyde Williams and Dept. of PE and Sports, Loughborough University

15 Organization and Training of World Swimming

Britain

Britain can consider itself to be the founder of the competitive sport of swimming. It therefore had a headstart over other nations but was unable to maintain this for even a short period of time. The reason was a mediocre climate combined with a lack of the necessary indoor pools. Australia, the U.S.A., and other European countries quickly caught us up.

Britain continued to languish as an occasional medal-winning country at the Olympics until 1956 when Judy Grinham's win in the 100 metres backstroke ended a long period of no medals since 1908. In 1960 Britain won one gold medal through Anita Lonsbrough in the 200 metres breaststroke and the standards set by Ian Black, Judy Grinham, Margaret Edwards and others at the successful 1958 European Championships continued.

However, Britain regressed once more in the 1960s and we were limited to the silver medal successes of Bobby McGregor (in 1964) and Martyn Woodruff (in 1968) despite swimmers such as Diane Harris and Stella Mitchell on breaststroke and Jill Norfolk on backstroke setting world records over yard distances. Our swimmers were often equal in technique but lacked both the conditioning and the starting and turning ability of other countries.

Something had to be done if we were to catch up. The A.S.A. introduced a special investigative committee to look into all aspects of the sport and they made recommendations in the Martin Report in January 1970. Very few of their recommendations were taken up. However, professional coaching started to spread

and the 1970s saw many local authorities charge fees and employ coaches for the first time. Local authority cutbacks in the 1980s curtailed this development to a certain extent.

Never the less Britain surged during the 1970s. The surge followed in the wake of a relatively poor showing in the 1972 Olympics. David Wilkie, Duncan Goodhew, Sharron Davies and Adrian Moorhouse have become better known, although swimming remains a sport that only attracts coverage when the Olympics are taking place.

The finances of the A.S.A. have developed since the introduction of B.B.C. television rights and of the A.S.A. Awards Schemes which have awarded many badges.

The A.S.A.

The A.S.A., founded in 1869, was the first swimming association founded in the world. The A.S.A. Committee is comprised of two representatives from its five constituent districts — the North, South, West, Midlands and the North-East. For international purposes, they are joined by representatives from Scotland and Wales to form the Amateur Swimming Federation of Great Britain. There are over 1700 clubs in the A.S.A.

Although the men's events have increased in number from 6 to 13 and the women's from 5 to 13, the slight increase in the number of Olympic finalists between 1948 and 1994 has

British finalists in Olympic Games (since 1948)

MEN

	1948	1952	1956	1960	1964	1968	1972	1976	1980	1984	1988	1992
1st								1	1		1	
2nd					1	1	1	1	1		1	
3rd								1	1	2	1	1
4th				2		2			1	2		
5th		1					1			2		1
6th		2	2					1	3	1		2
7th	3			1	1		1	2	1	1	3	2
8th	1			1	1		2		2		1	1
Total	4(6)	3(6)	2(7)	4(8)	3(10)	3(14)	5(15)	6(13)	10(13)	8(15)	7	7(15)

(Total no. of events in brackets)

WOMEN

	1948	1952	1956	1960	1964	1968	1972	1976	1980	1984	1988	1992
1st		1	1								0	0
2nd			1						2	1	0	0
3rd	1	1	1	1						3	0	0
4th	1			1	1				3		0	0
5th		1	1	1	2	2				1	0	0
6th	1		2	2	2	2		1	2	3	0	0
7th		1			1	2		2		3	0	0
8th		1	2		1	1	1	1	1	1	0	0
Total	3(5)	4(5)	7(6)	7(7)	7(8)	7(13)	1(14)	4(13)	8(13)	12(14)	0(15)	0(15)
Grand total	7	7	9	11	10	10	6	11	18	20	7	7

in 1988 and 1992. British women's swimming has dropped sharply in the last two Olympics with the country no longer in the top league of women's swimming.

In Britain age-group swimming was introduced on a national basis in the 1960s and yet, interestingly, the average age of our Olympic teams remained much the same, as can be seen in the table below.

Women's swimming since 1980 has seen an increase in the age of team members, with a number of swimmers in their thirties at international level.

	1968 Men	1968 Women	1980 Men	1980 Women
Average age–years	20.1	17.4	20.53	17.56
Average weight–kg (lb)	76.7 (168.8)	60.3 (132.6)	77.0 (169.4)	57.5 (126.5)
Average height–m (in)	1.79 (70.77)	1.68 (66.3)	1.83 (72.1)	1.69 (66.6)

The age range was between 15 and 24 years in both cases but the majority of swimmers representing Britain were between 17 and 21. This contrasts with the findings of E. Jokl[1] who noted that the participants in the 1952 Helsinki Olympics ranged between 14 and 36 in the case of the women and between 13 and 45 for the men. The oldest British swimmer in the two later Olympics was some 12 years younger than the oldest competing male in Helsinki, but the youngest was two years older than the youngest male in Helsinki.

The popular misconception that swimmers are getting younger every day is not accurate. Some younger participants have been more successful and therefore more prominent. Despite age-group swimming, the trend in our teams has remained much the same since 1939.

Comparison of Olympic and British winning times (Time difference in brackets)

	1948	1952	1956	1960	1964	1968	1972	1976	1980	1984	1988
Men											
100 m freestyle											
	57.3	57.4	55.4	55.2	53.4	52.2	51.22	49.99	50.40	49.80	48.63
	1:01.0	58.9	58.3	59.1	53.5	53.5	54.70	53.11	51.88	50.93	51.18
	(3.7)	(1.5)	(2.9)	(3.9)	(0.1)	(1.3)	(3.48)	(3.12)	(1.48)	(1.13)	(2.55)
1500 m freestyle											
	19:18.5	18:30.0	17:58.9	17:19.6	17:01.7	16:38.9	15:52.58	15:02.40	14:58.27	15:05.20	15:00.48
	20:19.8	19:59.2	0	18:22.7	18:12.3	0	16:54.39	15:46.60	15:43.17	15:38.18	15:21.26
	(1:01.3)	(1:29.2)	(0)	(1:03.1)	(1:10.6)	(0)	(1:01.81)	(44.20)	(44.90)	(32.98)	(20.86)
100 m backstroke											
	1:06.4	1:05.4	1:02.2	1:01.9	No event	58.7	56.58	55.49	56.53	55.79	55.5
	1:09.1	1:07.8	1:05.6	1:04.7		1:02.8	1:01.25	1:00.34	58.38	58.07	58.02
	(2.7)	(2.4)	(3.4)	(2.8)	(0)	(4.1)	(4.67)	(4.85)	(1.85)	(2.28)	(2.98)
200 m breaststroke											
	2:39.3	2:34.4	2:34.7	2:37.4	2:27.8	2:28.7	2:21.55	2:15.11	2:15.85	2:13.34	2:13.52
	2:49.4	2:48.6	2:47.1	2:41.5	2:36.6	2:39.1	2:23.67	2:15.11	2:20.92	2:20.69	2:14.12
	(10.1)	(14.2)	(12.4)	(4.1)	(8.8)	(10.6)	(2.12)	(−)	(5.07)	(7.35)	(0.60)
Women											
100 m freestyle											
	1:06.3	1:06.8	1:02.0	1:01.2	59.5	1:00.0	58.59	55.65	54.79	55.92	54.93
	1:09.4	1:08.6	1:08.5	1:03.1	1:04.7	1:01.0	1:02.07	1:0031	57.88	58.09	57.81
	(3.1)	(1.8)	(6.5)	(1.9)	(5.2)	(1.0)	(3.48)	(4.66)	(3.09)	(2.17)	(2.88)
400 m freestyle											
	5:17.8	5:12.1	4:54.6	4:50.6	4:43.3	4:31.8	4:19.04	4:09.89	4:08.76	4:07.10	4:03.85
	5:22.5	5:16.6	5:23.6	4:59.7	4:52.0	5:02.7	4:39.1	4:30.05	4:19.99	4:16.41	4:16.66
	(4.7)	(4.5)	(29.0)	(9.3)	(8.7)	(30.9)	(20.96)	(31.16)	(11.23)	(9.31)	(12.81)
100 m backstroke											
	1:14.4	1:14.3	1:12.9	1:09.3	1:07.7	1:06.2	1:05.78	1:01.83	1:00.86	1:02.55	1:00.89
	1:18.3	1:17.5	1:12.9	1:10.8	1:09.5	1:12.0	1:10.43	1:06.66	1:05.56	1:04.47	1:04.27
	(3.9)	(3.2)	(−)	(1.5)	(1.8)	(5.8)	(4.65)	(4.83)	(4.70)	(1.92)	(4.38)
200 m breastroke											
	2:57.3	2:51.07	2:53.1	2:49.5	2:46.4	2:44.4	2:41.71	2:33.25	2:29.54	2:30.38	2:26.71
	3:06.1	2:57.6	2:56.1	2:49.5	2:49.0	2:51.2	2:47.42	2:38.26	2:36.32	2:35.51	2:36.14
	(8.9)	(5.9)	(3.0)	(−)	(2.6)	(6.8)	(5.71)	(5.01)	(6.78)	(5.13)	(9.43)

Britain and the rest of the world

The table on p. 201 shows the difference between the Olympic winning times and the times of the best British swimmers. A British time has never been more than 10 per cent slower than the winning time. The differential in the 1984 Olympics was smaller than the 1948 Olympics in all but one event. As a general rule, the gap between the best in Britain and the best in the world remains consistent, Britain neither improving nor getting worse.

U.S.A.

The domination of East German female swimming in the 1980s dented the USA's role as the world's most consistently outstanding nation. Already the best team in the world, United States swimming really took off in 1947 when Carl Bauer got the Amateur Athletic Union (A.A.U.) to agree to a system of competition graded by age. Prior to this he had tried and become convinced that this system of age-group competition would benefit not only his area of St Louis but the country as a whole.

It was felt that the control of movement from junior ranks to national championships was a monopoly and the Pacific Association was used as a test area in 1951. The age group explosion revolutionized American, and eventually world, swimming. Half a million American children registered for age-group events each year. Mary Lou Elsinius, who won a gold medal in the 1955 Pan American Games, was the first age-grouper to win a gold at a major games. By 1964 every American swimmer at the Tokyo Olympics had graduated through their age-group programme.

California benefited enormously from the age-group programme. Affluence resulted in many new swimming pools being built in the 1950s. As these pools were built so the concern for the safety of young children grew and the upshot was a new interest in California in the sport of swimming. North California had a large proportion of the 15,000 young swimmers involved in the age-group programme. Within the decade, there were a quarter of a million swimmers involved nationwide.

The U.S.A. were successful in the 1960s and 1970s because they were the first country to develop mass competitive participation. By 1968 they were able to win no less than 58 medals at the Olympics. They were also the first country to introduce nationwide professional coaching with pools available both early in the morning and after school exclusively for swimming training. Swimmers were training up to 4 hours per day in the 1960s. By 1970 82 out of 85 junior colleges had their own pools[2] and all universities had one.

The A.A.U. was formed in 1888 to be responsible for amateur sport in America and swimming has now been taken over by the organization American Swimming. Each swimmer pays a registration fee which is then distributed partly towards national funds, partly towards district associations. In the early 1970s nearly half the athletes registered by the A.A.U. were from the aquatic disciplines.

The American university system, which is run by the National Collegiate Athletic Association (N.C.A.A.), has been the envy of the world for a long time. Many universities have been able to offer either full or part academic scholarships based on swimming prowess. This has had the effect not only of keeping American men's swimming at the top but also of attracting top swimmers from all over the world to America because of the training advantages. As a result, the European men in Britain, Sweden and West Germany in particular have learnt and, as a rule, improved.

If we take the example of the writer of our foreword, James Counsilman. He coached Indiana University, one of the most successful universities of all time. At that time they had 36 men on their swimming team and 10 divers. Of these, five swimmers are on full scholarships whilst a number of other scholarships merely cover tuition fees and are therefore less. Their training programme begins at the end of September and ends in March with the N.C.A.A. Championships.

America still employs the 'farm team' system. Farm teams are clubs who are mainly interested in recreational swimming and are willing to feed an up-and-coming swimmer to a more competitive club. This was mimicked in the German Democratic Republic where swimmers were taken from recreational-orientated clubs and moved to national centres.

There are 13 regions in America swimming covering 50 states. Many pool complexes have been built, with Mission Viejo and the University of Texas being outstanding complexes. A great amount of money has been spent, for instance the Santa Clara International Swim Center cost £400,000 even in 1967. The complex is comprised of three outdoor pools.

However, the system that was the envy of the world has become its own enemy. Many girl swimmers dropped out of the age-group programmes before maturity and since 1972 U.S. swimming has been actively encouraging more swimmers to continue swimming at colleges and universities. U.S. Women's Swimming has been competitive with the rest

of the world without regaining the dominant position it enjoyed in the 1960s.

The men have also been challenged by Europe, Canada and, in particular, the Soviet Union and their slice of the gold medal cake diminished. The non-appearances of America at the 1980 Olympics and of the Soviet Union at the 1984 Olympics has made true comparison between the countries difficult. Meanwhile the ability of other countries in relation to the U.S.A. has been growing.

The table below emphasizes the position:

Gold medals won				
			Women	Men
1960	Rome	OG	5	4
1964	Tokyo	OG	6	7
1968	Mexico	OG	10	9
1972	Munich	OG	8	9
1973	Belgrade	WC	3	8
1975	California	WC	3	8
1976	Montreal	OG	1	12
1978	Berlin	WC	9	11
1980	Moscow	OG	None	None
1983	Ecuador	WC	2	6
1984	Los Angeles	OG	11	9
1986	Madrid	WC	2	5
1988	Seoul	OG	3	5

German Democratic Republic

The success of the G.D.R. until its integration with West Germany was the story of modern international swimming. It is attributable to all sorts of things but essentially stems from two important factors: first, the G.D.R.'s national policy of encouraging all people of all ages to take part *en masse* in sport; and second, the system of selection and the scientific approach by which they seek talent.

The D.T.S.B., the East German sports organization, involves 8,000 sports clubs and 2.6 million people (that amounts to 15 per cent of the total population). By 1976 there were 300,000 elected officials, 191,000 sports coaches and 93,000 judges. Interestingly, swimming didn't rank in the top six most popular sports which contrasts sharply with

Sports Council statistics in this country which show swimming to be the second most popular participatory sport. Over 60 per cent of East German schoolchildren took part in extra-curricular sport and more than 5 million people in any one year took part in a competitive sport of one sort or another. It's little wonder that since the G.D.R. first took part in the 1956 Olympics the number of medals won increased at each Olympics until 1988.

The East German Swimming Association (D.S.S.V.) had roughly 85,000 members in over 700 clubs making it their eighth most popular sport. The country had more than 2,000 swimming pools; facilities and opportunities abound for any talented performer. In 1954 there were only 41 indoor 50 m pools – by

1976 there were 129. A further ten pools were completed by 1980 in Berlin alone.

Swimming has been compulsory in schools since 1956 and recently it became part of the curriculum for six-years-olds to learn. Many of these young swimmers found themselves involved in competitive swimming through children's and youth *Spartakiads* – the East German equivalent of the U.S. age group system. The first outstanding swimmer to come through the system was the great back-stroker Roland Matthes, who became the first European to beat the minute in the 100 m backstroke in 1966.

Discovering talent began from the age of 7 to 8. Those without suitable talents are weeded out over a period of years. At the age of 9 or 10 the talented swimmers passed on to one of East Germany's 16 sports schools. By this time they were swimming between 500 and 600 miles a year. This moved up to about 700 miles by the time they were 12. Training was programmed to ensure that long distances were swum at high speed, ie aerobically.

The swimmers were re-tested physically every six weeks in order to adapt their training programme accordingly. The idea was that if training was not adjusted after this period then the swimmer was not benefiting from the training. Blood counts and muscle biopsis were made. At the East German Sports School at Halle meals were controlled via a computer which allowed the swimmers 5 meals a day – 3900 calories altogether with protein being 12 and 15 per cent of the diet and carbohydrates 60 per cent.

The East German rise

The G.D.R. women set new standards. The men's swimming never quite reached the same level. At the 1981 European Championships the women set a new record by winning the gold and silver in every individual event as well as both relays. By comparison, the men's team just won one gold in 1986 at the World Championships and one in 1988 at the Olympics.

The quality of East German swimming was underlined in the women's relay in the 1976 Olympics when they set a world record of 4:07.95, defeating the U.S.A. by nearly 7 seconds. Splits were as follows:

		Individual winning time
Back leg	1:02.23	1:01.83
Breaststroke	1:10.15	1:11.16
Butterfly	59.53	1:00.13
Freestyle	56.04	55.65
Total	4:07.95	4:08.77

The relay takeovers gave the advantage on the last three legs but the figures do demonstrate a level of overall quality that was amazingly repeated in 1980:

		Individual winning time
Back	1:01.51	1:00.86
Breast	1:09.46	1:10.22
Fly	1:00.14	1:00.42
Free	55.56	54.79
Total	4:06.57	4:06.29

The G.D.R. has taught the world that a fine combination of so far unforeseen strength and quality technique can overcome the vast mileage training programmes predominant in much of the world's women's swimming today. The East German women won every event at the 1985 European Championships in Sofia, Bulgaria. This not only confirmed their domination over Europe for more than a decade but also demonstrated their ability to overcome their non-participation in the Los Angeles Olympics.

The basic ideology in the G.D.R. was one in which the athlete can use his abilities for the betterment of the state. To this end the German University of Body Culture was established in 1950. Medics can specialize in sports medicine during a five-year university course. It's little wonder that in the G.D.R., top sportsmen were considered to be a separate class of human – a step towards what the state called 'the new socialist man'.

Medals Won			
Olympics	Men	Women	Combined no. of finalists
1956	0	0	
1960	0	0	
1964	0	0	
1968	2 gold 1 silver	2 silver 1 bronze	18
1972	2 gold 1 silver 1 bronze	4 silver 1 bronze	25
1976	1 bronze	11 gold 6 silver 1 bronze	37
1980	1 gold 2 silver 1 bronze	11 gold 8 silver 7 bronze	40
1984	1 gold 2 silver 2 bronze	10 gold 5 silver 7 bronze	
1988	Did not compete	Did not compete	

Russia

In the mid-1970s the then Soviet Union was the top European men's team but came some way behind the U.S.A. in world terms. Their women have been strong in breaststroke since 1964 but lack quality in any other event.

The Russian policy has been to make sure that their coaches are as qualified as possible: all swimming coaches are graduates with degrees from schools of physical education. In 1974 there were some 900 full-time qualified coaches working in 1200 indoor pools. Now the number of pools is nearer 1500. Strenuous efforts were made throughout the 1970s to gain greater knowledge and foreign coaches were brought in, such as Forbes and Ursula Carlile from Australia. Groups were sent on exchange training sessions to places like Mission Viejo in the U.S.A., and selected coaches were sent to meets and conferences throughout the world. Despite climatic difficulties, great progress has been made and Russia can now confidently challenge the U.S.A. in men's events.

Russia now possesses in Moscow the best pool complex in the world: the Olympic centre has no less than twelve pools of which four are 50 m in length. Moscow also has two 50 m pools at the Physical Culture Pool and the two Olympic pools – a massive amount of resources for training. The Moscow training complex has a hostel for 1,000 swimmers, some of whom live there and train all the year round, and the national team come together there four times a year.

Sport in general in Russia is structured so that there are twenty national sports societies representing workers in different industries. They all have a set of committees who run the clubs. The sports societies are financed by membership fees, state grants and spectator entrance fees. Like the original A.A.U. in the U.S.A., these societies are multisport-based.

The Moscow Dynamo Football Club is the best known feature of the Dynamo Sports Complex, but the Dynamo Swim Centre is older established. It includes a 50 m, a 25 m and a 17 m pool and one small teaching pool, along with two full-sized gymnasia. There are some 500 swimmers in the swimming school from 5 years of age and older with 15 full-time coaches, plus a doctor, masseur and technician.

The club is divided into five main groups:
1 The top ten breaststroke swimmers in Russia who train 9 to 11 times per week.
2 A group of twelve swimmers with two coaches who train 9 times per week.
3 A group of twelve swimmers of 13 years of age with two coaches who train 7 times per week.

4 Two groups of twenty swimmers of 11 years with four coaches. They train 6 times per week.

In addition there are twenty teaching groups. All groups do some land training but only the top perform strengthening work.

Most Dynamo swimmers attend normal schools which operate between 8.30 and 1 or 2 p.m. Relations are cooperative with schools so that swimming can be timetabled into the pupils' day. The Dynamo club even has its own tutors in order to ensure that no one misses out on education. A residential educational institution called the Internat is responsible for educating the swimmers, who come from all over Russia to attend the breaststroke school. Of the 40 top swimmers at Dynamo in 1981, 34 had been developed internally and six were top breaststrokers who had come from elsewhere.

In 1981 Russia produced a four-year national plan based on the findings of the Sports Scientific Research Committee and the Central Swimming Committee, which is mainly comprised of coaches. The plan was to cover swimming from top to bottom in every department. Copious scientific records are kept on all swimmers and recommendations made to the Head Soviet Coach, Sergei Vaitzekovski, who travels to the various swim centres promoting swimmers to the national squads and moving them to the towns accordingly.

There are four grades of coach in Russia: the top grade who are paid approximately 300 roubles per month; grade 1 at 220; grade 2 at 180; and no grade, who are normally students studying for their diploma.

The Russians have introduced new attention to detail in swimming, with enormous scientific resources assisting their efforts. Blood lactate tests are taken every three or four weeks and land work exercises are specially devised so as to be specific to their particular strokes. Although the first Russian world record breaker stretches back to 1947, the most famous is without doubt Vladimir Salnikov, who broke the world record in the 400 m seven times, the 800 m record on five occasions and the 1500 m three times. He was the first man under 15 minutes for 1500 m, the first under 3:50 for 400 m and under 8 minutes for 800 m.

Russian swimmers have always managed to remain in the sport until their late twenties and to stay at the top. Propenko, Pankin, Bure, Stepanova are all names who have managed to stay at the top simply because of the incentive of a better lifestyle by being a top sporting performer in their country. The average age of the Russian teams at the recent Olympics has been slightly higher than in other countries. For example, in Montreal the mean age of the men was 19 years. There were 23 teams members. The 21-strong women's team averaged 18 years.

The salient feature in Russian swimming today is the low swimmer/coach ratio per group in all their swimming centres. With a population the size of Russia there should be plenty of room for age group or junior wastage, but the Russian philosophy is to weed the no-hopers out early and to channel them into another activity where they have some talent. The coaches can then concentrate on the talented few. This directly contrasts with the U.S.A., Australia, Canada and Britain, all of whom are trying to make coaching commercially viable in a free enterprise environment with large squads.

Australia

Australia was one of the early participants in competitive swimming and has been constantly among the medals since the introduction of modern swimming. It was one of the first countries to introduce professional coaching and really surged as a nation prior to the 1956 Olympics in Melbourne. At these Olympics Australia won no less than eight gold medals.

Since that high point the Australians have been slipping. In 1960 they won five gold medals, the second most behind the U.S.A., but they had been expected to do better. In 1964 this became four and the drop has continued slowly ever since. Success in the early 1950s was partly due to the Olympics being held in Melbourne, but partly due to more advanced scientific testing and training allied to a glut of natural talent. Australian coaches were the first at this time to use the controlled interval method of training, which was copied from athletics. Here swimmers are asked to make repetitions over set distances with a set amount of rest. The aim is to repeat swim as close as possible to in a race situation. This method of training and pre-meet team get-togethers in excellent Australian weather helped to produce such stars as Jon Henricks, Murray Rose, the Konrads, David Theile and Dawn Fraser.

Australia as a country is a difficult one to control. The land mass is roughly the same area as the U.S. minus Alaska and yet the population is sparse. It has a population of about 12 million people, most of whom live close to the sea and are therefore swimming and water-safety conscious. But in recent years Australia has suffered because of her inability to educate and train the older swimmer at university level.

The Australian Swimming Union, an amateur-based organization, has overall responsibility for the sport and is comprised of the six state swimming unions, half of whom have their own professional secretary. The Swimming Union has grown to the extent that there were some 300 clubs by the start of the 1970s, about a fifth of the number in England alone. The Swimming Union has a registration system for each swimmer which part pays for administration and part for running competitions.

Until the 1970s the season began at the start of October and ended in April. Most of the competitions were held in 50 m open-air pools, the disadvantage of this being that out of season was becoming more of a problem as the long-course open-air pools were unusable even in Australia in the winter. In the mid-1970s 25 m winter competitions were introduced.

Age-group swimming spread from the U.S.A. to Australia in 1954 in preparation for the Melbourne Olympics. Junior and senior competitions were replaced by under 10, 12, 14 and 16 races. Allied with the abundance of 50 m pools, the situation was perfect for the great teams of the 1950s and 60s. Sydney has about 50 long-course pools and Melbourne in excess of 40, the majority unheated. Most of these facilities tended to lose money for the municipality and so professional coaching was given its head. Coaches have been allowed to lease facilities for three years or more for coaching and teaching programmes. The pools are now used from 5 o'clock, in the morning to 10 at night. Other coaches own their own pools, as in the U.S.A.

Swimming is an expensive sport in Australia and tends to rule out working-class participants simply because of high coaching fees. However, since the war there has been a great emphasis on teaching of swimming in schools. In Brisbane, for instance, most primary schools have their own 25 m teaching pool.

	Men 100 m free	Men 200 m free	Women 100 m free	Women 200 m free
1960	1st	NE	1st	NE
1964	NQ	NE	1st	NE
1968	1st	1st	NQ	7th
1972	5th	4th	3rd	1st
1976	NQ	NQ	NQ	NQ
1980	8th	3rd	NQ	NQ
1984	2nd	8th	5th	4th
1988	6th	1st	NQ	NQ
1992	2nd	8th	5th	4th

NE = No event   NQ = No qualifiers

The table on the left shows the highest Australian positions in recent Olympics.

	Men 400 m	Men 1500 m	Women 400 m	Women 800 m
1960	1st	1st	5th	NE
1964	3rd	1st	4th	NE
1968	4th	3rd	3rd	4th
1972	1st	2nd	1st	2nd
1976	NQ	3rd	NQ	4th
1980	7th	3rd	4th	1st
1984	3rd	8th	5th	4th
1988	2nd	NQ	5th	3rd
1992	3rd	8th	5th	4th

This table shows highest Australian positions for the middle and distance events.

By the 1970s the top Australian swimmers were covering 4 to $4\frac{1}{2}$ miles every morning between 5 and 7.30 a.m. on six or seven days a week and the same again after school in the evening. Forty to 45 miles per week, or 500 miles per year, produced and still is producing many as the finer technique demonstrated just after the war was less in evidence.

Australia would appear to have maintained traditional high standards in these events with there only being ten occasions when her swimmers dropped lower than fourth.

Canada

Canada emerged as a strong challenger in world swimming terms in the 1960s, moving up to fifth place in Mexico and remaining close to that position ever since. It has the disadvantage of small population in a large country (24 million), but has the advantage of good university backup in both its own country and in the neighbouring U.S.A., plus the most advanced administrative setup of any western swimming nation in relation to professional coaching and the amount of money coming into the sport.

Canada was one of the first countries to be influenced by the American two-season year with the short-course swimming taking place between October and April and the long-course in May to September. There is a strong emphasis on age-group competitions during the winter. The summer season is directed towards the national championships with few meets held at city or provincial level.

At grassroots level the teaching programme in Canada is the responsibility of the Red Cross organization, which receives a grant from most cities, and part of the teaching responsibility is borne by the Y.M.C.A. In Canada swimming is more developed than in Britain with no taxes levied on their buildings and most money coming from appeals. Both these organizations mirror similar work being carried out in the U.S.A., except that the spatial geography of Canada makes teaching and competing difficult. The effect on future competitive levels has taken some overcoming.

With the exception of George Hodgson who won the 400 m and 1500 m in the 1912 Olympics, Canada has been quite a late starter. The next gold medal was not won until 1980 when Victor Davies inherited the 200 m breaststroke I won in his home country in 1976. However, 1984 proved to be exceptional when Canada finished with four golds.

The Canadian Amateur Swimming Association (C.A.S.A.) was founded in 1909. There are ten provisional sections. In 1969 the status of the C.A.S.A. was altered so that a new organization was formed which was specifically responsible for swimming. With the other disciplines, this became the Aquatic Federation of Canada. The Canadian National Department of Health and Welfare assisted in the 1960s through its offices for fitness and amateur sport. The Canadian organization has moved along since then with a National Aquatics Administration in Ottawa and the country divided into administrative sections with professional secretariats.

The country now operates on a grants system where clubs who produce the best results get the greater financial injections. Large salaries have attracted top coaches from South Africa, Australia and Britain. Canada has been trying to reduce the number of swimmers of university age moving to America.

References
1 'Age and Physical Activity' by E. Jokl in *Coaching Newsletter* July 1957
2 Hamilton Bland Report 1969 for the Winston Churchill Memorial Trust

Appendix I: Swimming Champions

World championships

World Championships were first mooted after the I.O.C. started to place pressure on F.I.N.A. to reduce the number of Olympic swimming events. It was felt that a world competition was needed which was truly representative of all facets of the sport. To date championships have been held as follows:

Venue	Date
Belgrade, Yugoslavia	31 Aug–9 Sept 1973
Cali, Colombia	19–27 July 1975
West Berlin	18–28 Aug 1978
Guayaquil, Ecuador	29 July–8 Aug 1982
Madrid, Spain	13–23 Aug 1986
Perth, Australia	3–13 January 1991
Rome, Italy	1–11 September 1994

MEN

50 m Freestyle

1986	Tom Jager (U.S.A.)	22.49
1991	Tom Jager (U.S.A.)	22.16
1994	Alex Popov (Rus)	22.17

100 m Freestyle

1973	Jim Montgomery (U.S.A.)	51.70
1975	Andy Coan (U.S.A.)	51.25
1978	David McCagg (U.S.A.)	50.24
1982	Jorge Woithe (G.D.R.)	50.18
1986	Matt Biondi (U.S.A.)	48.94
1991	Matt Biondi (U.S.A.)	49.18
1994	Alex Popov (Rus)	49.12

200 m Freestyle

1973	Jim Montgomery (U.S.A.)	1:53.02
1975	Tim Shaw (U.S.A.)	1:51.04
1978	William Forrester (U.S.A.)	1:51.02
1982	Michael Gross (W. Ger)	1:49.84
1986	Michael Gross (W. Ger)	1:48.70
1991	Georgio Lamberti (Ita)	1:47.27
1994	Antti Kasvio (Fin)	1:47.32

400 m Freestyle

1973	Richard Demont (U.S.A.)	3:58.18
1975	Tim Shaw (U.S.A.)	3:54.88
1978	Vladimir Salnikov (U.S.S.R.)	3:51.94
1982	Vladimir Salnikov (U.S.S.R.)	3:51.30
1986	Rainer Henkel (W. Ger)	3:50.05
1991	Jorge Hoffman (Ger)	3:48.04
1994	Kieren Perkins (Aus)	3:43.80

1500 m Freestyle

1973	Stephen Holland (Aus)	15:31.85
1975	Tim Shaw (U.S.A.)	15:28.92
1978	Vladimir Salnikov (U.S.S.R.)	15:03.99
1982	Vladimir Salnikov (U.S.S.R.)	15:01.77
1986	Rainer Henkel (W. Ger)	15:05.31
1991	Jorge Hoffman (Ger)	14:50.36
1994	Kieren Perkins (Aus)	14:50.52

100 m Backstroke

1973	Roland Matthes (G.D.R.)	57.47
1975	Roland Matthes (G.D.R.)	58.15
1978	Robert Jackson (U.S.A.)	56.36
1982	Dirk Richter (G.D.R.)	55.95
1986	Igor Polianski (U.S.S.R.)	55.78
1991	Jeff Rouse (U.S.A.)	55.23
1994	Martin Lopez-Zubero (Spa)	55.17

200 m Backstroke

1973	Roland Matthes (G.D.R.)	2:01.87
1975	Zoltao Verraszto (Hun)	2:05.05
1978	Jesse Vassallo (U.S.A.)	2:02.16
1982	Richard Carey (U.S.A.)	2:00.82
1986	Igor Polianski (U.S.S.R.)	1:58.78
1991	Martin Lopez-Zubero (Spa)	1:59.52
1994	Vladimir Selkov (Rus)	

100 m Butterfly

1973	Bruce Robertston (Can)	55.69
1975	Gregory Jagenburg (U.S.A.)	55.63
1978	Joseph Bottom (U.S.A.)	54.30
1982	Matthew Gribble (U.S.A.)	53.88
1986	Pablo Morales (U.S.A.)	53.54
1991	Anthony Nesty (Sur)	53.29
1994	Rafal Szukala (Pol)	53.51

200 m Butterfly

1973	Robin Backhaus (U.S.A.)	2:03.32
1975	William Forrester (U.S.A.)	2:01.95
1978	Michael Bruner (U.S.A.)	1:59.38
1982	Michael Gross (W. Ger)	1:58.85
1986	Michael Gross (W. Ger)	1:56.53
1991	Melvin Stewart (U.S.A.)	1:55.69
1994	Denis Pankratov (Rus)	1:56.54

100 m Breaststroke

1973	John Henken (U.S.A.)	1:04.02
1975	David Wilkie (G.B.)	1:04.26
1978	Walter Kusch (W. Ger)	1:03.56
1982	Stephen Lundquist (U.S.A.)	1:02.75
1986	Victor Davis (Can)	1:02.71

| 1991 | Norbert Rozsa (Hun) | 1:01.45 |
| 1994 | Norbert Rozsa (Hun) | 1:01.24 |

200 m Breaststroke

1973	David Wilkie (G.B.)	2:19.28
1975	David Wilkie (G.B.)	2:18.23
1978	Nicholas Nevid (U.S.A.)	2:18.37
1982	Victor Davis (Can)	2:14.77
1986	Jozsef Szabo (Hun)	2:14.27
1991	Mike Barrowman (U.S.A.)	2:11.23
1994	Norbert Rozsa (Hun)	2:12.81

200 m Individual Medley

1973	Gunnar Larsson (Swe)	2:08.36
1975	Andras Hargitay (Hun)	2:07.72
1978	Graham Smith (Can)	2:03.65
1982	Alexander Sidorenko (U.S.S.R.)	2:03.30
1986	Tamas Darnyi (Hun)	2:01.57
1991	Tamas Darnyi (Hun)	1:59.36
1994	Jani Sievenen (Fin)	1:58.16

400 m Individual Medley

1973	Andras Hargitay (Hun)	4:31.11
1975	Andras Hargitay (Hun)	4:32.57
1978	Jesse Vassallo (U.S.A.)	4:20.05
1982	Ricardo Prado (Bra)	4:19.78
1986	Tamas Darnyi (Hun)	4:18.98
1991	Tamas Darnyi (Hun)	4:12.36
1994	Tom Dolan (U.S.A.)	4:12.30

4 × 100 m Freestyle Team

1973 U.S.A.   3:27.18
(Melvin Nash, Joseph Bottom, Jim Montgomery, John Murphy)
1975 U.S.A.   3:24.85
(Bruce Furniss, Andy Coan, Jim Montgomery, John Murphy)
1978 U.S.A.   3:19.74
(Dave McCagg, Ambrose Gaines, Jim Montgomery, Jack Babashoff)
1982 U.S.A.   3:19.26
(Christopher Cavanagh, Robin Leamy, David McCagg, Ambrose Gaines)
1986 U.S.A.   3:19.89
(Tom Jager, Matt Biondi, Mike Heath, Paul Wallace)
1991 U.S.A.   3:17.15
(Tom Jager, Shaun Jordan, Matt Biondi + 1)
1994 U.S.A.   3:16.90
(Jon Olsen, Gary Hall, Josh Davis, Ugur Taner)

4 × 200 m Freestyle Team

1973 U.S.A.   7:33.22
(Kurt Krumpholtz, Robin Backhaus, Richard Klatt, Jim Montgomery)

1975 U.S.A.   7:20.82
(Bruce Furniss, William Forrester, Robert Hackett, Ambrose Gaines)
1978 West Germany   7:39.44
(Klaus Steinbach, Werner Lampe, Peter Nocke, Geissler)
1982 U.S.A.   7:21.09
(Richard Saeger, Jeffrey Float, Kyle Miller, Ambrose Gaines)
1986 G.D.R.   7:15.91
(Sven Lodziewski, Lars Hinneburg, Thomas Flemming, Dirk Richter)
1991 Germany   7:13.50
(Peter Sitt, Steffan Zesner, Stefan Pfeiffer, Michael Gross)
1994 Sweden   7:17.74
(Anders Holmertz, Christer Wallin, Forlaner, Tommy Werner)

4 × 100 m Medley Team

1973 U.S.A.   3:49.49
(Mike Stamm, John Henken, Joseph Bottom, Jim Montgomery)
1975 U.S.A.   3:49.00
(John Murphy, Richard Collella, Gregory Jagenburg, Andrew Coan)
1978 U.S.A.   3:44.63
(Robert Jackson, Stephen Lundquist, Joseph Bottom, David McCagg)
1982 U.S.A.   3:40.84
(Richard Carey, Stephen Lunquist, Matthew Gribble, Ambrose Gaines)
1986 U.S.A.   3:41.25
(Dan Veatch, David Lundberg, Pablo Morales, Matt Biondi)
1991 U.S.A.   3:39.66
(Jeff Ouse, Eric Wunderluch, Mark Henderson, Matt Biondi)
1994 U.S.A.   3:37.74
(Jeff Rouse, Eric Wunderlich, Mark Henderson, Gary Hall)

WOMEN

50 m Freestyle

1986	Tamara Costache (Rum)	25.28
1991	Yong Zhuang (Chn)	25.47
1994	Jingyi Le (Chn)	24.51

100 m Freestyle

1973	Kornelia Ender (G.D.R.)	57.54
1975	Kornelia Ender (G.D.R.)	56.50
1978	Barbara Krause (G.D.R.)	55.68
1982	Birgit Meinike (G.D.R.)	55.79

1986	Kristin Otto (G.D.R.)	55.05
1991	Nicole Haislett (U.S.A.)	55.17
1994	Jingyi Le (Chn)	54.01

200 m Freestyle

1973	Keena Rothhammer (U.S.A.)	2:04.99
1975	Shirley Babashoff (U.S.A.)	2:02.50
1978	Cynthia Woodhead (U.S.A.)	1:58.53
1982	Anne-Marie Verstappen (Hol)	1:59.53
1986	Heike Friedrich (G.D.R.)	1:58.26
1991	Hayley Lewis (Aus)	2:00.48
1994	Franzeska Van Almsick (Ger)	1:56.78

400 m Freestyle

1973	Heather Greenwood (U.S.A.)	4:20.28
1975	Shirley Babashoff (U.S.A.)	4:16.87
1978	Tracey Wickham (Aus)	4:06.28
1982	Carmela Schmidt (G.D.R.)	4:08.98
1986	Heike Friedrich (G.D.R.)	4:07.45
1991	Janet Evans (U.S.A.)	4:08.63
1994	Aihua Yang (Chn)	4:09.64

800 m Freestyle

1973	Novello Calligaris (Ita)	8:52.97
1975	Jennifer Turrall (Aus)	8:44.75
1978	Tracey Wickham (Aus)	8:24.94
1982	Kimberley Linehan (U.S.A.)	8:27.48
1986	Astrid Strauss (G.D.R.)	8:28.24
1991	Janet Evans (U.S.A.)	8:24.05
1994	Janet Evans (U.S.A.)	8:29.85

100 m Backstroke

1973	Ulrike Richter (G.D.R.)	1:05.42
1975	Ulrike Richter (G.D.R.)	1:03.30
1978	Linda Jezek (U.S.A.)	1:02.55
1982	Kirstin Otto (G.D.R.)	1:01.30
1986	Barbara Mitchell (U.S.A.)	1:01.74
1991	Kristin Egerszegi (Hun)	1:01.78
1994	Cihong He (Chn)	1:00.57

200 m Backstroke

1973	Melissa Belote (U.S.A.)	2:20.52
1975	Birgit Treiber (G.D.R.)	2:15.46
1978	Linda Jezek (U.S.A.)	2:11.93
1982	Kornelia Sirch (G.D.R.)	2:09.91
1986	Kornelia Sirch (G.D.R.)	2:11.37
1991	Kristin Egerszegi (Hun)	2:09.15
1994	Cihong He (Chn)	2:07.40

100 m Butterfly

1973	Kornelia Ender (G.D.R.)	1:02.53
1975	Kornelia Ender (G.D.R.)	1:01.24
1978	Mary Joan Pennington (U.S.A.)	1:00.20
1982	Mary Meagher (U.S.A.)	59.41
1986	Kornelia Gressler (G.D.R.)	59.51
1991	Hong Qian (Chn)	59.68
1994	Limin Liu (Chn)	58.98

200 m Butterfly

1973	Rosemary Kother (G.D.R.)	2:13.76
1975	Rosemary Kother (G.D.R.)	2:13.82
1978	Tracy Caulkins (U.S.A.)	2:09.87
1982	Innes Geissler (G.D.R.)	2:08.66
1986	Mary Meagher (U.S.A.)	2:08.41
1991	Summer Sanders (U.S.A.)	2:09.24
1994	Limin Liu (Chn)	2:07.25

100 m Breaststroke

1973	Renate Vogel (G.D.R.)	1:13.74
1975	Hannelore Anke (G.D.R.)	1:12.72
1978	Julia Bogdanova (U.S.S.R.)	1:10.31
1982	Ute Geweniger (G.D.R.)	1:09.14
1986	Sylvia Gerasch (G.D.R.)	1:08.11
1991	Lindsay Frame (Aus)	1:08.81
1994	Samantha Riley (Aus)	1:07.69

200 m Breaststroke

1973	Renate Vogel (G.D.R.)	2:40.01
1975	Hannelore Anke (G.D.R.)	2:37.25
1978	Lina Kachushite (U.S.S.R.)	2:31.42
1982	Svetna Varganova (U.S.S.R.)	2:28.82
1986	Silkie Hoerner (G.D.R.)	2:27.40
1991	Elena Volkova (U.R.S.)	2:29.53
1994	Samantha Riley (Aus)	2:26.87

200 m Individual Medley

1973	Andrea Hubner (G.D.R.)	2:20.51
1975	Katharine Heddy (U.S.A.)	2:19.80
1978	Tracy Caulkins (U.S.A.)	2:14.07
1982	Petra Schneider (G.D.R.)	2:11.79
1986	Kristin Otto (G.D.R.)	2:15.56
1991	Li Lin (Chn)	2:13.40
1994	Bin Lu (Chn)	2:12.34

400 m Individual Medley

1973	Andrea Wegner (G.D.R.)	4:57.51
1975	Ulrike Tauber (G.D.R.)	4:52.76
1978	Tracy Caulkins (U.S.A.)	4:40.83
1982	Petra Schneider (G.D.R.)	4:36.10
1986	Kathleen Nord (G.D.R.)	4:43.75
1991	Li Lin (Chn)	4:41.45
1994	Guohong Dai (Chn)	4:39.14

4 × 100 m Medley Team

1973 G.D.R. 4:16.84
(Ulrike Richter, Renate Vogel, Rosemarie Kother, Kornelia Ender)

1975 G.D.R. 4:14.74
(Ulrike Richter, Hannelore Anke, Rosemarie Kother, Kornelia Ender)

1978 U.S.A. 4:08.21
(Linda Jezek, Tracy Caulkins, Mary Joan Pennington, Cynthia Woodhead)

1982 G.D.R. 4:05.88
(Kirstin Otto, Ute Geweniger, Innes Geissler, Brigit
Meinike)
1986 G.D.R. 4.04.82
(Kathrin Zimmermann, Sylvia Gerasch, Kornelia
Gressler, Kristin Otto)
1991 U.S.A. 4:06.51
1994 China 4:01.67
(Cihong He, Guahong Dai, Limin Lu, Jingyi Le)

4 × 100 m Freestyle Team

1973 G.D.R. 3:52.45
(Kornelia Ender, Andrea Eife, Sylvia Eichner,
Andrea Hubner)
1975 G.D.R. 3:49.37
(Kornelia Ender, Barbara Krause, Claudia Hempel,
Ute Bruckner)
1978 U.S.A. 3:43.43
(Tracy Caulkins, Stephanie Elkins, Cynthia
Woodhead, Jill Sterkel)
1982 G.D.R. 3:43.97
(Brigit Meinike, Karen Metschuk, Kirstin Otto,
Susanne Linke)
1986 G.D.R. 3:40.57
(Kristin Otto, Manuela Stellmach, Heike Friedrich,
Schulze)
1991 U.S.A. 3:43.26
(Nicole Haislett, Janet Evans, + 1, Jenny Cooper)
1994 China 3:37.91
(Jingyi Le, Ying Shan, Yang Le, Bin Lu)

4 × 200 m Freestyle Team

1986 G.D.R. 7:59.33
(Manuela Stellmach, Astrid Strauss, Heike Friedrich,
Nadja Bergknecht)
1991 Germany 8:02.56
(team names)
1994 China 7:57.96
(Ying Le, Aihua Yang, Guanbin Zhou, Bin Lu)

Olympic Games

The earliest celebration of the Olympic Games of
which there is a record is that of July 766 B.C. The
ancient Games were ended in A.D. 392 by the decree of
the Roman Emperor Theodosius.

No.	Venue	Date
I	Athens, Greece	5–15 Apr 1896
II	Paris, France	14 May–28 Oct 1900
III	St Louis, U.S.A.	1 July–28 Oct 1904
IV	London, England	27 Apr–29 Oct 1908
V	Stockholm, Sweden	5 May–22 July 1912
VI	Berlin, Germany	Not held 1916
VII	Antwerp, Belgium	20 Apr–12 Sept 1920
VIII	Paris, France	3 May–27 July 1924
IX	Amsterdam, Holland	28 July–12 Aug 1928
X	Los Angeles, U.S.A.	31 July–7 Aug 1932
XI	Berlin, Germany	2 Aug–16 Aug 1936
XII	Helsinki, Finland	Not held 1940
XIII	No venue	Not held 1944
XIV	London, England	29 July–14 Aug 1948
XV	Helsinki, Finland	19 July–3 Aug 1952
XVI	Melbourne, Australia	22 Nov–8 Dec 1956
XVII	Rome, Italy	25 Aug–11 Sept 1960
XVIII	Tokyo, Japan	10–24 Oct 1964
XIX	Mexico City, Mexico	12–27 Oct 1968
XX	Munich, West Germany	26 July–10 Aug 1972
XXI	Montreal, Canada	18–26 July 1976
XXII	Moscow, U.S.S.R.	19–28 July 1980
XXIII	Los Angeles, U.S.A.	19 July–5 Aug 1984
XXIV	Seoul, South Korea	17 Sept–2 Oct 1988
XXV	Barcelona, Spain	25 July–00 ??? 1992

Swimming for men was included in the first Games
of the modern era, in Athens in 1896. Two events for
women (100 and 4 × 100 m freestyle) were added for
Stockholm in 1912.

The only swimmer to win the same individual title
at three successive Games is Dawn Fraser (Aus) who
won the 100 m in 1956, 1960 and 1964. The first to win
four golds at a single Games was Don Schollander
(U.S.A.) in the 100 m, 400 m, 4 × 100 m and 4 × 200 m
in 1964.[1]

The technical conditions for the breaststroke championships have varied according to the developments of
the stroke (see chapters on breaststroke and butterfly).[1]

KEY

Bu = won using overwater arm recovery before separation of
breaststroke and butterfly on 1 January 1954
Uw = won swimming long distances underwater before this
was ruled out on 1 January 1957

MEN

50 m Freestyle

1988	Biondi, Matt (U.S.A.)	22.14
1992	Alex Popov (C.S.I.)	21.91

100 m Freestyle

1896	Hajos, Alfred (Hun)	1:22.2
1904*	Halmay, Zoltan (Hun)	1:02.8
1908	Daniels, Charles (U.S.A.)	1:05.6
1912	Kahanamoku, Duke (U.S.A.)	1:03.4
1920	Kahanamoku, Duke (U.S.A.)	1:01.4
1924	Weissmuller, Johnny (U.S.A.)	59.0
1928	Weissmuller, Johnny (U.S.A.)	58.6
1932	Miyazaki, Yasuki (Jap)	58.2
1936	Csik, Ferenc (Hun)	57.6

*100 yds

1948	Ris, Wally (U.S.A.)	57.3
1952	Scholes, Clarke (U.S.A.)	57.4
1956	Henricks, Jon (Aus)	55.4
1960	Devitt, John (Aus)	55.2
1964	Schollander, Don (U.S.A.)	53.4
1968	Wenden, Mike (Aus)	52.2
1972	Spitz, Mark (U.S.A.)	51.22
1976	Montgomery, Jim (U.S.A.)	49.99
1980	Woite, Jorge (G.D.R.)	50.40
1984	Gaines, Ambrose (U.S.A.)	49.80
1988	Biondi, Matt (U.S.A.)	48.63
1992	Popov, Alex (C.S.I.)	49.02

200 m Freestyle

1900	Lane, Freddy (Aus)	2:52.2
1904*	Daniels, Charles (U.S.A.)	2:44.2
1908–64	event not held	
1968	Wenden, Mike (Aus)	1:55.2
1972	Spitz, Mark (U.S.A.)	1:52.78
1976	Furniss, Bruce (U.S.A.)	1:50.29
1980	Koplialkov, Sergei (U.S.S.R.)	1:49.81
1984	Gross, Michael (West Ger)	1:47.44
1988	Armstrong, Duncan (Aus)	1:47.25
1992	Sodovy, Eugene (C.S.I.)	1:46.70

*100 yds

400 m Freestyle

1904*	Daniels, Charles (U.S.A.)	6:16.2
1908	**Taylor, Henry (G.B.)**	**5:36.8**
1912	Hodgson, George (Can)	5:24.4
1920	Ross, Norman (U.S.A.)	5:26.8
1924	Weissmuller, Johnny (U.S.A.)	5:04.2
1928	Zorilla, Alberto (Arg)	5:01.6
1932	Crabbe, Buster (Clarence) (U.S.A.)	4:48.4
1936	Medica, Jack (U.S.A.)	4:44.5
1948	Smith, Bill (U.S.A.)	4:41.0
1952	Boiteux, Jean (Fra)	4:30.7
1956	Rose, Murray (Aus)	4:27.3
1960	Rose, Murray (Aus)	4:18.3
1964	Schollander, Don (U.S.A.)	4:12.2
1968	Burton, Mike (U.S.A.)	4:09.0
1972	Cooper, Bradley (Aus)	4:00.27
1976	Goodell, Brian (U.S.A.)	3:51.93
1980	Salnikov, Vladimir (U.S.S.R.)	3:51.31
1984	Dicarlo, George (U.S.A.)	3:51.23
1988	Dassler, Uwe (G.D.R.)	3:46.95
1992	Sadovy, Eugene (C.S.I.)	3:45.00

*440 yds

1500 m Freestyle

1904*	Rausch, Emil (Ger)	27:18.2
1908	**Taylor, Henry (G.B.)**	**22:48.4**
1912	Hodgson, George (Can)	22:00.0

*one mile (1,609 m)

1920	Ross, Norman (U.S.A.)	22:23.2
1924	Charlton, (Boy) Andrew (Aus)	20:06.6
1928	Borg, Arne (Swe)	19:51.8
1932	Kitamura, Kusuo (Jap)	19:12.4
1936	Terada, Noboru (Jap)	19:13.7
1948	McLane, Jimmy (U.S.A.)	19:18.5
1952	Konno, Ford (U.S.A.)	18:30.0
1956	Rose, Murray (Aus)	17:58.9
1960	Konrads, John (Aus)	17:19.6
1964	Windle, Bobby (Aus)	17:01.7
1968	Burton, Mike (U.S.A.)	16:38.9
1972	Burton, Mike (U.S.A.)	15:52.58
1976	Goodell, Brian (U.S.A.)	15:02.40
1980	Salnikov, Vladimir (U.S.S.R.)	14:58.27
1984	O'Brien, Michael (U.S.A.)	15:05.20
1988	Salnikov, Vladimir (U.S.S.R.)	15:00.40
1992	Perkins, Kieren (Aus)	14:43.48

100 m Backstroke

1904*	Brack, Walter (Ger)	1:16.8
1908	Bieberstein, Arno (Ger)	1:24.6
1912	Hebner, Harry (U.S.A.)	1:21.2
1920	Kealoha, Warren (U.S.A.)	1:15.2
1924	Kealoha, Warren (U.S.A.)	1:13.2
1928	Kojac, George (U.S.A.)	1:08.2
1932	Kiyokawa, Masaji (Jap)	1:08.6
1936	Kiefer, Adolph (U.S.A.)	1:05.9
1948	Stack, Allen (U.S.A.)	1:06.4
1952	Oyakawa, Yashinobu (U.S.A.)	1:05.7
1956	Theile, David (Aus)	1:02.2
1960	Theile, David (Aus)	1:01.9
1964	event not held	
1968	Matthes, Roland (G.D.R.)	58.7
1972	Matthes, Roland (G.D.R.)	56.58
1976	Naber, John (U.S.A.)	55.49
1980	Baron, Bengt (Swe)	56.53
1984	Carey, Richard (U.S.A.)	55.79
1988	Suzuki, Dachi, (Jap)	55.05
1992	Tewkesbury, Mark (Can)	53.98

*100 yds

200 m Backstroke

| 1900 | Hoppenber, Ernst (Ger) | 2:47.0 |

From left to right:
Henry Taylor,
Boy Charlton,
Arne Borg,
Buster Crabbe,
David Wilkie.

1904–60	event not held	
1964	Graef, Jed (U.S.A.)	2:10.3
1968	Matthes, Roland (G.D.R.)	2:09.6
1972	Matthes, Roland (G.D.R.)	2:02.82
1976	Naber, John (U.S.A.)	1:59.19
1980	Wladar, Sandor (Hun)	2:01.93
1984	Carey, Richard (U.S.A.)	2:00.23
1988	Polianski, Igor (U.S.S.R.)	1:59.37
1992	Lopez-Zubero, Martin (Spa)	1:58.47

100 m Breaststroke

1968	McKenzie, Don (U.S.A.)	1:07.7
1972	Taguchi, Nobutaka (Jap)	1:04.94
1976	Henken, John (U.S.A.)	1:03.11
1980	**Goodhew, Duncan (G.B.)**	**1:03.34**
1984	Lunquist, Stephen (U.S.A.)	1:01.65
1988	**Moorhouse, Adrian (G.B.)**	**1:02.04**
1992	Diebel, Nelson (U.S.A.)	1:01.50

200 m Breaststroke

1908	**Holman, Frederick (G.B.)**		**3:09.2**
1912	Bathe, Walter (Ger)		3:01.8
1920	Malmroth, Hakan (Swe)		3:04.4
1924	Skelton, Robert (U.S.A.)		2:56.6
1928	Tsuruta, Yoshiyuki (Jap)		2:48.8
1932	Tsuruta, Yoshiyuki (Jap)		2:45.4
1936	Hamuro, Tetsou (Jap)		2:42.5
1948	Verdeur, Joe (U.S.A.)	Bu	2:39.3
1952	Davies, John (Aus)	Bu	2:34.4
1956	Furukawa, Masaru (Jap)	Uw	2:34.7
1960	Mulliken, Bill (U.S.A.)		2:37.4
1964	O'Brien, Ian (Aus)		2:27.8
1968	Munoz, Felipe (Mex)		2:28.7
1972	Henken, John (U.S.A.)		2:21.55
1976	**Wilkie, David (G.B.)**		**2:15.11**
1980	Zhulpa, Robertas (U.S.S.R.)		2:15.85
1984	Davis, Victor (Can)		2:13.34
1988	Szabo, Josef (Hun)		2:13.52
1992	Barrowman, Mike (U.S.A.)		2:10.16

100 m Butterfly

1968	Russell, Doug (U.S.A.)	55.9
1972	Spitz, Mark (U.S.A.)	54.27
1976	Vogel, Matthew (U.S.A.)	54.35
1980	Arviddson, Par (Swe)	54.92
1984	Gross, Michael (West Ger)	53.08
1988	Nesty, Anthony (Sur)	53.00
1992	Morales, Pablo (U.S.A.)	53.32

200 m Butterfly

1956	Yorzyk, Bill (U.S.A.)	2:19.3
1960	Troy, Mike (U.S.A.)	2:12.8
1964	Berry, Kevin (Aus)	2:06.6
1968	Robie, Carl (U.S.A.)	2:08.7
1972	Spitz, Mark (U.S.A.)	2:00.70
1976	Bruner, Michael (U.S.A.)	1:59.23
1980	Fesenko, Sergei (U.S.S.R.)	1:59.76
1984	Sieben, John (Aus)	1:57.04
1988	Gross, Michael (West Ger)	1:56.94
1992	Stewart, Melvin (U.S.A.)	1:56.26

200 m Individual Medley

1968	Hickcox, Charles (U.S.A.)	2:12.0
1972	Larsson, Gunnar (Swe)	2:07.17
1976–80	event not held	
1984	Baumann, Alexander (Can)	2:01.42
1988	Darnyi, Tamas (Hun)	2:00.17
1992	Darnyi, Tamas (Hun)	2:00.76

400 m Individual Medley

1964	Roth, Dick (U.S.A.)	4:45.4
1968	Hickcox, Charles (U.S.A.)	4:48.4
1972	Larsson, Gunnar (Swe)	4:31.98
1976	Stracan, Rodney (U.S.A.)	4:23.68
1980	Sidorenko, Alexander (U.S.S.R.)	4:22.89
1984	Baumann, Alexander (Can)	4:17.41
1988	Darnyi, Tamas (Hun)	4:14.75
1992	Darnyi, Tamas (Hun)	4:14.23

4 × 100 m Freestyle Relay

1964	United States	3:33.2
	(Clarke, Steve; Austin, Mike; Illman, Gary; Schollander, Don)	
1968	United States	3:31.7
	(Zorn, Zac; Rerych, Steve; Spitz, Mark; Walsh, Ken)	

The 1964 U.S. team (*left to right*): Saari, Schollander, Clark, Ilman.

1972	United States (Edgar, Dave; Murphy, John; Heidenrich, Jerry; Spitz, Mark)	3:26.42	1932	Japan (Miyazaki, Yasuki; Yokoyama, Takashi; Yusa, Masanori; Toyoda, Hisakichi)	8:58.4
1976–80	event not held		1936	Japan (Yusa, Masanori; Sugiura, Shigeo; Arai, Shigeo; Taguchi, Masaharu)	8:51.5
1984	United States (Gaines, Ambrose; Heath, Michael; Bondi, Matthew; Cavanagh, Christopher)	3:19.03	1948	United States (Ris, Wally; Wolf, Wallace; McLane, Jimmy; Smith, Bill)	8:46.0
1988	U.S.A. (Hudepohl, Jeff; Biondi, Matt; Jager, Tom; Olsen, Jon)	3:16.53	1952	United States (Moore, Wayne; Woolsey, Bill; Konno, Ford; McLane, Jimmy)	8:31.1
1992	U.S.A. (Jacobs, Christopher; Dalbey, Troy; Jager, Tom; Biondi, Matt)	3:16.74	1956	Australia (O'Halloran, Kevin; Devitt, John; Rose, Murray; Henricks, Jon)	8:23.6

4 × 200 m Freestyle Relay

1908	**Great Britain** **(Derbyshire, Rob; Radmilovic, Paul;** **Foster, Willie; Taylor, Henry)**	**10:55.6**	1960	United States (Harrison, George; Blick, Dick; Troy, Mike; Farrell, Jeff)	8:10.2
1912	Australasia (Healy, Cecil (Aus); Champion, Malcolm (N.Z.); Boardman, Leslie (Aus); Hardwick, Harold (Aus))	10:11.2	1964	United States (Clark, Steve; Saari, Roy; Ilman, Gary; Schollander, Don)	7:52.1
1920	United States (McGillivray, Perry; Kealoha, Pua; Ross, Norman; Kahanamoku, Duke)	10:04.4	1968	United States (Nelson, John; Rerych, Steve; Spitz, Mark; Schollander, Don)	7:52.3
1924	United States (O'Connor, Wallace; Glancy, Harry; Breyer, Ralph; Weissmuller, Johnny)	9:53.4	1972	United States (Kinsella, John; Tyler, Fred; Genter, Steve; Spitz, Mark)	7:35.78
1928	United States (Clapp, Austin; Laufer, Walter; Kojac, George; Weissmuller, Johnny)	9:36.2	1976	United States (Bruner, Mike; Furniss, Bruce; Naber, John; Montgomery, Jim)	7:23.22

1980	U.S.S.R.	7:23.50
	(Kopliakov, Sergei; Salnikov, Vladimir; Stukolkin, Igor; Krylor, Ivan)	
1984	United States	7:15.69
	(Heath, Michael; Hayes, Bruce; Float, Jeffrey; Larson, David)	
1988	U.S.A.	7:12.51
	(Dalbey, Troy; Celinski, Matthew; Gjertsen, Douglas; Biondi, Matt)	
1992	C.I.S.	7:11.95
	Lepikov, Dmitri; Pychenko, Vladimir; Taianovitch, Veniamin; Sadovyi, Eugeny)	

4 × 100 m Medley Relay

1960	United States	4:05.4
	(McKinney, Frank; Hait, Paul; Larson, Lance; Farrell, Jeff)	
1964	United States	3:58.4
	(Mann, Tom; Craig, Bill; Schmidt, Fred; Clark, Steve)	
1968	United States	3:54.9
	(Hickcox, Charles; McKenzie, Don; Russell, Doug; Walsh, Ken)	
1972	United States	3:48.16
	(Stamm, Mike; Bruce, Tom; Spitz, Mark; Heidenreich, Jerry)	
1976	United States	3:42.22
	(Naber, John; Henken, John; Vogel, Matt; Montgomery, Jim)	
1980	Australia	3:45.70
	(Kerry, Mark; Evans, Peter; Tonelli, Mark; Brooks, Neil)	
1984	United States	3:39.30
	(Carey, Richard; Lundquist, Stephen; Morales, Pablo; Gaines, Ambrose)	
1988	U.S.A.	3:36.93
	(Berkoff, David; Schroeder, Richard; Biondi, Matt; Jacobs, Christopher)	
1992	U.S.A.	3:36.93
	(Rouse, Jeff; Diebel, Nelson; Morales, Pablo; Olsen, Jon)	

WOMEN

50 m Freestyle

| 1988 | Otto, Kristin (G.D.R.) | 25.49 |
| 1992 | Yang, Wenyi (Chn) | 24.79 |

100 m Freestyle

1912	Durack, Fanny (Aus)	1:22.2
1920	Bleibtrey, Ethelda (U.S.A.)	1:13.6
1924	Lackie, Ethel (U.S.A.)	1:12.4
1928	Osipowich, Albina (U.S.A.)	1:11.0

Judy Grinham.   Anita Lonsbrough.

1932	Madison, Helene (U.S.A.)	1:06.8
1936	Mastenbrock, Rie (Neth)	1:05.9
1948	Andersen, Greta (Den)	1:06.3
1952	Szoke, Katalin (Hun)	1:06.8
1956	Fraser, Dawn (Aus)	1:02.0
1960	Fraser, Dawn (Aus)	1:01.2
1964	Fraser, Dawn (Aus)	59.5
1968	Henne, Jan (U.S.A.)	1:00.0
1972	Neilson, Sandra (U.S.A.)	58.59
1976	Ender, Kornelia (G.D.R.)	55.65
1980	Krause, Barbara (G.D.R.)	54.79
1984	Hogshead, Nancy (U.S.A.)	55.92
	and Steinseifer, Carrie (U.S.A.)	
1988	Otto, Kristin (G.D.R.)	54.93
1992	Zhuang, Yang (Chn)	54.64

200 m Freestyle

1968	Meyer, Debbie (U.S.A.)	2:10.5
1972	Gould, Shane (Aus)	2:03.56
1976	Ender, Kornelia (G.D.R.)	1:59.26
1980	Krause, Barbara (G.D.R.)	1:58.33
1984	Wayte, Mary (U.S.A.)	1:59.23
1988	Friedrich, Heike (G.D.R.)	1:57.65
1992	Nicole Haislett (U.S.A.)	1:57.90

400 m Freestyle

1924	Norelius, Martha (U.S.A.)	6:02.2
1928	Norelius, Martha (U.S.A.)	5:42.8
1932	Madison, Helene (U.S.A.)	5:28.5
1936	Mastenbrook, Rie (Neth)	5:26.4
1948	Curtis, Ann (U.S.A.)	5:17.8
1952	Gyenge, Valeria (Hun)	5:12.1
1956	Crapp, Lorraine (Aus)	4:54.6
1960	Von Saltza, Chris (U.S.A.)	4:50.6
1964	Duenkel, Ginny (U.S.A.)	4:43.3
1968	Meyer, Debbie (U.S.A.)	4:31.8
1972	Gould, Shane (Aus)	4:19.04
1976	Thumer, Petra (G.D.R.)	4:09.89
1980	Diers, Innes (G.D.R.)	4:08.76
1984	Cohen, Tiffany (U.S.A.)	4:07.10
1988	Evans, Janet (U.S.A.)	4:03.85
1992	Hase, Dagmar (Ger)	4:07.18

800 m Freestyle

1968	Meyer, Debbie (U.S.A.)	9:24.0
1972	Rothmammer, Keena (U.S.A.)	8:53.68
1976	Thumer, Petra (G.D.R.)	8:37.14
1980	Ford, Michelle (Aus)	8:28.90
1984	Cohen, Tiffany (U.S.A.)	8:24.95
1988	Evans, Janet (U.S.A.)	8:20.20
1992	Evans, Janet (U.S.A.)	8:25.52

100 m Backstroke

1924	Bauer, Sybil (U.S.A.)	1:23.2
1928	Braun, Marie (Neth)	1:22.0
1932	Holm, Eleanor (U.S.A.)	1:19.4
1936	Senff, Nina (Neth)	1:18.9
1948	Harup, Karen (Den)	1:14.4
1952	Harrison, Joan (SAf)	1:14.3
1956	**Grinham, Judy (G.B.)**	**1:12.9**
1960	Burke, Lynn (U.S.A.)	1:09.3
1964	Ferguson, Cathie (U.S.A.)	1:07.7
1968	Hall, Kaye (U.S.A.)	1:06.2
1972	Belote, Melissa (U.S.A.)	1:05.78
1976	Richter, Ulrike (G.D.R.)	1:01.83
1980	Reinisch, Rica (G.D.R.)	1:00.86
1984	Andrews, Theresa (U.S.A.)	1:02.55
1988	Otto, Kristin (G.D.R.)	1:00.89
1992	Egerszegi, Kristin (Hun)	1:00.68

200 m Backstroke

1968	Watson, Lorraine (U.S.A.)	2:24.8
1972	Belote, Melissa (U.S.A.)	2:19.19
1976	Richter, Ulrike (G.D.R.)	2:13.43
1980	Reinisch, Rica (G.D.R.)	2:11.77
1984	De Rover, Jolande (Hol)	2:12.38
1988	Egerszegi, Kristin (Hun)	2:09.29
1992	Egerszegi, Kristin (Hun)	2:07.96

100 m Breaststroke

1968	Bjedov, Djurdica (Yugo)	1:15.8
1972	Carr, Cathy (U.S.A.)	1:13.58
1976	Anke, Hannelore (G.D.R.)	1:11.16
1980	Geweniger, Ute (G.D.R.)	1:10.22
1984	Van Stavern, Petra (Hol)	1:09.88
1988	Dangalakova, Tania (U.S.S.R.)	1:07.95
1992	Rudkovsaia, Elena (C.S.I.)	1:08.00

200 m Breaststroke

1924	**Morton, Lucy (G.B.)**	**3:33.2**
1928	Schrader, Hilde (Ger)	3:12.6
1932	Dennis, Clare (Aus)	3:06.3
1936	Maehata, Hideko (Jap)	3:03.6
1948	Van Vliet, Nel (Neth)	2:57.2
1952	Szekely, Eva (Hun)	*Bu* 2:51.7
1956	Happe, Ursula (W. Ger)	2:53.1
1960	**Lonsbrough, Anita (G.B.)**	**2:49.5**
1964	Prosumenschikova, Galina (U.S.S.R.)	2:46.4
1968	Wichman, Sharon (U.S.A.)	2:44.4
1972	Whitfield, Beverley (Aus)	2:41.71

1976	Koshevaia, Marina (U.S.S.R.)	2:33.35
1980	Kachushite, Lina (U.S.S.R.)	2:29.54
1984	Ottenbrite, Anne (Can)	2:30.38
1988	Hoerner, Silke (G.D.R.)	2:26.71
1992	Iwasaki, Kyoko (Jap)	2:26.65

100 m Butterfly

1956	Mann, Shelley (U.S.A.)	1:11.0
1960	Schuler, Carolyn (U.S.A.)	1:09.5
1964	Stouder, Sharon (U.S.A.)	1:04.7
1968	McClements, Lynn (Aus)	1:05.5
1972	Aoki, Mayumi (Jap)	1:03.34
1976	Ender, Komelia (G.D.R.)	1:01.13
1980	Metschuck, Karen (G.D.R.)	1:00.42
1984	Meagher, Mary (U.S.A.)	59.26
1988	Otto, Kristin (G.D.R.)	59.00
1992	Qian, Hong (Chn)	58.62

200 m Butterfly

1968	Kok, Ada (Neth)	2:24.7
1972	Moe, Karen (U.S.A.)	2:15.57
1976	Pollack, Andrea (G.D.R.)	2:11.41
1980	Geissler, Innes (G.D.R.)	2:10.44
1984	Meagher, Mary (U.S.A.)	2:06.90
1988	Nord, Kathleen (G.D.R.)	2:09.51
1992	Sanders, Summer (U.S.A.)	2:08.67

200 m Individual Medley

1968	Kolb, Claudia (U.S.A.)	2:24.7
1972	Gould, Shane (Aus)	2:23.07
1976–80	event not held	
1984	Caulkins, Tracy (U.S.A.)	2:12.64
1988	Hunger, Daniela (G.D.R.)	2:12.59
1992	Lin, Li (Chn)	2:11.65

400 m Individual Medley

1964	De Varona, Donna (U.S.A.)	5:18.7
1968	Kolb, Claudia (U.S.A.)	5:08.5
1972	Neall, Gail (Aus)	5:02.97
1976	Tauber, Ulrike (G.D.R.)	4:42.77
1980	Schneider, Petra (G.D.R.)	4:36.29
1984	Caulkins, Tracy (U.S.A.)	4:39.24
1988	Evans, Janet (U.S.A.)	4:37.76
1992	Egerszegi, Kristin (Hun)	4:36.54

4 × 100 m Freestyle Relay

1912	**Great Britain**	**5:52.8**
	(Moore, Bella; Steer, Irene; Speirs, Annie; Fletcher, Jennie)	
1920	United States	5:11.6
	(Bleibtrey, Ethelda; Schroth, Frances; Guest, Irene; Woodbridge, Margaret)	
1924	United States	4:58.8
	(Ederle, Gertrude; Wehselau, Marlechen; Lackie, Ethel; Donelly, Euphrasia)	

1928	United States	4:47.6
	(Lambert, Adelaide; Osipowich, Albina; Garatti, Eleanora; Norelius, Martha)	
1932	United States	4:38.0
	(McKim, Josephine; Garatti-Saville, Eleanor; Johns, Helen; Madison, Helene)	
1936	Netherlands	4:36.0
	(Selbach, Jopie; Wagner, Catherina; Den Ouden, Willy; Mastenbroek, Rie)	
1948	United States	4:29.2
	(Corridon, Marie; Kalama, Thelma; Helser, Brenda; Curtis, Ann)	
1952	Hungary	4:24.4
	(Novak, Ilona; Temes, Judit; Novak, Eva; Szoke, Katalin)	
1956	Australia	4:17.1
	(Fraser, Dawn; Leech, Faith; Morgan, Sandra; Crapp, Lorraine)	
1960	United States	4:08.9
	(Spillane, Joan; Stobs, Shirley; Wood, Carolyn; Von Saltza, Chris)	
1964	United States	4:03.8
	(Stouder, Sharon; De Varona, Donna; Watson, Pokey; Ellis, Kathy)	
1968	United States	4:02.5
	(Barkman, Jane; Gustavson, Linda; Pedersen, Sue; Henne, Jan)	
1972	United States	3:55.19
	(Neilson, Sandra; Kemp, Jenny; Barkman, Jane; Babashoff, Shirley)	
1976	United States	3:44.82
	(Belote, Melissa; Carr, Cathy; Dearduff, Deana; Neilson, Sandra)	
1980	German Democratic Republic	3:42.71
	(Diers, Innes; Husenbeck, Heike; Krause, Barbara; Metschuck, Karen)	
1984	United States	3:43.43
	(Hogshead, Nancy; Steinseifer, Carrie; Torres, Dara; Johnson, Jenna)	
1988	German Democratic Republic	3:40.63
	(Otto, Kristin; Meissner, Katrin; Hunger, Daniela; Stellmach, Manuela)	
1992	United States	3:39.46
	(Haislett, Nicole; Torres, Dara; Martino, Angel; Thompson, Jennifer)	

4 × 100 m Medley Relay

1960	United States	4:45.9
	(Burke, Lynn; Kemper, Patty; Schuler, Carolyn; Von Saltza, Chris)	
1964	United States	4:33.9
	(Ferguson, Cathy; Goyette, Cynthia; Stouder, Sharon; Ellis, Kathy)	

1968	United States	4:28.3
	(Hall, Kaye; Ball, Catie; Daneils, Ellie; Pedersen, Sue)	
1972	German Democratic Republic	4:20.75
	(Richter, Ulrike; Anke, Hannelore; Pollack, Andrea; Ender, Kornelia)	
1976	United States	4:07.95
	(Peynton, Kim; Boglioli, Wendy; Sterkel, Jill; Babashoff, Shirley)	
1980	German Democratic Republic	4:06.67
	(Reinisch, Rica; Geweniger, Ute; Pollack, Andrea; Metschuck, Karen)	
1984	United States	4:08.34
	(Andrew, Theresa; Caulkins, Tracy; Meagher, Mary; Hogshead, Nancy)	
1988	East Germany	4:03.74
	(Otto, Kristin; Hoerner, Silke; Weigang, Birte; Meissner, Katrin)	
1992	United States	4:02.54
	(Loveless, Lea; Nall, Anita; Ahmann-Leighton, Chris; Thompson, Jennifer)	

EVENTS NO LONGER HELD

50 yd Freestyle

1904	Halmay, Zoltan (Hun)	28.0
	(After swim-off with Scott Leary (U.S.A.))	

500 m Freestyle

1896	Neumann, Paul (Aut)	8:12.6

880 yd Freestyle

1904	Rausch, Emil (Ger)	13:11.4

1000 m Freestyle

1900	**Jarvis, John (G.B.)**	**13:40.0**

1200 m Freestyle

1896	Hajos, Alfred (Hun)	18:22.2

4000 m Freestyle

1900	**Jarvis, John (G.B.)**	**58:24.0**

400 m Breaststroke

1904	Zacharias, Georg (Ger)	*7:23.6
1912	Bathe, Walther (Ger)	6:29.6
1920	Malmroth, Haken (Swe)	6:31.8

*440 yd

100 m for sailors (of ships anchored in the port of Piraeus)

1896	Malokinis, Jean (Ger)	2:20.4

200 m Obstacle Swimming

1900 Lane, Freddy (U.S.A.)   2:28.4

60 m Underwater Swimming

1900 De Vauderville, Charles (Fr)   1:53.4

Plunging

1904 Dickey, Paul (U.S.A.)   62 ft 6 ins

4 × 50 yd Freestyle Relay

1904 New York A.C. (U.S.A.)*   2:04.6
      (Ruddy, Joseph; Goodwin, Leon;
      Handley, Louis de B; Daniels, Charles)

*The only Games when non-national teams have been allowed
to participate

5 × 40 m Freestyle Relay

1900 Germany   19 pts
      (Hoppenberg, Ernst; Hainle, Max; Von
      Petersdorff, Herbert; Schone, Max;
      Frey, Julius)

Interim Games

After the failure of the 1904 Games in St Louis, European Olympic leaders pressed for a sports festival for their athletes, most of whom had been unable to participate in the United States. Greece, the home of the ancient Olympic Games and hosts to the first Games of the modern era in 1896, offered to stage such a meeting. In fact their event in 1906, in Athens, proved as big a disappointment as St Louis and attracted only a few national representatives. As a result these Interim Games were refused recognition as an Olympiad, although F.I.N.A. list the 1906 winners among their Olympic roll of honour, as follows[1]:

100 m Freestyle

Daniels, Charles (U.S.A.)   1:13.0

400 m Freestyle

Scheff, Otto (Aut)   6:22.8

One mile

Taylor, Henry (G.B.)   **28:28.0**

1000 m Freestyle Relay

Hungary   17:16.2

1 *Encyclopaedia of Swimming*

European Championships
MEN

50 m Freestyle

1987	Woite, Jorge (G.D.R.)	22.66
1989	Trachenko, Vladimir (U.R.S.)	22.64
1991	Rudolph, Nils (Ger)	22.33
1993	Popov, Alex (U.R.S.)	22.27
1995	Popov, Alex (U.R.S.)	22.25

100 m Freestyle

1926	Barany, Istvan (Hun)	1:01.0
1927	Borg, Arne (Swe)	1:00.0
1931	Barany, Istvan (Hun)	59.8
1934	Csik, Ferenc (Hun)	59.7
1938	Hoving, Karl (Neth)	59.8
1947	Jany, Alex (Fr)	56.9
1950	Jany, Alex (Fr)	57.7
1954	Nyeki, Imre (Hun)	57.7
1958	Pucci, Paolo (It)	56.3
1962	Gottvalles, Alain (Fr)	55.0
1966	**McGregor, Bobby (G.B.)**	**53.7**
1970	Rousseau, Michael (Fr)	52.9
1974	Nocke, Peter (W. Ger)	52.18
1977	Nocke, Peter (W. Ger)	51.55
1981	Johannson, Per (Swe)	50.55
1983	Johansson, Per (Swe)	50.20
1985	Caron, Stefan (Fra)	50.20
1987	Lodziewski, Stefan (G.D.R.)	49.79
1989	Lamberti, Georgio (Ita)	49.24
1991	Popov, Alex (U.R.S.)	49.18
1993	Popov, Alex (U.R.S.)	49.15
1995	Popov, Alex (U.R.S.)	49.10

200 m Freestyle

1970	Fassnacht, Hans (W. Ger)	1:55.2
1974	Nocke, Peter (W. Ger)	1:53.10
1977	Nocke, Peter (W. Ger)	1:51.72
1981	Kopliakov, Sergei (U.S.S.R.)	1:51.23
1983	Gross, Michael (W. Ger)	1:47.87
1985	Gross, Michael (W. Ger)	1:47.95
1987	Holmertz, Anders (Swe)	1:48.44
1989	Lamberti, Georgio (Ita)	1:46.69
1991	Wojdat, Arthur (Pol)	1:48.10
1993	Kasvio, Antti (Fin)	1:47.11
1995	Sievenen, Jani (Fin)	1:48.98

400 m Freestyle

1926	Borg, Arne (Swe)	5:14.2
1927	Borg, Arne (Swe)	5:08.6
1931	Barany, Istvan (Hun)	5:04.0
1934	Taris, Jean (Fr)	4:55.5
1938	Borg, Bjorn (Swe)	4:51.6
1947	Jany, Alex (Fr)	4:35.2
1950	Jany, Alex (Fr)	4:48.0
1954	Csordas, Gyorgy (Hun)	4:38.8

1958	Black, Ian (G.B.)	4:31.3
1962	Bontekoe, Johan (Neth)	4:25.6
1966	Wiegand, Frank (G.D.R.)	4:11.1
1970	Larsson, Gunnar (Swe)	4:02.6
1974	Samsanov, Alexander (U.S.S.R.)	4:02.11
1977	Ruskin, Sergei, (U.S.S.R.)	3:54.83
1981	Petric, Borut (Yugo)	3:51.63
1983	Salnikov, Vladimir (U.S.S.R.)	3:49.80
1985	Dassler, Uwe (G.D.R.)	3:51.52
1987	Dassler, Uwe (G.D.R.)	3:48.95
1989	Wodjat, Arthur (Pol)	3:47.78
1991	Sadovy, Eugene (U.R.S.)	3:49.02
1993	Kasvio, Antti (Fin)	3:47.81
1995	Zeisner, Stefan (Ger)	3:50.35

1500 m Freestyle

1926	Borg, Arne (Swe)	21:29.2
1927	Borg, Arne (Swe)	19:07.2
1931	Halassy, Oliver (Hun)	20:49.0
1934	Taris, Jean (Fr)	20:01.5
1938	Borg, Bjorn (Swe)	19:55.6
1947	Mitro, Gyorgy (Hun)	19:28.0
1950	Lehmann, Heinz (Ger)	19:48.2
1954	Csordas, Gyorgy (Hun)	18:57.8
1958	Black, Ian (G.B.)	18:05.8
1962	Katona, Jozsef (Hun)	17:49.5
1966	Belits-Geiman, Semyon (U.S.S.R.)	16:58.5
1970	Fassnacht, Hans (W. Ger)	16:19.2
1974	Pfeutze, Frank (G.D.R.)	15:54.97
1977	Salnikov, Vladimir (U.S.S.R.)	15:16.45
1981	Salnikov, Vladimir (U.S.S.R.)	15:09.17
1983	Salnikov, Vladimir (U.S.S.R.)	15:08.84
1985	Dassler, Uwe (G.D.R.)	15:08.56
1987	Henkel, Rainer (W. Ger)	15:02.23
1989	Hoffman, Jorge (G.D.R.)	15:01.52
1991	Hoffman, Jorge (Ger)	15:02.27
1993	Hoffman, Jorge (Ger)	15:13.31
1995	Zeisner, Stefan (Ger)	15:11.25

100 m Backstroke

1926	Frohlich, Gustav (Ger)	1:16.0
1927	Lundahl, Eksil (Swe)	1:17.4
1931	Deutsch, Gerhard (Ger)	1:14.8
1934	Besford, John (G.B.)	1:11.7
1938	Schlauch, Hans (Ger)	1:09.0
1947	Vallerey, Georges (Fr)	1:07.6
1950	Larsson, Goran (Swe)	1:09.4
1954	Bozon, Gilbert (Fr)	1:05.1
1958	Christophe, Robert (Fr)	1:03.1
1962–66	event not held	
1970	Matthes, Roland (G.D.R.)	58.9
1974	Matthes, Roland (G.D.R.)	58.21
1977	Rolko, Miloslav (Cze)	58.35
1981	Wladar, Sandor (Hun)	56.72
1983	Richter, Dirk (G.D.R.)	56.10
1985	Polianski, Igor (U.S.S.R.)	55.24
1987	Zabolotnov, Sergei (U.S.S.R.)	56.06

1989	Lopez-Zubero, Martin (Spa)	56.44
1991	Lopez-Zubero, Martin (Spa)	55.30
1993	Lopez-Zubero, Martin (Spa)	55.03
1995	Selkov, Vladimir (U.R.S.)	55.48

200 m Backstroke

1962	Barbier, Leonid (U.S.S.R.)	2:16.6
1966	Gromack, Yuri (U.S.S.R.)	2:12.9
1970	Matthes, Roland (G.D.R.)	2:08.8
1974	Matthes, Roland (G.D.R.)	2:04.64
1977	Verraszto, Zoltan (Hun)	2:03.88
1981	Wladar, Sandor (Hun)	2:00.80
1983	Zabolotnov, Sergei (U.S.S.R.)	2:01.00
1985	Polianski, Igor (U.S.S.R.)	1:58.50
1987	Zabolotnov, Sergei (U.S.S.R.)	1:59.35
1989	Battistelli, Stefano (Ita)	1:59.96
1991	Lopez-Zubero, Martin (Spa)	1:58.66
1993	Selkov, Vladimir (U.R.S.)	1:58.09
1995	Selkov, Vladimir (U.R.S.)	1:58.48

100 m Breaststroke

1970	Pankin, Nicolai (U.S.S.R.)	1:06.8
1974	Pankin, Nicolai (U.S.S.R.)	1:05.63
1977	Moerken, Gerald (W. Ger)	1:02.86
1981	Kis, Ivan (Hun)	1:03.44
1983	Zhulpa, Roberta (U.S.S.R.)	1:03.32
1985	Moorehouse, Adrian (G.B.)	1:02.99
1987	Moorehouse, Adrian (G.B.)	1:02.13
1989	Moorehouse, Adrian (G.B.)	1:01.71
1991	Rozsa, Norbert (Hun)	1:01.49
1993	Guttler, Kaoly (Hun)	1:01.04
1995	de Burghgraeve, Fred (Bel)	1:01.12

200 m Breaststroke

1926	Rademacher, Erich (Ger)	2:52.6
1927	Rademacher, Erich (Ger)	2:55.2
1931	Reingoldt, Toivo (Fin)	2:52.2
1934	Sietas, Erwin (Ger)	2:49.0
1938	Balke, Joachim (Ger)	2:45.8
1947	Romain, Roy (G.B.)	Bu 2:40.1
1950	Klein, Herbert (W. Ger)	Bu 2:38.6
1954	Bodinger, Klaus (G.D.R.)	2:40.9
1958	Kolesnikov, Leonid (U.S.S.R.)	2:41.1
1962	Prokopenko, Georgy (U.S.S.R.)	2:32.8
1966	Prokopenko, Georgy (U.S.S.R.)	2:30.0
1970	Katzur, Klaus (G.D.R.)	2:26.0
1974	Wilkie, David (G.B.)	2:20.42
1977	Morken, Gerard (W. Ger)	2:16.78
1981	Zhulpa, Robertas (U.S.S.R.)	2:16.15
1983	Moorehouse, Adrian (G.B.)	2:17.49
1985	Volkov, Dmitry (U.S.S.R.)	2:19.53
1987	Szabo, Josef (Hun)	2:13.87
1989	Gillingham, Nick (G.B.)	2:12.90
1991	Gillingham, Nick (G.B.)	2:12.55
1993	Gillingham, Nick (G.B.)	2:12.49
1995	Forneev, Andrei (U.R.S.)	2:12.64

100 m Butterfly

1970	Lampe, Hans (W. Ger)	57.6
1974	Pyttel, Roger (G.D.R.)	55.90
1977	Pyttel, Roger (G.D.R.)	55.49
1981	Markovsky, Alexander (U.S.S.R.)	54.89
1983	Gross, Michael (W. Ger)	54.00
1985	Gross, Michael (W. Ger)	54.02
1987	**Jameson, Andy (G.B.)**	**53.62**
1989	Szukala, Rafael (Pol)	54.47
1991	Kulikov, Vladislav (U.R.S.)	54.22
1993	Szukala, Rafael (Pol)	53.41
1995	Pankratov, Denis (U.R.S.)	52.32

200 m Butterfly

1954	Tumpek, Gyorgy (Hun)	2:32.2
1958	**Black, Ian (G.B.)**	**2:21.9**
1962	Kuzmin, Valentin (U.S.S.R.)	2:14.2
1966	Kuzmin, Valentin (U.S.S.R.)	2:10.2
1970	Poser, Udo (E. Ger)	2:08.4
1974	Hargtay, Andras (Hun)	2:03.80
1977	Kraus, Michael (W. Ger)	2:00.40
1981	Gross, Michael (W. Ger)	1:59.19
1983	Gross, Michael (W. Ger)	1:57.05
1985	Gross, Michael (W. Ger)	1:56.65
1987	Gross, Michael (W. Ger)	1:57.59
1989	Darnyi, Tamas (Hun)	1:58.87
1991	Esposito, Frank (Fra)	1:59.59
1993	Pankratov, Denis (U.R.S.)	1:56.25
1995	Pankratov, Denis (U.R.S.)	1:56.24

200 m Individual Medley

1970	Larsson, Gunnar (Swe)	2:09.3
1974	**Wilkie, David (G.B.)**	**2:06.32**
1977	Hargitay, Andras (Hun)	2:06.82
1981	Sidorenko, Alexander (U.S.S.R.)	2:03.41
1983	Franceschi, Giovanni (It)	2:02.48
1985	Darnyi, Tamas (Hun)	2:03.23
1987	Darnyi, Tamas (Hun)	2:00.56
1989	Darnyi, Tamas (Hun)	2:01.03
1991	Sorensen, Lars (Den)	2:02.63
1993	Sievenen, Jani (Fin)	1:59.50
1995	Sievenen, Jani (Fin)	1:58.61

400 m Individual Medley

1962	Androssov, Gennadi (U.S.S.R.)	5:01.5
1966	Wiegand, Frank (G.D.R.)	4:47.9
1970	Larsson, Gunnar (Swe)	4:36.2
1974	Hargitay, Andras (Hun)	4:28.89
1977	Fesenko, Sergei (U.S.S.R.)	4:26.83
1981	Fesenko, Sergei (U.S.S.R.)	4:22.77
1983	Franceschi, Giovanni (It)	4:20.41
1985	Darnyi, Tamas (Hun)	4:20.70
1987	Darnyi, Tamas (Hun)	4:15.42
1989	Darnyi, Tamas (Hun)	4:15.25
1991	Sacchi, Lucca (It)	4:17.81
1993	Sievenen, Jani (Fin)	4:15.51
1995	Sievenen, Jani (Fin)	4:14.75

4 × 100 m Freestyle Relay

1962	France (Gropaiz, Gerard; Christophe, Robert; Curtillet, Jean-Pasqual; Gottvalles, Alain)	3:43.7
1966	East Germany (Weigand, Frank; Poser, Udo; Gregor, Horst; Sommer, Peter)	3:36.8
1970	U.S.S.R. (Bure, Vladimir; Mazanov, Victor; Kulikov, Georgi; Ilichev, Leonid)	3:32.3
1974	West Germany (Steinbach, Klaus; Schiller, Gerhard; Meier, Kessler; Nocke, Peter)	3:30.61
1977	West Germany (Steinbach, Klaus; Schmidt, Andreas; Konnecker, Jurgen; Nocke, Peter)	3:26.57
1981	U.S.S.R. (Krayusik, Sergei; Kopliakov, Sergei; Markovsky, Alexander; Smiryagin, Alexander)	3:21.48
1983	Soviet Union	3:20.88
1985	West Germany	3:22.18
1987	East Germany	3:19.17
1989	West Germany	3:19.68
1991	U.R.S.	3:17.11
1993	U.R.S.	3:18.80
1995	U.R.S.	0:00.00

4 × 200 m Freestyle Relay

1926	Germany (Heitmann, August; Berges, Friedel; Rademacher, Joachim; Heinrich, Herbert)	9:57.2
1927	Germany (Heitmann, August; Berges, Friedel; Rademacher, Joachim; Heinrich, Herbert)	9:49.6
1930	Hungary (Szabados, Laszlo; Szekely, Andras; Wanie, Andras; Barany, Istvan)	9:34.0
1934	Hungary (Grof, Odon; Csik, Ferenc; Marothy, Andras; Lengyel, Arpad)	9:30.2
1938	Germany (Birr, Wener; Plath, Werner; Heimlich, Arthur; Freese, Hans)	9:17.6
1947	Sweden (Olsson, Per Olaf; Ostrand, Per Olaf; Lunden, Martin; Johansson, Olle)	9:00.5
1950	Sweden (Synnerholm, Tore; Larsson, Goran; Ostrand, Per Olaf; Johansson, Olle)	9:06.5
1954	Hungary (Till, Laszlo; Kadas, Geza; Domotor, Zoltan; Nyeki, Imre)	8:47.8

1958	U.S.S.R.	8:33.7
	(Nikolaev, Gennadi; Luzkovski, Jozsef; 2 NAMES MISSING)	
1962	Sweden	8:14.8
	(Rosendhal, Hans; Svensson, Mats; Bengtsson, Lars-Erik; Lindberg, Per Ole)	
1966	U.S.S.R.	8:00.2
	(Ilichev, Leonid; Belits-Geiman, Semyon; Pletnev; Novikov, Eugeny)	
1970	West Germany	7:49.5
	(Lampe, Werner; von Schilling, Olaf; Meeuw, Folkert; Fassnacht, Hans)	
1974	West Germany	7:39.70
	(Steinback, Klaus; Lampe, Werner; Meeuw, Folkert; Nocke, Peter)	
1977	U.S.S.R.	7:28.21
	(Rastatov, Vladimir; Rusin, Sergei; Kopliakov, Sergei; Krilov, Alexander)	
1981	U.S.S.R.	7:24.41
	(Shemetov, Vladimir; Salnikov, Vladimir; Chaev, Alexander; Kopliakov, Sergei)	
1983	West Germany	7:20.40
1985	West Germany	7:19.23
1987	West Germany	7:13.10
1989	Italy	7:15.39
1991	U.R.S.	7:16.96
1993	U.R.S.	7:15.84
1995	Germany	0:00.00

4 × 100 m Medley Relay

1958	U.S.S.R.	4:16.5
	(Barbier, Leonid; Minaschkin, Vladimir; Semjenkov, Vitali; Polevoi, Viktor)	
1962	German Democratic Republic	4:09.0
	(Dietze, Henninger; Egon; Gregor, Horst; Wiegand, Frank)	
1966	U.S.S.R.	4:02.4
	(Mazanov, Victor; Prokopenko, Georgy; Kuzmin, Valentin; Ilichev, Leonid)	
1970	German Democratic Republic	3:54.4
	(Matthes, Roland; Katzur, Klaus; Poser, Udo; Unger, Lutz)	
1974	West Germany	3:51.57
	(Steinbach, Klaus; Kusch, Walter; Meeuw, Folkert; Nocke, Peter)	
1977	West Germany	3:48.73
	(Steinbach, Klaus; Morken, Gerrard; Krause, Michael; Nocke, Peter)	
1981	U.S.S.R.	3:44.23
	(Sidorenko, Alex; Miskarov, Alex; Dombrovsky, Alex; Smiriagon, Alex)	

1983	U.S.S.R.	3:43.99
1985	West Germany	3:43.59
1987	U.S.S.R.	3:41.51
1989	U.R.S.	3:41.44
1991	U.R.S.	3:40.68
1993	U.R.S.	3:38.90
1995	U.R.S.	3:38.11

WOMEN

50 m Freestyle

1987	Costache, Tamara (Rom)	25.50
1989	Plewinski, Catherine (Fr)	25.63
1991	Osygus, Sylvia (Ger)	25.80
1993	van Almsick, Franziska (Ger)	25.53
1995	Oloffson, Linda (Swe)	25.76

100 m Freestyle

1927	Vierdag, Marie (Neth)	1:15.0
1931	Godard, Yvonne (Fr)	1:10.0
1934	Den Ouden, Willy (Neth)	1:07.1
1938	Hveger, Ragnhild (Den)	1:06.2
1947	Nathansen, Fritze (Den)	1:07.8
1950	Schumacher, Irma (Neth)	1:06.4
1954	Szoke, Katalin (Hun)	1:05.8
1958	Jobson, Kate (Swe)	1:04.7
1962	Pechstein, Heidi (G.D.R.)	1:03.3
1966	Grunert, Martine (G.D.R.)	1:01.2
1970	Wetzko, Gabrielle (G.D.R.)	59.6
1974	Ender, Kornelia (G.D.R.)	56.96
1977	Krause, Barbara (G.D.R.)	56.55
1981	Metschuck, Karen (G.D.R.)	55.74
1983	Meineke, Birgit (G.D.R.)	55.18
1985	Friedrich, Heike (G.D.R.)	55.71
1987	Otto, Kristin (G.D.R.)	55.38
1989	Meissner, Katrin (G.D.R.)	55.38
1991	Plewinski, Catherine (Fr)	56.20
1993	van Almsick, Franziska (Ger)	54.57
1995	van Almsick, Franziska (Ger)	55.34

200 m Freestyle

1970	Wetzko, Gabriele (G.D.R.)	2:08.2
1974	Ender, Kornelia (G.D.R.)	2:03.22
1977	Thumer, Petra (G.D.R.)	2:00.29
1981	Schmidt, Carmelia (G.D.R.)	2:00.27
1983	Meineke, Birgit (G.D.R.)	1:59.45
1985	Friedrich, Heike (G.D.R.)	1:59.55
1987	Friedrich, Heike (G.D.R.)	1:58.24
1989	Stellmach, Manuela (G.D.R.)	1:58.93
1991	Jacobsen, Ute (Den)	2:00.29
1993	van Almsick, Franziska (Ger)	1:57.97
1995	Kielgass, Kerstin (Ger)	2:00.56

400 m Freestyle

| 1927 | Braun, Marie (Neth) | 6:11.8 |

1931	Braun, Marie (Neth)	5:42.0
1934	Mastenbroek, Rie (Neth)	5:27.4
1938	Hveger, Ranghild (Den)	5:09.0
1947	Harup, Karen (Den)	5:18.2
1950	Andersen, Greta (Den)	5:30.9
1954	Sebo, Agota (Hun)	5:14.4
1958	Koster, Jan (Neth)	5:02.6
1962	Lasterie, Adrie (Neth)	4:52.4
1966	Mandonnaud, Claude (Fr)	4:48.2
1970	Sehmisch, Elke (G.D.R.)	4:32.9
1974	Franke, Angelika (G.D.R.)	4:17.83
1977	Thumer, Petra (G.D.R.)	4:08.91
1981	Diers, Innes (G.D.R.)	4:08.58
1983	Strauss, Astrid (G.D.R.)	4:08.07
1985	Strauss, Astrid (G.D.R.)	4:09.22
1987	Friedrich, Heike (G.D.R.)	4:06.39
1989	Moehring, Anke (Ger)	4:05.84
1991	Dalby, Irene (Nor)	4:11.63
1993	Hasse, Dagmar (Ger)	4:10.47
1995	van Almsick, Franziska (Ger)	4:08.37

800 m Freestyle

1970	Neugebauer, Karin (G.D.R.)	9:29.1
1974	Dorr, Kornelia (G.D.R.)	8:52.45
1977	Thumer, Petra (G.D.R.)	8:38.32
1981	Schmidt, Carmelia (G.D.R.)	8:32.79
1983	Strauss, Astrid (G.D.R.)	8:32.12
1985	Strauss, Astrid (G.D.R.)	8:32.45
1987	Moehring, Anke (G.D.R.)	8:19.53
1989	Moehring, Anke (G.D.R.)	8:23.99
1991	Dalby, Irene (Nor)	8:32.08
1993	Henke, Jana (Ger)	8:32.47
1995	Jung, Julia (Ger)	8:36.08

100 m Backstroke

1927	Den Turk, Willy (Neth)	1:24.6
1931	Braun, Marie (Neth)	1:22.8
1934	Mastenbroek, Rie (Neth)	1:20.3
1938	Kint, Cor (Neth)	1:15.0
1947	Harup, Karen (Den)	1:15.9
1950	Van der Horst, Ria (Neth)	1:17.1
1954	Wielema, Geertje (Neth)	1:13.2
1958	**Grinham, Judy (G.B.)**	**1:12.6**
1962	Van Velsen, Ria (Neth)	1:10.5
1966	Caron, Christine (Fr)	1:08.1
1970	Lekveishvili, Tina (U.S.S.R.)	1:07.8
1974	Richter, Ulrike (G.D.R.)	1:03.0
1977	Treiber, Birgit (G.D.R.)	1:02.63
1981	Kleber, Ina (G.D.R.)	1:02.81
1983	Kleber, Ina (G.D.R.)	1:01.79
1985	Weigang, Brigit (G.D.R.)	1:02.16
1987	Otto, Kristin (G.D.R.)	1:01.86
1989	Otto, Kristin (G.D.R.)	1:01.86
1991	Egerszegi, Kristin (Hun)	1:00.31
1993	Egerszegi, Kristin (Hun)	1:00.83
1995	Jacobsen, Mette (Den)	1:02.46

200 m Backstroke

1970	Gyarmati, Andrea (Hun)	2:25.5
1974	Richter, Ulrike (G.D.R.)	2:17.35
1977	Treiber, Birgit (G.D.R.)	2:13.10
1981	Polit, Koreen (G.D.R.)	2:12.50
1983	Sirch, Kornelia (G.D.R.)	2:12.05
1985	Sirch, Kornelia (G.D.R.)	2:10.89
1987	Sirch, Kornelia (G.D.R.)	2:10.20
1989	Hase, Dagmar (G.D.R.)	2:12.46
1991	Egerszegi, Kristin (Hun)	2:06.62
1993	Egerszegi, Kristin (Hun)	2:09.12
1995	Egerszegi, Kristin (Hun)	2:07.24

100 m Breaststroke

1970	Stephanova, Galina (U.S.S.R.)	1:15.6
1974	Justin, Christel (W. Ger)	1:12.55
1977	Bogdanova, Julia (U.S.S.R.)	1:11.89
1981	Geweniger, Ute (G.D.R.)	1:08.60
1983	Geweniger, Ute (G.D.R.)	1:08.51
1985	Gerasch, Sylvia (G.D.R.)	1:08.62
1987	Hoerner, Silke (G.D.R.)	1:07.91
1989	Boernike, Susanne (G.D.R.)	1:09.55
1991	Rudkoskaia, Elena (U.R.S.)	1:09.05
1993	Gerasch, Sylvia (Ger)	1:10.05
1995	Becue, Brigitte (Belg)	1:09.30

200 m Breaststroke

1927	Schrader, Hilda (Ger)	3:20.4
1931	**Wolstenholme, Celia (G.B.)**	**3:16.2**
1934	Genenger, Martha (Ger)	3:09.1
1938	Sorensen, Inge (Den)	3:05.4
1947	Van Nliet, Nel (Neth)	2:56.6
1950	Vergauwen, Raymonde (Belg)	3:00.1
1954	Happe, Ursula (W. Ger)	2:54.9
1958	Den Haan, Ada (Neth)	2:52.0
1962	**Lonsbrough, Anita (G.B.)**	**2:50.2**
1966	Prosumenschikova, Galina (U.S.S.R.)	2:40.8
1970	Stepnanova (Prosumenschikova) Galina (U.S.S.R.)	2:40.7
1974	Linka, Carla (G.D.R.)	2:34.99
1977	Bogdanova, Julia (U.S.S.R.)	2:35.04
1981	Geweniger, Ute (G.D.R.)	2:32.41
1983	Geweniger, Ute (G.D.R.)	2:30.64
1985	Bogomilova, Tamila (U.S.S.R.)	2:28.57
1987	Hoerner, Silke (G.D.R.)	2:27.49
1989	Boernike, Susanne (G.D.R.)	2:27.77
1991	Rudkovskaia, Elena (U.R.S.)	2:29.50
1993	Becue, Brigitte (Belg)	2:31.18
1995	Becue, Brigitte (Belg)	2:27.66

100 m Butterfly

1954	Langenau, Jutta (G.D.R.)	1:16.6
1958	Lagerberg, Tineke (Neth)	1:11.9
1962	Kok, Ada (Neth)	1:09.0
1966	Kok, Ada (Neth)	1:05.6
1970	Gyarmati, Andrea (Hun)	1:05.0
1974	Kother, Rosemarie (G.D.R.)	1:01.99

1977	Pollack, Andrea (G.D.R.)	1:00.61
1981	Geweniger, Ute (G.D.R.)	1:00.40
1983	Geissler, Ines (G.D.R.)	1:00.31
1985	Grebler, Karen (G.D.R.)	59.46
1987	Otto, Kristin (G.D.R.)	59.52
1989	Plewinski, Catherine (Fr)	59.08
1991	Plewinski, Catherine (Fr)	1:00.32
1993	Plewinski, Catherine (Fr)	1:00.13
1995	Jacobsen, Mette (Den)	1:00.64

200 m Butterfly

1970	Linder, Helga (G.D.R.)	2:20.2
1974	Kother, Rosemarie (G.D.R.)	2:14.45
1977	Fiebig, Anette (G.D.R.)	2:12.77
1981	Geissler, Ines (G.D.R.)	2:08.50
1983	Polit, Kornelia (G.D.R.)	2:07.82
1985	Alex, Jacquelin (G.D.R.)	2:11.78
1987	Nord, Kathleen (G.D.R.)	2:08.85
1989	Nord, Kathleen (G.D.R.)	2:09.33
1991	Jacobsen, Ute (Den)	2:12.87
1993	Egerszeki, Kristin (Hun)	2:10.71
1995	Smith, Michelle (Ire)	2:11.60

200 m Individual Medley

1970	Grunert, Martine (G.D.R.)	2:27.6
1974	Tauber, Ulrike (G.D.R.)	2:18.97
1977	Tauber, Ulrike (G.D.R.)	2:15.95
1981	Geweniger, Ute (G.D.R.)	2:12.64
1983	Geweniger, Ute (G.D.R.)	2:10.07
1985	Nord, Kathleen (G.D.R.)	2:16.07
1987	Sirch, Kornelia (G.D.R.)	2:15.04
1989	Hunger, Daniele (G.D.R.)	2:13.26
1991	Hunger, Daniele (G.D.R.)	2:15.53
1993	Hunger, Daniele (Ger)	2:15.33
1995	Smith, Michelle (Ire)	2:15.27

400 m Individual Medley

1962	Lasterie, Adrie (Neth)	5:27.8
1966	Heukels, Betty (Neth)	5:25.0
1970	Stoltz, Evelyn (G.D.R.)	5:07.9
1974	Tauber, Ulrike (G.D.R.)	4:52.42
1977	Tauber, Ulrike (G.D.R.)	4:45.22
1981	Schneider, Petra (G.D.R.)	4:39.30
1983	Nord, Kathleen (G.D.R.)	4:39.95
1985	Nord, Kathleen (G.D.R.)	4:47.08
1987	Lung, Noemi (Rum)	4:20.21
1989	Hunger, Daniele (G.D.R.)	4:41.82
1991	Egerszeki, Kristin (Hun)	4:39.78
1993	Egerszeki, Kristin (Hun)	4:39.55
1995	Egerszeki, Kristin (Hun)	4:40.33

4 × 100 m Freestyle Relay

1927	**Great Britain**	**5:11.6**
	(Laverty, Marion; King, Ellen;	
	Davies, Valerie; Cooper, Joyce)	
1931	Netherlands	4:55.0
	(Baumeister, Truus; Den Ouden, Willy;	
	Vierdag, Marie; Braun, Marie)	

1934	Netherlands	4:41.5
	(Spelbach, Jopie; Den Ouden, Willy;	
	Timmermann, Ans; Mastenbroek, Rie)	
1938	Denmark	4:31.4
	(Arndt, Eva; Ove-Petersen, Birte; Kraft,	
	Gunvor; Hveger, Ragnhild)	
1947	Denmark	4:32.3
	(Andersen, Greta; Harup, Karen;	
	Svendsen, Eva; Nathansen, Fritze)	
1950	Netherlands	4:33.9
	(Mauser, Ann; Vaessen, Marie-Louise;	
	Termeulen, Hannie; Schumacher, Irma)	
1954	Hungary	4:30.6
	(Gyenge, Valeria; Temes, Judit; Sebo,	
	Agota; Szoke, Katalin)	
1958	Netherlands	4:22.9
	(Schimmel, Corrie; Kraan, Gretje;	
	Lagerberg, Tinke; Gastelaars, Cockie)	
1962	Netherlands	4:15.1
	(Gastelaars, Cockie; Lasterie, Adrie;	
	Terpstra, Erica; Tigelaar, Ineke)	
1966	U.S.S.R.	4:11.3
	(Sipchenko, Natalia; Rudenka, Antonia;	
	Ustinova, Natalia; Sosnova, Tamara)	
1970	German Democratic Republic	4:00.8
	(Wetzko, Gabriele; Komor, Iris;	
	Schmisch, Elke; Schulze, Carola)	
1974	German Democratic Republic	3:52.48
	(Ender, Kornelia; Franke,	
	Angelika; Eife, Andrea; Hueber	
	Andrea)	
1977	German Democratic Republic	3:49.52
	(Trieber, Ulrike; Wachtler, Birgit;	
	Priemer, Petra; Krause, Barbara)	
1981	German Democratic Republic	3:44.37
	(Meinike, Birgit; Metschuck, Karen;	
	Diers, Innes; Linke, Carmela)	
1983	German Democratic Republic	3:44.72
1985	German Democratic Republic	3:44.48
1987	German Democratic Republic	3:42.58
1989	German Democratic Republic	3:42.46
1991	Holland	3:45.36
1993	Germany	3:41.69
1995	Germany	3:43.22

4 × 200 m Freestyle Relay

1983	German Democratic Republic	8:02.27
1985	German Democratic Republic	8:03.82
1987	German Democratic Republic	7:55.47
1989	German Democratic Republic	7:58.54
1991	Denmark	8:05.90
1993	Germany	8:03.12
1995	Germany	0:00.00

4 × 100 m Medley Relay

1958	Netherlands	4:52.9
	(De Nijs, Lennie; Den Haan, Ada; Voorbij, Atie; Gastelaars, Cockie)	
1962	German Democratic Republic	4:40.1
	(Schmidt, Ingrid; Goebel, Barbara; Noak, Ute; Pechstein, Heidi)	
1966	Netherlands	4:36.4
	(Sikkens, Coby; Kok, Gretta; Kok, Ada; Beumer, Toos)	
1970	German Democratic Republic	4:30.1
	(Hofmeister, Barbara; Schuchardt, Brigette; Lindner, Helga; Wetzko, Gabriele)	
1974	German Democratic Republic	4:13.78
	(Richter, Ulrike; Vogel, Renata; Kother, Rosemary; Ender, Kornelia)	
1977	German Democratic Republic	4:14.35
	(Richter, Ulrike; Nitschke, Carola; Pollack, Andrea; Krause, Barbara)	
1981	German Democratic Republic	4:09.72
	(Kleber, Ina; Geweniger, Ute; Geissler, Innes; Metschuck, Karen)	
1983	German Democratic Republic	4:05.79
1985	German Democratic Republic	4:06.93
1987	German Democratic Republic	4:04.05
1989	German Democratic Republic	4:07.40
1991	German Democratic Republic	4:08.55
1993	Germany	4:06.91
1995	Germany	4:09.97

Appendix 2: Milestones in Swimming

Fastest sidestroker ever	Emil Rausch 1904 Olympic winner
Furthest breaststroker	Capt Matthew Webb, crossing the English Channel 1875
Fastest Trudgeon crawl	Norman Ross 1920 triple winner
Fastest English overarm	John A. Jarvis 1900 triple winner
Fastest 8-beat crawl swimmer	Gertrude Ederle Olympics and English Channel
Fastest woman	Sybil Bauer first woman to beat an existing man's world record (backstroke)
Most versatile	Katherine Rawls won U.S. Nationals in all but backstroke and tower diving
Most gold medals in one Olympics	Mark Spitz – 7 in 1972
Medals in most Olympics	Zolten Halmay – 5 Olympics 1896–1908
Most Olympic medals won	Mark Spitz – 4 in 1968 plus 7 in 1972
Most consecutive National A.A.U. Championships, one stroke	Michael 'Turk' McDermott – breaststroke (9)
World records lasting longest (men)	Adolph Kiefer – 12 years, 100 m backstroke in 1:04.8 from 18 Jan 1936 to 23 June 1948
(women)	Barney Kieran – 16 years, mile in 23:16.8 from 1908 to 1924
Olympic record lasting longest	Dawn Fraser – O.R. for 100 m freestyle in 1:02.0 from 1956 to 1972
Longest periods undefeated	30 years – George Hodgson over 400 and 1500 m
Longest periods undefeated	10 years – Johnny Weissmuller in freestyle
Longest periods undefeated	8 years – Katherine Rawls in individual medley
All available freestyle world records at one time	Ragnhild Hveger – 19 in 1940
Only triple repeat Olympic winner	Dawn Fraser – 100 m freestyle 1956, 1960, 1964
First man to break 1 minute 100 m freestyle	Johnny Weissmuller – 58.6 on 9 July 1922
First woman to break 1 minute 100 m freestyle	Dawn Fraser – 59.9 on 27 October 1962
First man to break 2 minutes 200 m freestyle	Don Schollander – 1:58.8 on 27 July 1963
First woman to break 2 minutes 200 yd freestyle	Penny Estes
Record lasting longest	48 years – Matthew Webb only man to swim English Channel 1875 to 1923
Recognised modern world records lasting longest	18 years – Ragnhild Hveger 200 m freestyle in 2:21.7 from 1938 to 1956

Index